Preface Books

A series of scholarly and critical studies of major writers intended for those needing modern and authoritative guidance through the characteristic difficulties of their work to reach an intelligent understanding and enjoyment of it.

General Editor: MAURICE HUSSEY

A Preface to Wordsworth (*Revised ed.*)   JOHN PURKIS
A Preface to Donne (*Revised ed.*)   JAMES WINNY
A Preface to Jane Austen (*Revised ed.*)   CHRISTOPHER GILLIE
A Preface to Pope   I. R. F. GORDON
A Preface to Hardy   MERRYN WILLIAMS
A Preface to James Joyce   SYDNEY BOLT
A Preface to Hopkins   GRAHAM STOREY
A Preface to Conrad   CEDRIC WATTS
A Preface to Lawrence   GĀMINI SALGĀDO
A Preface to Forster   CHRISTOPHER GILLIE
A Preface to Auden   ALLAN RODWAY
A Preface to Dickens   ALLAN GRANT
A Preface to Shelley   PATRICIA HODGART
A Preface to Keats   CEDRIC WATTS
A Preface to George Eliot   JOHN PURKIS
A Preface to Orwell   DAVID WYKES
A Preface to Henry James   S. GORLEY PUTT
A Preface to Milton (*Revised ed.*)   LOIS POTTER

A Preface to Orwell

David Wykes

Longman, London and New York

LONGMAN GROUP LIMITED
Longman House
Burnt Mill, Harlow, Essex, CM20 2JE, England
and associated companies throughout the world

Published in the United States of America
by Longman Inc. New York

© Longman Group Limited 1987

First published 1987

British Library Cataloguing in Publication Data
Wykes, David
   A preface to Orwell.
   1. Orwell, George—Criticism and
interpretation
   I. Title
   823'.912   PR6029.R8Z/

   ISBN 0-582-35193-6

Library of Congress Cataloging in Publication Data
Wykes, David.
   A preface to Orwell.

   (Preface books)
   Bibliography: p.
   Includes index.
   Summary: A biography of George Orwell and an examina-
tion of his major works.
   1. Orwell, George, 1903–1950.   2. Authors, English—
20th century—Biography.   [1. Orwell, George, 1903–1950.
2. Authors, English]   I. Title.
   PR6029.R8Z954   1987   828'.91209   [B]   [92]   86-64
   ISBN 0-582-35193-6

ISBN 0 582 35193 6

Set in Baskerville 169 10/11pt.
Produced by Longman Group (FE) Ltd.
Printed in Hong Kong.

Contents

LIST OF ILLUSTRATIONS   vii
ACKNOWLEDGEMENTS   viii
FOREWORD   ix
REFERENCES   x

PART ONE: THE WRITER IN HIS SETTING

1 *Writing*   2
The writer   2
The writings   3
The English People   8
The pleasures of reading Orwell   22

2 *Life*   25
A chronology: the lives of Blair and Orwell   25
The good fit: Orwell and Adlerian psychology   37

3 *Repute*   45
'Orwellian': a mythology   45
Orwell's sincerity: *Homage to Catalonia*   50
Unofficial history   57

4 *Attitudes, beliefs and ideas*   61
Human relationships   61
Colonialism   63
'The terribly difficult issue of class'   66
Socialism   72
Power: 'a boot stamping on the human face'   76
History: predicting the past   79
Language and style   82
The religious sense of life   94

PART TWO: THE LITERARY CHARACTER OF ORWELL

5 *Novels, essays and criticism*   100
'Writer' as 'novelist'   100
Orwell's theory of the novel   100
The Orwell novel: *Coming Up for Air*   105
Essays   109
'How the Poor Die'   112
Criticism   118
Literary criticism   118
'From an anthropological point of view'   120

6   *The great fictions*: *Animal Farm and 1984*   124
Not really novels   124
Animal Farm: artistry   124
Animal Farm: propaganda   128
Allegorical ingenuity   129
Hard questions   130
1984: Shape and definition   134
Julia   139
Prophecy: 'a novel about the future'   145

PART THREE: REFERENCE SECTION

Gazetteer   150
   United Kingdom   150
   Abroad   158
Short biographies   163
Parties, movements, ideologies and events   171
Bibliography   181
   Further reading   181
   References and citations   183
   Before 1984: utopias and prophecies of political doom   185
Indices   188

List of illustrations

Abstract 1932 by Wyndham Lewis	cover picture
George Orwell	frontispiece
Unemployed miners searching a tip for coal, 1935	6
Thomas Rowlandson, *Portsmouth Point*	11
Henry Moore, *Pit Boys at the Pithead*, 1942	19
John Minton, *Hop picking near Maidstone*, 1945	21
Mr Blair and Mrs Blair with Eric	26
George Orwell with Richard Blair, 1946	33
Orwell's house in Jura	35
St Cyprian's School, Eastbourne	40
Eton College bathers on the beach near Athens	43
Spanish Civil War posters supporting the Republican cause	51
Orwell's Spain, 1936–1937	53
Orwell in Marrakech, 1938	67
Down and out in Paris and in London	70
Wigan in 1939	108
Clandestine edition, Warsaw, 1979	125
Two scenes from the 1954 BBC adaptation of *1984*	141
Clandestine Polish stamp: Cracow Solidarity branch	147
Plaque in Hampstead unveiled in 1969	153
Blair's grave	156
Eileen Blair	162
Sonia Orwell	165

Acknowledgements

Maurice Hussey, General Editor of this series, made unusual contributions to this book, his greatest accomplishment being to get the procrastinating author to finish it. In addition, he reshaped the overlong manuscript, chose pictures, contributed the bibliography of 'utopias and prophecies of political doom', and retained his author's affection, respect, and gratitude.

Jay Wright typed the manuscript with encouraging speed, accuracy, and enthusiasm.

We are grateful to the following for permission to reproduce copyright material by George Orwell:
Author's agents on behalf of the estate of the late Sonia Brownwell Orwell and Martin Secker & Warburg Ltd and Harcourt Brace Jovanovich Inc for extracts from *A Clergyman's Daughter, Down and Out in London and Paris, The Road to Wigan Pier, Burmese Days, Keep the Aspidistra Flying, Coming Up for Air, Animal Farm, Homage to Catalonia, Nineteen Eighty-Four, The Collected Essays, Journalism and Letters of George Orwell*, Vols I, II, III and IV.

We are grateful to the following for permission to reproduce photographs:
BBC, page 141; BBC Hulton Picture Library, pages 70 and 108; British Library, pages 125 and 147; Daily Telegraph Colour Library, page 35 (photo George Wright); Eastbourne Central Library, page 40; Ediciones Catedra, SA, Madrid, page 51; Fox/Photosource, page 6; *Hampstead and Highgate Express*, page 153; Orwell Archive, University College London, pages ii (photo Vernon Richards), 26 (lower photo Avril Dunn), 33 (photo Vernon Richards), 43 (photo Denys King-Farlow), 67, 162 (photo Avril Dunn) and 165; Portsmouth City Museums, page 11; Alan Spence Photography, page 156; Wakefield City Art gallery and Henry Moore, page 19.

The painting *Abstract 1932* by Wyndham Lewis is reproduced on the cover by permission of Kettering Borough Council.

Foreword

George Orwell's place in our literary and cultural history showed no sign of diminution between 1950 when he died (and was buried under his original name Eric Blair) and the mystic year of 1984. He is still much discussed and read so that he is present in the mind's eye with his cigarette, and his typewriter pounding away. His numerous short works show him articulating virtually every idea that came into his head from toads to Tolstoy and a task that any interpreter has is to sort through this mass and present the core of these opinions as the central all-connecting threads in Orwell's meaning for posterity. David Wykes has presented these in a scholarly and evocative manner through the author's own words and his alert judgement as a specialist in the literature of the period. The core of this *Preface* will probably prove to be sections on 'Attitudes, beliefs and ideas' in Part One and the later supplement on 'Parties, movements, ideologies and events', since it is just here that the new reader is inclined to be hazy and imprecise. The studies of the two 'not really novels' are equally helpful.

Many critics have taken up the comparisons between Orwell and Swift or Dickens but at the end of Part Two we are given an image of Orwell in the tradition of Dante. If he was a socialist who was inherently anti-Marx, anti-Lenin, anti-Stalin and anti-Trotsky he can be allowed as an unbeliever 'with a religious temperament' to have a leaning towards Christianity; even if in his case he was looking for a way to reconcile its moral principles with a disbelief in the afterlife, a position which is probably secretly maintained by several modern ecclesiastics. These points are among many that Professor Wykes explains most carefully and persuasively.

In the judgement of W. F. Bolton (in *The Language of 1984*): 'Orwell is not well served or best understood by admiration of him as a prophet, a linguistic sage, an abstract thinker or a tragic hero.' Here are still more parts of the jigsaw, and every reader will need to ponder, then, exactly what it is that makes Orwell into a 'necessary man', in the phrase by David Wykes. In the process so much more of the fiction, the reporting and the documentary that made up his range as man of letters will be surely sought out and read. To find the correct perspective and context we shall be indebted to the many points of reference that are established throughout this study.

MAURICE HUSSEY
General Editor

References

Since Orwell's work exists across the English-speaking world in a multitude of editions and paginations, I have identified quotations from Orwell by indicating *chapter* numbers in the case of novels and books of reportage, and—in the case of the *Collected Essays, Journalism and Letters*—by giving the volume number followed by the number of the item within the volume, and—where subsections are numbered—by the subsection within the item. Thus '4/86/iii' refers to the third subsection of item 86, 'Such, such, were the joys', in volume 4 of the *Collected Essays, Journalism and Letters*, published by Secker and Warburg and Penguin in Britain, and by Harcourt Brace Jovanovich in the United States.

I dedicate my part in this book to my mother and to the memory of my father, Frank Perry Wykes

DAVID WYKES is Professor of English at Dartmouth College, Hanover, New Hampshire, having previously taught at the universities of Nottingham, Trondheim and Oxford. Dr Wykes is the author of *A Preface to Dryden* (1977, but now unfortunately out of print) in the present series.

Part One
The Writer in his Setting

1 Writing

The writer

George Orwell is not, in the common acceptance of the term, a 'difficult' writer. He held to a concept of the writer's function that always turned him away from the esoteric, and he was by his nature a believer in the moral value of clarity. Nor was he, as his critics have gratefully noted, a genius. He had to seek for his talent, to discover his strength by trials and errors, and carefully nurture its growth. Orwell never possessed a literary kingdom as his own unchallengeable right nor made himself the unavoidable ancestor of the generations who follow him. Since his literary engagement with life was essentially political—once he had found his true direction—there has to be some doubt about his future reputation and readership. Is this writing that will outlive the particular conditions that brought it into being?

Yet Orwell's importance as one of the salient figures of twentieth-century British life is certain. His life and work will be necessary for any sound understanding of it. His work, that is to say, has great documentary value; it is a means to an understanding of something beside itself. This is not generally held to be the highest species of literary worth, but valuable nevertheless. So one intention of this book is to examine the documentary nature and quality of Orwell's work, to make available a proper understanding of the document which *is* that work.

Orwell's life as a writer has great representative value. Without being himself a theorist of literature—indeed, he reveals a rather English discomfort with theorizing of any kind—Orwell acts out in his literary person some of the great debates of modern literary theory. The most striking of these is the problem of the artist's engagement with public life and of the place of art in that life. Orwell seems to have accepted the predominant view of modern aesthetics in the West that a work of art exists to be itself, that its existence is an end, not a means. Yet the subjects that seized his creative interest as his career unfolded carried him irresistibly away from that position. He found that his work had to become instrumental, that his reason for writing was to change the world. Sometimes he saw this as the betrayal of an ideal and as the misapplication of his talent. At other times he claimed defiantly that 'all art is propaganda' and that in this age his avoidance of politics would have been a greater betrayal, had it not been impossible.

In 1946, Orwell stated that for the last ten years he had wanted 'to make political writing an art', that is somehow to make art as a means also art as an end, to annihilate the class distinction that literary opinion had come to accept as natural. This particular effort is an element that runs through his career, and this book will study its evolution.

Orwell's work, like Solzhenitsyn's, makes us aware that if we are free to put aside the problem of political writing as art, then that is simply our good fortune. In Orwell's lifetime, the first half of this century, the problem forced itself on the writer, the critic, and the reader. If it has ceased to do so, the respite is likely to be brief, and Orwell's case—the story of his whole life and career, not just a couple of his books—will be urgently needed again. He is a necessary man.

The writings

Orwell had to be a writer, as he explains in the essay of 1946, 'Why I Write', which serves as the introduction to the *Collected Essays, Journalism and Letters*. He knew it from a very early age, and when he tried to abandon the idea he was conscious that he was outraging his true nature. 'Why I Write', therefore, really explains why Orwell became the kind of writer he did, and its range of motives and insights concerning the literary personality of Orwell anticipates all that the literary biographer is able to say about him: the 'power of facing unpleasant facts', the 'literary ambitions . . . mixed up with the feeling of being isolated and undervalued', the desire 'to push the world in a certain direction', the starting point in 'the feeling of partisanship, a sense of injustice'. 'Why I Write' is indispensable, and basically self-explanatory.

In a couple of respects only does it need a gloss. It was written late in Orwell's career, and it implies a kind of certainty about the shape of that career which is misleading. In 1946 Orwell knew what kind of writer he was and why, but it had taken him a long time to come to that certainty. By emphasizing the political commitment of his writing, Orwell inadvertently contrives to under-emphasize, although he is careful to include, what he calls 'the aesthetic motive' of his work. His deepest commitment of all was to writing. He had decided that political purpose was essential if he was to write well, and so despised his own work where that commitment was lacking, but he makes it clear that those negative judgements are aesthetic ones. The aesthetic motive, the desire to make the writing as good as it could be, was as strong or stronger than the political motive. His praise for Arthur Koestler's 'grownupness' as a political writer concentrates on Koestler's having 'digested his material' and his subsequent, and rarer, ability to 'treat it on the aesthetic level' (3/68). For a twentieth-century writer to keep out of politics was, for Orwell, to fail the demands of his age: 'Nowadays the present and the future are too terrifying to be escaped from . . . .' What he perhaps insufficiently stresses is that the writer who meets the political demands of his vocation in our century still has to meet the timeless demand of art.

Orwell did so most famously in a pair of works of fiction that are not quite novels: *Animal Farm* and *1984*. But it is another paradox of his paradoxical career that he succeeded most often in meeting the joint demands of politics and art in a literary form that nowadays engages aesthetic judgements amidst great uncertainties. Orwell's best writing is most consistently found in his essays where he draws on his interpretations of his life and his reading. One must go there to find him at his best, as writer and as the student of his times. This book about Orwell, therefore, makes the four volumes of *Collected Essays, Journalism and Letters* its central text and chief resource.

If we see Orwell's writing career as he never could, as one suddenly completed by his untimely death in 1950, its shape seems to suggest a long period of searching and experiment followed by discovery and success with his last two books of fiction. *Animal Farm* and *1984* were certainly successful in a manner unprecedented in Orwell's career, and the displeasure he took in the existence of certain of his earlier books (refusing permission to reprint them) strongly suggests that he saw his own output as having that shape. But if it is to be described as a career of 'apprenticeship in failure', followed by a 'breakthrough into success' then we should be careful to clarify the nature of the 'failure', since it is of an unusual kind.

The books Orwell published in the 1930s conform to patterns. The pattern of the journey, for instance, is prominent. He journeyed to Burma, to Paris, to Wigan, to Spain, and each journey produced a book. In his novels, the characters may travel; Dorothy Hare does, in *A Clergyman's Daughter*, on a journey of escape into self-exploration, and George Bowling does, in *Coming Up for Air*, in search of the past. (Only *Keep the Aspidistra Flying* avoids this pattern.) Then there is the pattern of explanation, of Orwell's books as basically concerned to display and explain the conditions of life for people placed in specific physical and moral locations. All of Orwell's books—of the 1930s and later—fit this pattern of exposition.

Both patterns, however, indicate elements in Orwell's literary make-up that he had to transform in order to achieve the successes of *Animal Farm* and *1984*. First, both patterns derive from Orwell's strongly empirical and experimental mind. He had to have experienced what he was writing about, but he finally discovered that such truthfulness did not need to involve similarity of material circumstance. He could write fiction, that is to say, without giving it the closeness of autobiography that marks all of his novels of the 1930s. The journeys that brought his books into being did not have to be incorporated into the books.

Moreover, he could meet his fundamental need to *explain* in his writing, his complete commitment to literary exposition, by modifying the conventional realistic novel, as he does in *1984*, or by choosing a non-realistic, allegorical form (the beast fable in *Animal Farm*). Realism was very important to him, as we shall see, and his belief in the value of the novel was quite as sincere, but because of his need to be a writer who explained, certain formal aspects of the realistic novel inevitably cramped him. Plot, for instance, was a difficulty for Orwell. He wanted to show how people lived—the lives of British and Burmese in Burma, or the life of a struggling writer in London. Essentially he wanted to cut a slice through life, to reveal its true nature, its basic if surprising ordinariness. But the novel demanded, in its tragic mode, catastrophe, and in its comic mode some kind of final turn into happy resolution. Orwell meeting these demands gives us the not-quite-right endings of his novels: Flory's suicide, Gordon's decision to embrace the aspidistra, the returns of Dorothy Hare and George Bowling (preceded, in Bowling's case, by the 'false catastrophe' of the RAF's bombing of Lower Binfied). As *Animal Farm* and *1984* show, the kind of ending that would work for Orwell was the drama of recognition, the animals looking from man to pig or Winston's true love for Big Brother, recognition that gathers into one great irony the book's completed lines of development. (Another great instance of this kind of ending is the reader's realization at the end of Solzhenitsyn's *One Day in the Life of Ivan Denisovich* that this really has been 'almost a happy day' in Shukov's life.) Such endings, though they surprise the reader, offer the surprise of recognition. They tell us what we have known all along but only now do we recognize it. There is nothing arbitrary about them.

In his non-fictional works, however, those book-length essays sometimes called 'documentaries'—*Down and Out in Paris and London, The Road to Wigan Pier, Homage to Catalonia*—Orwell could exploit the method employed by many realistic novelists he admired; he found the extraordinary in the ordinary. Coal-mining, for instance, is drab, taken-for-granted, necessary, but—as labour—'as much beyond my power as it would be to perform on the flying trapeze or to win the Grand National'. He presents mining as surreal heroism, stressing its absolute necessity to civilization, the amazing demands on the miners, and the general desire of everyone else to ignore it, like a guilty secret. A hotel kitchen, a hop garden, or a colliery spoil bank can be the locale for such revelations. In the novel, however, the extraordinary in the ordinary was harder to handle. Orwell's most ambitious attempt,

Unemployed miners searching a tip of coal, 1935, one of the illustrations in the first edition of The Road to Wigan Pier

the Trafalgar Square sequence in *A Clergyman's Daughter*, can never free itself from the dominance of James Joyce's *Ulysses*. *Keep the Aspidistra Flying* depends totally upon the personality of Gordon Comstock, which is finally unable to convince the reader that this particular angle of vision is quite valid. The greatest success is *Coming Up for Air*, where the mental world of George Bowling is 'visionary' in ways that are fairly convincing, though Orwell nevertheless felt that he needed the bombs to drop.

Orwell's novels of the 1930s may be described as experiments even though they are not on the whole what is normally meant by 'experimental'. They exerted their strongest influence when they were reprinted as a result of his later popularity and in spite of his repudiation of *A Clergyman's Daughter* and *Keep the Aspidistra Flying* as 'weak silly books'. All the early novels seemed important to those young writers who had to endure being labelled 'Angry Young Men'. Their anger, much like Orwell's until he found out that he was a socialist, tended to be an attitude or cast of mind rather than something with clear objectives. Their only political attitude, like his for a long time, was an imprecise leftism. The principal characters in the early novels of Kingsley Amis and John Wain and in the plays, especially *Look Back in Anger*, of John Osborne, were fairly well-educated and by choice *déclassé*, vocal and vehement in criticism, but contemptuous of the 'pseudo' and the consciously intellectual. The literary method was a realistic adherence to the details of middle-class life.

These writers found Orwell established on the territory they wanted for themselves, and they accepted him as a kindred spirit. John Osborne, for instance, several times causes Jimmy Porter to quote from the essay 'England Your England' in *Look Back in Anger*. Gordon Comstock's social *milieu*, the monologues of George Bowling, and the wanderings of Dorothy Hare were all re-enacted. The biggest difference was that the 'Angries' found more comedy in their characters' situations than Orwell did, but this difference is, on inspection, one of degree. Orwell's sardonic irony could easily be transformed into the sardonic comedy of Kingsley Amis. Jim Dixon's unforgettable attempt to rectify a disaster of burnt bedclothes by using a razor blade to cut out the burnt bits exists in full potential in Gordon Comstock's surreptitious tea-making.

> He tiptoed down, clutching the damp bundle of tea-leaves against his breast. The W. C. was on the second floor. At the angle of the stairs he halted, listened a moment longer. Ah! another clatter of crockery.
>
> All clear! Gordon Comstock, poet ('of exceptional promise,' *The Times Lit. Supp.* had said), hurriedly slipped into the W. C., flung his tea-leaves down the waste-pipe, and pulled the plug.

The English People

'How can one make a pattern out of this muddle?' (2/17/i)

In September 1943 the publishers Collins of London commissioned Orwell to write the text of *The English People*, one of their series of illustrated books, 'Britain in Pictures'. Orwell finished it by May 1944, though it was not published until 1947. *The English People* is a longish essay, about thirty-two pages of text. Much of it is a reworking of ideas from a 1941 piece, 'The Lion and the Unicorn: Socialism and the English Genius'. It is something Orwell drew from stock, yet on the subject of the English people his stock of ideas was rich. The essay allowed him to express himself cogently on what were then, and for the major part of his career, his main themes. To start with it is to go to the centre of Orwell's intellectual and emotional character, and to discover there some paradoxes.

The essay begins with a paradox. 'In peace time, it is unusual for foreign visitors to this country to notice the existence of the English people.' This miracle of imperceptiveness turns, of course, on the definition of 'people', and Orwell at once makes it clear that he means the common people, the working masses who make up seventy-five per cent of the population, and not therefore the 'property-owning classes' who normally absorb the attention of the visitor, causing him to 'ignore the other forty-five million' and to define as typically English the habits and attitudes of a mere quarter of the population. 'Even the prevailing physical type does not agree with the caricatures, for the tall, lanky physique which is traditionally English is almost confined to the upper classes.'

The overt paradox of this has a covert accompaniment, for these words were not written by a man 'rather small, with short limbs and brisk movements' belonging by birth and upbringing to the often invisible forty-five million. For Orwell was an Old Etonian, an ex-officer of the Indian Imperial Police, with 'the tall lanky physique' conforming to the caricatures of the 'typically English'. The voice which so firmly undertakes here to assert for the mass of the unpropertied English its claim to be *the* English people always murmured 'Eton' to those who knew. The 'language of the BBC' which 'is barely intelligible to the masses' was at this time Orwell's professional dialect, since he then worked as a Talks Producer in the Indian Section of the BBC Eastern Service. (He quit that job in November 1943 and became literary editor of *Tribune*, a weekly paper on the left wing of the Labour movement.) As the essay advances, one other great paradox unfolds. This is clearly the work of an intellectual, one who lives the life of the mind, yet the only group of which he speaks with vigorous detestation is the intelligentsia.

It will be rightly concluded that Orwell had turned his life into paths which were not the easiest, the 'natural' ones for him. To a remarkable extent, the man who wrote *The English People* had decided consciously what kind of man he wanted to be and what opinions to hold. They were not the customary ones of his 'class and station', for he had rejected his class and his station. He had chosen a new name: 'George Orwell' was the pseudonym of Eric Blair. These decisions were impelled by powerful psychological pressures, and to learn about Orwell is to find out about the pressures and his response to them. One of Orwell's most interesting creations is George Orwell, but the very first thing one wants to know about a writer is simply what he writes about. *The English People*, this 'commissioned booklet' as one of his editors calls it (in 1947 Orwell himself called it 'a silly little book'), can nevertheless be a guide to the salient features of Orwell's literary mind.

The topic for Orwell is given life by his sense of injustice. Though the essay is almost totally free of the tone or attitudes one might associate with such a purpose, its objective at bottom is to right a wrong, to give back to the English working masses the importance, and indeed the power, which Orwell sees as theirs by right but stolen from them. They are the 'real English', and Orwell speaks for them. His words imply, besides, his basic democracy and his socialism. The injustice is one of numbers. Forty-five million people are ignored in favour of a much smaller property-owning class. (On 3 June 1940 Orwell noted in his diary a letter in the *Daily Telegraph* from Lady Oxford on the subject of war economies: 'Since most London houses are deserted there is little entertaining . . . in any case, most people have to part with their cooks and live in hotels.' He remarked: 'Apparently nothing will ever teach these people that the other 99% of the population exists.')

The essay is divided into subsections, and the titles given to those divisions are in themselves the skeleton of Orwell's social beliefs: 'The Moral Outlook of the English People', 'The Political Outlook of the English People', 'The English Class System', 'The English Language', 'The Future of the English People'. Almost everything Orwell ever wrote, and certainly everything that was important to him, could be fitted under one of these headings.

In the very first section, 'England at First Glance', Orwell tries to see his subject through the eyes of 'a foreign observer, new to England, but unprejudiced, and able because of his work to keep in touch with ordinary, useful, unspectacular people'. The characteristics of the English, as tabulated from this observer's impressions, make a surprising list: 'artistic insensibility, gentleness, respect for legality, suspicion of foreigners, sentimentality about animals, hypocrisy, exaggerated class distinctions, and an obsession with sport'. Only one item on the list, the rather strange 'gentleness', is uncompromisingly positive.

He then devotes a paragraph to each of his items (composition teachers love Orwell) and that modifies the apparent antagonism a bit. 'Respect for legality' does turn out to mean respect for (an albeit imperfect) law, and although the obsession with sport is real, it is 'not carried to quite such imbecile lengths' as the popular papers suggest. Even so, five pages into his essay, Orwell seems to be presenting data generally tending to indict rather than compliment the English people. The foreign observer may have cast a colder eye than Orwell intended when he set him to work.

At this stage, Orwell faces up to some doubts about his own procedure, putting them into the mind of his foreigner. 'But then probably a thought would strike him: is there such a thing as "the English character"? Can one talk about nations as though they were individuals? And supposing that one can, is there any genuine continuity between the England of today and the England of the past?' The response Orwell makes to his own questions is typical of his attitudes. Instead of arguing these points rationally and theoretically, he works out an answer which seems at first to be hardly logical at all. Orwell describes the past image of the common people which can be derived from 'old prints in the book-shop windows', and accepts that a hundred years earlier English life was distinguished by its brutality: 'an almost unending round of fighting, whoring, drunkenness, and bull-baiting'. (Orwell's unquestioning acceptance of the accuracy of this image is one of the oddities of the essay.) Still relying on the prints (he seems to have Rowlandson chiefly in mind), he concludes that even the physique of the English has changed. 'Where are they gone, the hulking draymen and low-browed prize-fighters, the brawny sailors with their buttocks bursting out of their white trousers, and the great overblown beauties with their swelling bosoms, like the figure-heads of Nelson's ships?' The gusto of this description is the strength of Orwell's argument. The 'connecting thread that runs through English life from the sixteenth century onwards' may be hard to find, to display empirically, 'but all English people who bother about such subjects feel that it exists'. The people in Rowlandson's prints do not reappear in the figures of English people in the 1940s, but they are accepted, embraced with zest, as typically English. Orwell supplies his foreigner's conclusion: 'a profound, almost unconscious patriotism and an inability to think logically are the abiding features of the English character . . . .'

The paradox here of patriotism and illogicality, an apparent contradiction concealing a real truth, is encountered everywhere in Orwell. His life was full of paradoxes and he made use of them in his art. (The opening lines of his works often exploit paradox: 'As I write, highly civilised human beings are flying overhead, trying

Thomas Rowlandson, Portsmouth Point

to kill me.' 'Saints should always be judged guilty until proved innocent.') Yet Orwell does not embrace the paradox as a kind of philosophical principle, as a belief that there is an order to the universe concealed beneath its surface. The paradoxes of G. K. Chesterton approach this level of importance in his thought, but Orwell's involvement (almost entanglement) in paradoxes has no transcendental meaning. His willingness to be paradoxical and to accept paradoxes is an insistence that truth is unlikely to be found by methods of simplication. If one sees truths on both sides of a contradiction, then the contradiction may be apparent only, for a deeper truth can absorb both surface truths. Sometimes Orwell was wrong, seeing paradox, fundamental unity, where only contraries existed. But more often he was right in struggling to reach the one truth which subsumed two apparently opposed positions. In political argument, simplication is strength, but Orwell impresses as a political arguer by rejecting easy simplication of theory while rejecting, too, all escape routes of obscurity. If he is entangled, muddled, he can see, as we can, what is entangling him.

These first few pages of *The English People* are as distinctively Orwell's as his fingerprints. The large identifying marks have already been indicated: the concerns with injustice and democracy, the socialism based on a hatred of the alienating powers of wealth, the suspicion of logic and theory which deny the complexities and entanglements of real life and hence a suspicion of intellectuals, the logicians and theorists. And there are other themes which in these pages have minor functions, though they are major elements over the whole span of Orwell's career.

One is history, the past as an intellectual and emotional foundation for the present and the only possible guide to the future. As we have seen, Orwell hauls the past almost by violence into the opening pages of *The English People*. Its importance to him overrides strict considerations of logic or literary form. His enjoyment in conjuring up a sort of archetype of the Rowlandson print is not, however, a sentimental indulgence. Orwell wants to establish as an important element in his argument the mid-twentieth-century 'gentleness' of the English people, extending even to a change of physique, which he sees as an achievement contrasting with the past. ('Within living memory . . . an eminent jurist, asked to name a typically English crime, could answer, "Kicking your wife to death".') What is characteristic is Orwell's insistence on the presence of the past; to ignore it, or—worse—deliberately distort it, were for him great intellectual crimes.

Two further points should be made, both a bit odd but both characteristic. We have seen that he comes to praise the English working class, but seems paradoxically, to be making a case against them. This, of course, is the Orwell form of paradox. He cannot state the truth of his love without the truth of working class xenophobia, insensitivity to aesthetic values, and so on. His seeming hardness towards the thing he loves is closely related to his hardness towards himself. When explaining himself, Orwell looks first for the discreditable motives for his deeds and traits and assumes always that such motives exist, even though they may not predominate. This tendency has, no doubt, psychological interest; we could find something discreditable in it. But, of course, Orwell's heroic status depends absolutely on his quite unfeigned unawareness of himself as a hero. One moment of self-congratulation would destroy it all. But Orwell seems to have been incapable of that. His attitude cannot be called modesty, since that implies suppressing awareness of one's worth. Orwell seems to have felt he was a failure, so we are happy to accept him as a success. Another paradox.

The second point is Orwell's use of 'English' and avoidance of 'British'. Patriotism for him had no imperialistic component. In *The English People* he proposes what has lately been called 'devolution': 'Both Scotland and Wales could and should be a great deal more autonomous than they are at present.' But his insistence on 'England' and 'English' was owing to more than a recognition that Scotland and Wales were distinct entities. At school he had felt that a 'curious cult of Scotland' was employed as one of the mechanisms of injurious social differentiation: 'Scotland was a private paradise which a few initiates could talk about and make outsiders feel small.'' (4/86/v) Although Orwell openly put no blame for this upon Scots themselves, his distaste did extend to them. 'I am glad you make a point of calling them "Scotchmen" and not "Scotsmen" as they like to be called. I find this a good easy way of annoying them.' (1/81) 'Britain' was a federation of which Orwell's own England was merely a part, and probably for him the name itself was a synthetic re-creation, having none of the weight and authenticity of 'England'. But Orwell's prejudice was not rooted enough to prevent him from making his last home in the Hebrides, where I suspect he did not call the people 'Scotchmen'.

MORAL IS POLITICAL   After 'England at First Glance' Orwell devotes the first two sections of the essay proper to moral outlook and political outlook. For Orwell it was inevitable that these two should come first, and to his readers it is just as inevitable that the two categories should be blurred, each overlapping the other. Orwell tried whenever opportunity came or could be found to resist the separation of the two, and the very structure of his writing here resists it.

He begins by describing the general apathy of his English people towards formal religion ('Only about ten per cent of them ever go near a place of worship except to be married and buried') and the reduction of religious feeling to a set of basic ethical tenets. But then paradox asserts itself. The English common people are, in one important respect, 'more Christian than the upper classes': 'they have held on to the one [doctrine] that the Church never formulated, because taking it for granted', by which he means 'the modern cult of power worship', the belief that might is right. The intelligentsia is deeply infected with this idea (Orwell comes close here to conflating the intelligentsia and the upper classes); since Carlyle's time it has taken its ideas from Europe and has been tainted by 'habits of thought that derive ultimately from Machiavelli'. In international politics, the English tend to side with the underdog, and Orwell pays them a paradoxical compliment: 'in this matter the English common people have lagged behind their century. They have failed to catch up with power politics, "realism", *sacro egoismo*, and the doctrine that the end justifies the means.' This laggardliness and these failures might be called 'backhanded insults', English irony in a typically Orwell form. And the subject matter has, of course, become political morality.

Orwell considers what might be called the received opinion about English liberties. Is the Englishman's home his castle?

The answer is, in 'an age of conscription and identity cards', not really. 'But the hatred of regimentation, the feeling that your spare time is your own and that a man must not be persecuted for his opinions, is deeply ingrained . . .' and undestroyed by wartime conditions.

Is the British press free? The answer is not really, because of centralized ownership and public lack of interest in preserving a free press. Yet few people are afraid to speak their political opinions aloud and few want to silence others. Indeed, 'the real totalitarian atmosphere, in which the State endeavours to control people's thoughts as well as their words, is hardly imaginable' (Orwell, of course, later imagined and imaged it.)

Are people tolerant, willing to hear both sides? Yes, but the cause is less a matter of principle than 'the prevailing lack of intellectuality'. Here Orwell brings into the open another aspect (paradoxical in form) of English political life. 'The English are not sufficiently interested in intellectual matters to be intolerant about them.' As Lionel Trilling has remarked, Orwell in his later years comes close to following Walter Bagehot, the nineteenth-century writer, who saw political virtue in what he called '*stupidity*, a concern for one's private material interests as a political motive which was preferable to an intellectual, theoretical interest'. Orwell does not elaborate on this position; he does not make it in itself a theory or pursue it as a paradox. But he goes with Bagehot in seeing real advantages for the general liberty of English life in the failure of people (outside the 'island of bigotry' which is the intelligentsia) to be unconcerned about party lines and 'contradictions' and 'deviations'. Orwell sums up on this topic in a passage beginning with a sentence of compliment taking, very characteristically, negative form: 'The English people are not good haters, their memory is very short, their patriotism is largely unconscious, they have no love of military glory and not much admiration for great men. They have the virtues and the vices of an old-fashioned people. To twentieth-century political theories they oppose not another theory of their own, but a moral quality which must be vaguely described as decency.' In fact, of course, Orwell has managed to assert not an opposition of moral to political, but an identity of the two. 'Gentleness' and 'decency' are the political theory of an old-fashioned people.

A BLOODLESS REVOLUTION The section on 'political outlook' ('outlook', of course, is well chosen—not 'system', not 'theory', certainly not 'philosophy') inevitably repeats some of the points which have been made earlier. Orwell has decency and gentleness as the foundations on which his account of working class 'political outlook' must rest, and this furnishes another paradox. The main political demand of the English people (and of George Orwell) is for 'profound changes', and Orwell interprets this as a demand for a revolution. So it must be a gentle and decent revolution.

But was Orwell right in assessing the English people's desire for 'profound changes' as a 'demand for revolution', albeit a gentle and decent one? He imagines a question put to the whole nation: 'What do you want from politics?' and gives the answer himself: 'Economic security, a foreign policy which will ensure peace, more social equality, and a settlement with India'. This does not sound like a revolutionary programme, and, although there would be much argument about the degree of implementation, it is undeniable that England since 1944 has moved in these directions. Changes which Orwell might have agreed to call profound or drastic have occurred. Yet it seems unlikely that he would have accepted this as the English revolution. In *The English People* he defines *his* revolution by implication and in diffuse ways, but its fundamentals, which he felt he shared with the mass of the English, were easily named: 'freedom and equality' were what Orwell believed in, and to judge him aright one must accept them as ideas of persisting validity and vitality to him. Socialism and liberalism were beliefs which he consistently upheld and fought hard to reconcile if they began to war upon each other. 'In England, if anywhere, it would be possible to abolish poverty without destroying liberty.'

CLASS   Orwell rejected class war, but made war upon class. From the beginning to the end of his career as a writer, he was absorbed with the workings of the English class system. Essentially, his view was that it was a mechanism of injustice, and the section he devotes to it in *The English People* is really subordinate to 'The Political Outlook of the English People', since the desire for 'more social equality' means for Orwell the abolition of class distinctions. But so powerful was the idea of class in Orwell's mind that, justly, it gets its own section of the book.

To outsiders, to Americans, for example, who may deny that there is a 'class system' in the USA, the detailed ramifications of English class-consciousness are sometimes bewildering, sometimes the 'dirty secret' of English literature, where, of course, these preoccupations are most often encountered. To understand Orwell and not bring class into consideration is, however, impossible; to wish that he would give it a rest is to ask him to change his nature.

Orwell is true to himself in being fascinated by the oddness of the English class system, its refusal, in fact to be logically systematic, and in his willingness to be just to the thing he hates. He describes in outline what he calls 'an industrial and capitalist country . . . haunted by the ghost of a caste system', but points out the quirkiness of the system's failure to 'correspond to economic distinctions'. An army officer earning £1000 a year is the social superior of a shopkeeper with twice as much. Class distinctions, he discovers, are snobbery 'mixed up with a kind of idealism, a feeling that style and tradition are more important than money'. The 'comparative integrity of the British ruling class—for when all is said and done they have not behaved so contemptibly as their European opposite numbers [Orwell had earlier noted with approval that 'Several dukes, earls and what nots were killed in the recent campaign in Flanders'] is probably bound up with their idea of themselves as feudal landowners'. To Orwell, this is a pastoral daydream, widely shared by the middle classes, but he does justice to its idealistic component. It helps produce the integrity he has noted. He is comforted to see wide-spread evidence of the growth of a technologically-oriented middle class 'not much interested in [its] own social status' and in the tendency of the working class and middle class eventually to merge, but he records also, with evident regret, but very firmly, that 'One cannot altogether acquit the English working class either of snobbishness or of servility'. They are disposed 'to accept class distinctions as permanent, and even to accept the upper classes as natural leaders', Churchill being the obvious example. To Orwell, opposition without blind hatred or bias was the ideal of political commitment. He realizes it in 'The English Class System'.

LANGUAGE   The justification for a section devoted to 'The English Language' is much more difficult to appreciate, particularly given the nature of Orwell's actual commentary here. Obviously, in writing of the English people, language is relevant, but no more relevant than many topics on which he is silent. But it is not true to say that Orwell, who was obsessed with ideas about language in his later years, simply allowed his obsession to force its way irrelevantly into this particular text. Orwell's concern, which is seen clearly at one of its evolutionary stages in *The English People*, basically became the political importance of language. That topic is not yet fully developed, but its relevance is greater than at first sight appears (since this is generally a political essay) though one is much better able to appreciate that if one knows that Orwell's line of thought eventually led to Newspeak.

Orwell describes the range, flexibility, and grammatical simplicity which have enabled English to become a world-wide language, but characteristically he puts his main emphasis on the disadvantages of these qualities. English is so simple that it inhibits the learning of foreign tongues, and, most ominous of all, English has 'a capacity for debasement'.

Orwell believed that English had entered a period of 'temporary decadence' attributable to a variety of causes. Decadence can be seen in vagueness, obscurity, decorative adjectives, the encroachment of Latin and Greek, and most of all in 'the worn-out phrases and dead metaphors with which the language is cluttered up'. As secondary causes, Orwell instances jargon ('English is peculiarly subject to jargons') and 'standard English', 'this dreary dialect', which relies heavily on ready-made phrases. Another cause is English's borrowings from American, 'a bad influence' which has had a 'debasing effect'.

Reading Orwell's catalogue, one cannot doubt his seriousness, but on this occasion his attribution of a first cause seems a mite factitious. He blames it on the class system. ' "Educated" English has grown anaemic because for long past it has not been reinvigorated from below.' Orwell argues that the vitality of the language is due to its imagery, and that the desirable imagery is simple and concrete and comes from those 'in contact with physical reality'. 'The English language suffers when the educated classes lose touch with the manual workers.'

The reinvigoration of the language requires that words and idioms be allowed to circulate freely among all sections of the population: 'Language ought to be the joint creation of poets and manual workers, and in modern England it is difficult for these two classes to meet.' This section is full of fascinating ideas which must be examined fully when we return to Orwell and language. The obsession with language and class existed for good reason, and eventually Orwell developed from it some of his most impressive insights (see also p. 82, 'Language and style').

THE FUTURE   Since Orwell's fame is based on *1984*, it might seem obvious that he would devote his final section to 'The Future of the English People'. Yet he was not what has lately been called a 'futurologist' or 'futurist'. He was interested in the future because he believed in the necessity of politics, and *1984* is squarely in the tradition of the utopia/dystopia in being a book about a political future. 'To take a rational political decision one must have a picture of the future'. (3/68) A politician for Orwell was one who worked to realize such a picture, and so Orwell himself, as a frequent writer on political subjects, repeatedly tried to imagine what was to come.

This indispensable element of political thought was troublesome and complex for Orwell because of his own psychological make-up. He wanted to believe in progress, and sought out evidence that it existed. Yet he did not have the comfortable mental facility of shutting out evidence to the contrary, indeed he was compelled to seek out such evidence by the related traits of self-depreciation and pessimism in his nature. The belief in progress, so essential and so easy for many on the Left in politics, was one that Orwell had to fight to retain, and the fact that *1984* was his last book has led to the belief—wrong, I would maintain—that at the end of his life he had lost all belief in progress.

It is necessary to grasp that progress for Orwell was not an easy belief but a real one nevertheless, since otherwise one might too easily conclude that 'The Future of the English People' is a very uncharacteristic piece. In it, Orwell sets out the 'special part' that the English can play in the world to come. They are to provide a model of bloodless revolution in which liberty and democracy are preserved. The basis in the English character for this assumption of the model rôle is, again, gentleness. 'The outstanding and—by contemporary standards—highly original quality of the English is their habit of *not killing one another*.' Orwell sees a working democracy in England as a moral and political blueprint whose imitation by other nations will give England the kind of pre-eminence which is otherwise no longer possible, a replacement for the imperial rôle. 'The world is sick of chaos and it is sick of dictatorship. Of all peoples the English are likeliest to find a way of avoiding both.'

To assume this rôle, Orwell asserts, England must undergo the great political change predicated throughout his book, with power in the hands of 'the ordinary English in the street'. Then, in a conclusion that blends Orwell's patriotism with Orwell's vision of

Henry Moore, Pit Boys at the Pithead, *1942, one of the illustrations in the first edition of* The English People

18

the English revolution, the question will be answered 'whether England is to survive as a great nation or not. And if the answer is to be "Yes", it is the common people who must make it so'. Here, the relevance to *1984* should be clear. Instead of the best possible future for the English, reverse it and find the worst. *1984* is a very English book.

ENGLAND IN PICTURES When *The English People* was finally published in 1947, Orwell was quite recently famous as the author of *Animal Farm*. This was useful to the publishers since they obviously felt some difficulty about presenting this book in a series in which calls for revolution were not expected. The blurb they wrote for the dust-jacket juggles manfully and clumsily with the problem Orwell had provided. (It may be unique in suggesting another book as antidote to itself.)

Animal Farm is (misleadingly) 'that brilliant satire on revolution' and Orwell's 'capacity to look with critical eyes upon his fellow citizens . . . is part of his love for them'.

Those who read this book may find much to make them angry—much with which they will disagree. But it is always better to be self-critical and to leave praise to others. Those who want kind words will find them abundantly in such a book as Mr Alfred Perles' recent *Round Trip*.

Having, in the first paragraph, said that Orwell 'should need no introduction', this most edgy blurb in the third paragraph says:

Mr George Orwell is a distinguished political journalist—distinguished especially for his honesty of opinion. This is a book with a particular political bias and should provoke those of contrary opinion to examine their own beliefs without sentimentality or hypocrisy.

Caveat emptor. Orwell's hack work in this context clearly had some power to disconcert.

That same power extends in one other direction. *The English People* has eight colour plates and seventeen black and white illustrations. All of these reproduce oil or watercolour paintings and drawings of English subjects by a variety of artists, some still well known: *Saturday Afternoon, A Derbyshire Village* by L. S. Lowry; *Hop Picking* by John Minton; *Miners at the Pithead* by Henry Moore; *Pub in Canning Town* by Henry Lamb; *Evening by the River, Salisbury in Wartime* by Edward Ardizzone. One cannot complain that the subjects of the paintings go against the grain of Orwell's text. Yet between the fact of these illustrations and what Orwell wrote there is, somehow, a great gulf fixed.

Orwell's text—one might say Orwell's character—seems to demand photographs, and not 'good' photographs either, but news-

John Minton, Hop picking near Maidstone, *1945, another of the illustrations in the first edition of* The English People. *This picture recalls the hop picking in* A Clergyman's Daughter.

21

paper photographs and stills from newsreels. Collins supplied illustrations which aspire, sometimes successfully, to beauty. Yet the beauty of Orwell's writing is oddly self-denying. In a fine, trenchant review of J. B. Priestley (1930, 1/7) Orwell wrote a sentence which ought to be right but which sounds in his mouth quite wrong: 'a novelist is not required to have good intentions but to convey beauty.' Now 'good intentions' are proverbially hellish, yet without denigration 'good intentions' seem to me to fit Orwell better than 'convey beauty'. Successful works of art always manage to be glamorous, however unglamorous their subjects or stern their creators. This is a difficult topic to handle, but Orwell's writing contrives, in perhaps the most mysterious paradox of all, to have the glamour of success and yet be unglamorous. The failure of these well-chosen illustrations to 'fit' Orwell's text points out one of his most characteristic but elusive qualities.

The pleasures of reading Orwell

In 1949 V. S. Pritchett began a review thus: '*Nineteen Eighty-Four* is a book that goes through the reader like an east wind, cracking the skin, opening the sores . . . .' The image is exactly right for the variety of discomfort rising to pain which Orwell offers to us. There is only rarely the grandeur of tragedy. Tragedy doesn't nag, isn't 'gritty'. In tragedy worlds end, and with the survivors we gaze on the ruins. Orwell's more often seems to be the universe of Murphy's Law: if things can go wrong, they will go wrong, and at the worst possible time. The emblem for this could be an incident in *Homage to Catalonia* (VII). In a raid on the Fascist trenches, Orwell's unit captures a large telescope, an object of enormous value in the 'weapon-starved' army of the Republic. 'We brought it out in triumph and leaned it against the parapet, to be carried off later.' Anyone acquainted with Orwell's universe would know, if he took pause for consideration, what will happen. In the confusion of the fighting the telescope has to be left behind. Its enormous desirability simply intensifies the occasion for regret, and there is an almost comic irony as the apparently inherent inevitability of it all emerges. Of course the telescope will be lost; this is the world of George Orwell.

The Telescope Syndrome crops up often, but its presence never—except perhaps in *1984*—gives the dominant tone to Orwell's world. It is a pessimistic world and it creates gloomy expectations; if things can go wrong they will. Yet Orwell is an undespairing pessimist. In 'Why I Write' he attributed to himself, as one of his strengths, 'a power of facing unpleasant facts'. The facts really are unpleasant, but the power is that of the facing. He is true to his truth; he has integrity. One result is that his vision has an uncompromising single-mindedness that leaves him open to parody. Orwell is *always* the schoolboy who notices the turd floating in the swimming-bath. When he looks at snow, one can anticipate what he will see.

> Snow is always dirty, except just after it has fallen. I have noticed this even in the high peaks of the Atlas mountains, miles from human habitation. The everlasting snow which looks so virginal, is in fact distinctly grimy when you get close to it. (4/74)

There is a drift towards self-parody, but it exists because Orwell must get close to things, face the unpleasant facts. The effect, however, is finally the paradoxical one he found defined by Henry Miller: 'What he seems to be saying is that if one stiffens oneself by the contemplation of ugliness, one ends by finding life not less but more worth living.' That was his own discovery. His love of being alive and his interest in the lives people are allowed to live or are prevented from living animate even his darkest passages. When he was shot through the throat in Spain, one of his reactions was 'a violent resentment at having to leave this world which, when all is said and done, suits me so well'.

The unpleasant fact and the love of life can positively jostle one another, as they do in a letter to Brenda Salkeld in 1934.

> This age makes me so sick that sometimes I am almost impelled to stop at a corner and start calling down curses from Heaven like Jeremiah or Ezra or somebody—'Woe upon thee, O Israel, for thy adulteries with the Egyptians' etc etc. The hedgehogs keep coming into the house, and last night we found in the bathroom a little tiny hedgehog no bigger than an orange. The only thing I could think was that it was a baby of one of the others, though it was fully formed—I mean, it had its prickles. (1/57)

The prophet of doom with an interest in hedgehogs is an engaging figure; both sides of him were equally real. He said in 'Why I Write', 'So long as I remain alive and well I shall continue to feel strongly about prose style, to love the surface of the earth, and to take pleasure in solid objects and scraps of useless information. It is no use trying to suppress that side of myself.' That side of him is well represented in his writings, but critics' estimates of him are apt to leave it out of account. The truth is that Orwell's political vision always incorporates a sensitivity to what we now call 'the quality of life'. Politics finds meaning in the details of the lives of individuals. Winston Smith has a dream of a Golden Country, which he is only once enabled to visit, and that dream is a real element in the book's political discussion. Orwell writing about roses or hedgehogs or 'Some Thoughts on the Common Toad' (4/40) is not in fact turning from the serious side of life but expanding the definition of what is serious. 'I think that by retaining one's childhood love of such things as trees, fish, butterflies and . . . toads, one makes a peaceful and decent future a little more probable.'

The pleasures of Orwell, then, have opposing and complementary sources. There is his power of facing truly unpleasant facts, balanced by his frequent reminders that life is worth living—and if worth living, worth improving. The fame of *1984* tends to alter the balance in the public mind, but it is right to remember that even without *1984* Orwell would be a fine and still necessary writer, and that the necessity of him is mainly a function of his artistry.

To go further, he is a writer who is well served by the anthology. Yet to read through the four volumes of the *Collected Essays, Journalism, and Letters* is to discover how often, particularly in casual pieces of journalism, Orwell produced something—a paragraph or a sentence—that sinks into the memory. The least frequently defined of his gifts as a writer is his ability to project a personality, to create a particular voice that one recognizes and trusts as Orwell's. The odd incompatibility of *Down and Out in Paris and London* with the rest of his work is owed, as Alex Zwerdling has suggested, to the failure to create such a voice. But by the time of *The Road to Wigan Pier* it existed. Here the unmistakable Orwell describes the kitchen table in the most famous tripe shop in English literature.

> I never saw this table completely uncovered, but I saw its various wrappings at different times. At the bottom there was a layer of old newspapers stained by Worcester Sauce; above that a sheet of sticky white oil cloth; above that a green serge cloth; above that a coarse linen cloth, never changed and seldom taken off. Generally the crumbs from breakfast were still on the table at supper. I used to get to know individual crumbs by sight and watch their progress up and down the table from day to day. (I)

The systematic objectivity of the archaeological strata, followed by the Dickensianly progressive crumbs, is so irresistible that it's hard not to feel manipulated; the virtuoso effect is perhaps a little too powerful. Some of the horrors of *The Road to Wigan Pier* are a bit overwritten or too deft in this way, as are some of the 'positive' passages, the 'working class interior', for example (VII). But these are the vice of a great virtue. Orwell has discovered his voice, his particular angle of vision—and delights in it, perhaps a bit too much.

In retrospect, to agree with Orwell all the time is utterly impossible and there are things anyone will wish Orwell had never said. But in general his writing offers the pleasure of a special certainty, as close to absolute as one can get: the confidence of knowing that this is what one man really thinks and feels.

2 Life

A chronology: the lives of Blair and Orwell

The left-hand column below sets out a chronology of the life of Eric Blair and the career of George Orwell. The right-hand column indicates historical events, particularly those with any special relevance to Orwell's writing.

The chronology of the life, read against the 'other events', emphasizes that Orwell was a late starter whose involvement with the formative public happenings of his generation was both anomalous and typical. Too young for the First World War, for instance, he also missed, because he was in Burma, the event that politically polarized so many of his generation: the General Strike of 1926. Yet, 'between the wars', he managed to get into the most educational and perhaps most mythological of twentieth-century conflicts, the Spanish Civil War. Similarly, the chronology shows rather vividly that in his last years, when he was writing *1984*, his concern with current events, particularly those associated with the Labour Government of 1945, was much reduced. Many of the important happenings of those last years go unmentioned in Orwell's writing.

To emphasize that Orwell's life was his laboratory, I have mentioned the writing he derived from an event together with the occurrence. Dates following titles are those of publication.

BLAIR AND ORWELL	OTHER EVENTS
1903 25 June, Eric Arthur Blair born Motihari, Bengal, India, Father (Richard) serving in Indian Civil Service.	1903 First flight by the Wright brothers. London Congress of Russian Social Democratic Party splits into Menshevik and Bolshevik factions, the latter led by Lenin and Trotsky.
1904 Mrs Blair returns to England with the children, and until 1911 Eric lives with his family at Henley-on-Thames.	1904 Shaw, *Man and Superman.*
	1905 Revolutionary uprisings in Russia after defeat by Japan. Einstein's Special Theory of Relativity.

Mr Blair and Mrs Blair with Eric

BLAIR AND ORWELL	OTHER EVENTS
	1906 Launch of *HMS Dreadnought*.
	1907 Kipling, Nobel Prize for Literature. W. H. Auden born.
	1909 Stephen Spender born.
	1910 E. M. Forster, *Howards End*.
1911 September, Eric Blair starts at St Cyprian's School, Eastbourne ('Such, such were the joys', 1952).	1911 D. H. Lawrence, *The White Peacock*.
	1912 Lenin editor of *Pravda*. Sinking of the *Titanic*. D. H. Lawrence, *Sons and Lovers*.
	1913 The Webbs found the *New Statesman*.
1914 2 October, Eric Blair's poem. 'Awake! Young Men of England' published in local paper.	1914 28 June, assassinations at Sarajevo. July, declarations of war
	1915 Somerset Maugham, *Of Human Bondage*
1916 Christmas, Blair leaves St Cyprian's.	1916 H. G. Wells, *Mr Britling Sees it Through*.
1917 Lent term as a scholar of Wellington College. May, begins at Eton, King's Scholar.	1917 Kerensky, Russian premier. October Revolution in Petrograd. Lenin Chief Commissar. T. S. Eliot, *Prufrock and Other Observations*.
	1918 11 November, Armistice. G. M. Hopkins, *Poems*.
	1919 G. B. Shaw, *Heartbreak House*.
	1920 Adler, 'The Practice and Theory of Individual Psychology'.
1921 Christmas, leaves Eton.	1921 BBC founded. D. H. Lawrence, *Women in Love*.
1922 November, Blair arrives in Mandalay as a	1922 Eliot, *The Waste Land*. Joyce, *Ulysses*.

recruit for the Indian
Imperial Police. Serves
at several posts until
leave in August 1927.
('A Hanging', 1931;
Burmese Days, 1934;
'Shooting an Elephant',
1936).

1923 Yeats, Nobel Prize for
Literature.
1924 Lenin died.
Ramsay MacDonald
forms first Labour
Government in Britain.
1925 Hitler, *Mein Kampf.*
1926 General Strike in
Britain, 3–12 May.
Stalin establishes his
power in USSR.
1927 Trotsky expelled from
Communist Party.
Snow

1928 January, Blair leaves
the Imperial Police.
Autumn, living in
London. Until 1932,
makes expeditions to
educate himself on the
conditions of the
underclass of English
society ('The Spike',
'Hop-picking', 1931;
'Clink', 'Common
Lodging Houses', 1932).
Spring until late 1929:
living and writing in
Paris, V^e *arrondissement.*
First professional
articles in Paris papers.
1929 February, pneumonia,
Hôpital Cochin, Paris
('How the Poor Die',
1946).
Autumn, working as
dishwasher and kitchen-
hand, Paris (*Down and
Out in Paris and London*,
1933). Return to
England.
1930 Blair works as a private
schoolmaster and tutor,
goes on tramping and
hop-picking expeditions,

1929 Trotsky expelled from
USSR. 24 October,
Wall St crash. British
unemployment rate
12.2%.
Robert Graves, *Goodbye
to All That.*

1930 W. H. Auden, *Poems.*
General world-wide
economic depression.
1932 Oswald Mosley forms

publishes articles and reviews, writes *Down and Out* which is rejected by several publishers until Gollancz takes it. Blair adopts the pseudonym of 'George Orwell'. Writing *Burmese Days*.

1933 School-teaching, writing, and further pneumonia.

1934 Writing almost full-time; *A Clergyman's Daughter* (1935). Living at Southwold, Suffolk, with parents. October, moves to Hampstead, part-time work in a bookshop ('Bookshop Memories', 1936).

1935 Writing *Keep the Aspidistra Flying*.

1936 February, March, gathering material in North of England for *The Road to Wigan Pier* (1937), commissioned by Gollancz. April, moves to Wallington, Herts. Writing *The Road to Wigan Pier*. 9 June, marries Eileen O'Shaughnessy. December, leaves for Spain, joins militia of POUM (Partido Obrero de Unificación

British Union of Fascists. 2.8 million unemployed in Britain.

1933 Hitler chancellor of Germany. Nazis establish first concentration camps. Book burnings. H. G. Wells, *The Shape of Things to Come*.

1934 Kirov assassinated in Leningrad; purge of Soviet Communist Party begins.

1936 January, George V dies. Edward VIII abdicates. December, George VI. May, Italy annexes Ethiopia. Gollancz founds the Left Book Club. July, army revolt against Republican Government in Spain begins a civil war. October, Franco appointed head of Fascist Government. November, siege of Madrid. Roosevelt elected to second term. Penguin Books begins selling sixpenny

Marxista).

paperbacks.
First Butlin's holiday
camp opened at Skegness.

1937 At the front, mainly
with the Workers
United Marxist Party
(POUM) militia in
Aragon; corporal.
April, on leave in
Barcelona, intending to
join International
Brigade in Madrid.
Communist *attentat* in
Barcelona against
revolutionary parties,
including POUM.
Orwell's presence is a
decisive moment in his
life, making him an
opponent of Stalinist
Communism.
10 May, returns to
front; second lieut.
20 May, wounded in
the throat.
16 June, POUM
outlawed by Spanish
Republican
Government. Orwell
and his wife hide from
the police, escape to
France, 23 June.
July, at Wallingford,
writing *Homage To
Catalonia*.
September, Secker and
Warburg agree to
publish the book after
Gollancz refuses for
political reasons.

1937 Show trials and purge
of generals in USSR.
Neville Chamberlain,
prime minister.
Air Raid Precautions
introduced in Britain.
April 26, German
bombers destroy
Guernica.
Koestler, *Spanish
Testament*.

1938 March, ill with TB.
April, *Homage to
Catalonia* published.
13 June, joins Independent

1938 March, Hitler annexes
Austria.
September, Munich
agreements.

Labour Party (ILP).
September 1938–March
1939, in Morocco for
reasons of health
('Marrakech', 1939).
Writing *Coming Up for
Air* (1939).

1939 June, death of Orwell's
father Richard Blair.
Orwell's attempts to get
into the war are
rebuffed.
Writes *Inside the Whale*
(essays, 1940).
Early in the war, leaves
the ILP.

1940 First contributions to
Horizon and *Tribune*.
Living in London.
Theatre critic for *Time
and Tide*. Joins the
Home Guard. Writing
The Lion and the Unicorn
(1941).

Nearly one third of
Czechoslovakia is given
to Germany. Beginnings
of the Volkswagen, the
ball-point pen, and
instant coffee.
Evelyn Waugh, *Scoop*.

1939 28 March, Madrid falls
to Franco, end of
Spanish War, approx-
imately one million
dead.
23 August, non-
aggression pact between
Nazi Germany and
Soviet Russia.
1 September, Germany
attacks Poland.
3 September, Britain
and France declare war
on Germany. Churchill,
First Lord of the
Admiralty.
Einstein writes to
Roosevelt on possible
military use of nuclear
fission.
Food rationing in
Britain.
Henry Miller, *Tropic of
Capricorn*.
17 September, USSR
attacks Poland.

1940 March, Katyn Forest
massacre of 10,000
Polish officers.
7 May, Chamberlain
resigns, Churchill prime
minister.
10 May, German
blitzkrieg.
29 May, Dunkirk
evacuation begins.
22 June, German-

French armistice.
15 August, Battle of
Britain at its peak.
21 August, Trotsky
assassinated in Mexico.
November, Roosevelt
elected to third term.
10 November, Coventry
bombed. 4,550 killed in
November air-raids on
Britain.

1941 First 'London Letters'
to *Partisan Review* in
New York.
August, begins work for
the BBC, Talks Dept,
Indian Service, and
publishes many articles
and reviews.

1941 6 April, Germans
invade Greece and
Yugoslavia.
20 May, German
invasion of Crete.
22 June, German
invasion of Russia.
7 December, Japanese
attack Pearl Harbor.
8 December, USA
declares war on Japan.
Koestler, *Darkness at
Noon.*
Welles, *Citizen Kane.*

1942 June, US naval victory
at Midway.
August, Battle of
Stalingrad begins.
2 December, first
controlled, self-sustaining
nuclear chain reaction,
University of Chicago.
24 December, first
surface-to-surface
guided missile test at
Peenemunde by Von
Braun.

1943 March, Orwell's mother
dies.
23 November, Orwell
leaves Home Guard for
medical reasons.

1943 February, German
surrender at Stalingrad.
July, Allied invasion of
Sicily.
Late November,

George Orwell with Richard Blair, 1946

	BLAIR AND ORWELL		OTHER EVENTS
	24 November, resigns from BBC. Appointed literary editor of *Tribune*. Begins writing *Animal Farm* (1945).		Teheran Conference, Roosevelt, Stalin, Churchill. T. S. Eliot, *Four Quartets*.
1944	February, finished *Animal Farm*. *The English People* (1947). June, the Orwells adopt a baby, Richard Horatio Blair. Several publishers (including T. S. Eliot for Faber and Faber) reject *Animal Farm* on political grounds. October, Secker and Warburg agree to publish *Animal Farm*.	1944	4 June, fall of Rome to Allies. 6 June, D Day, Normandy. 25 August, liberation of Paris. September, German missile attacks on Britain. November, Roosevelt elected to a fourth term.
1945	February, Orwell resigns as literary editor of *Tribune*. 29 March, Orwell in Cologne as war correspondent for the *Observer* returns to England on learning that his wife has died during an operation. April and May, in France, Germany, and Austria as a war correspondent. July, first attempt at writing *1984*. 17 August, *Animal Farm* published. September, first visit to Jura in the Hebrides.	1945	February, Yalta Conference. 12 April, death of Roosevelt. Truman President. 25 April, Americans and Russians meet on the Elbe. 30 April, Hitler kills himself. 8 May, Allied victory in Europe. July, Labour victory in British general election. 6 August, atomic bombing of Hiroshima. 9 August, atomic bombing of Nagasaki. 14 August, end of war in the Pacific.
1946	February, *Critical Essays*	1946	January, first session of

Orwell's house in Jura

published.
May, at Barnhill, Jura.
August, *Animal Farm*
published in USA.
Book of the Month
selection, sells half a
million copies. Orwell
at work on *1984*.
October, in London.

1947 April, to Jura, writing
or revising 'Such, such
were the joys'. Illness.
October, finishes draft
of *1984*.
December, in hospital
for TB, Glasgow.

1948 February, begins second
draft of *1984*.
July, returns to Jura.
September, health
deteriorates.
November, finishes *1984*.

1949 January, at Cotswold
Sanatorium, Cranham,
Glos.
June, *1984* published,
Book of the Month
selection, USA.
September, seriously ill,
transferred to
University College

UN General Assembly
in London.
5 March, Churchill's
'Iron Curtain' speech.
September, verdicts at
the Nuremberg trials.
National Health Service
Act.
Coal industry
nationalized.

1947 15 August,
independence for India.
Burma an independent
republic. Severe winter
causes great agricultural
losses in Britain.

1948 British railways
nationalized.
30 January, Gandhi
assassinated.
14 May, state of Israel
proclaimed, first Arab-
Israeli war begins.
June, Yugoslavia
expelled from the
Cominform.
24 July, Berlin
blockaded by the
Russians. Airlift.
November, Truman
elected president.
Norbert Wiener,
Cybernetics.
Pound, *The Pisan Cantos*.

1949 January, Communists
take over in China.
4 April, NATO Treaty
signed.
May, Berlin blockade
lifted.
September, USSR
detonates an atomic
bomb.

Hospital, London.
13 October, marries
Sonia Brownell.
1950 21 January, Orwell
dies; buried at Sutton
Courtenay, Berkshire,
as Blair.

Clothes rationing ends
in UK.

The good fit: Orwell and Adlerian psychology

Orwell's biographers are well supplied with facts, but his life seems markedly infertile as regards a particular form of myth often cultivated in twentieth-century life stories. The available facts seem to offer few handholds for the psychological biographer. To find Freudian or Jungian shaping forces beneath the events of Orwell's life cannot be impossible, since these greatest of our mythographers claim universal application for their patterns, but it does seem true that, if we think of Orwell's life as a narrative text, we cannot expect an illuminating interpretation of it from a Freudian or Jungian critic.

The narrative of Orwell's life, however, is not utterly closed to psychological reading, for Freud and Jung are not the only available interpreters. The psychology of Alfred Adler (1870–1937), who is—most suitably—the least fashionable member of the 'big three' of psychological theory, proves adept as the interpreter of certain salient features of Orwell's personality. To attempt an Adlerian reading of Orwell's development can provide at this point a summary perspective on the personality.

Orwell was not neurotic, and it should be understood that, in trying to show how his personality makes a 'good fit' with Adler's theories, we are studying the development and adaptations of a basically healthy individual. Orwell overcame a series of obstacles which life placed in his way and which, unsurmounted, might well have left him the victim of neurosis. Those conquests or adaptations make sense best when they are placed in Adlerian categories; the events seem to choose an Adlerian line of explanation.

Adler is the most amenable of the great psychological theorists for a study of Orwell's life in great part because he relied less on 'depth' in analysis and more on the subject's remembered circumstances, particularly the social relationships. An account like 'Such, such were the joys', an adult recollection of the years from eight to fourteen, would have seemed less important to many analysts than to those of an Adlerian bent. Orwell in that essay often seems to be assembling his recollections as if for an Adlerian analyst, though there is not much evidence to suggest that he knew about Adler or his theories.

One handicap carried by the would-be Adlerian literary biographer is that Adler's ideas are often best understood—because more systematically set out, better written, in fact—in the work of his disciples than in his own writings. In some respects one can call Adler a psychological theorist with little apparent gift for theorizing—a paradox that in fact supports his 'fit', his applicability to Orwell's case. Of the 'big three', he was the one without grandeur, though not free of pretensions. Other general points of contact and affinity between the two men are Socialism and a strong advocacy of reforms in society, an emphasis on the importance of education, and a down-playing of the dominant rôle of drives and instincts, including the sexual ones. (Orwell never wrote about this, but the details of his life seem to support the idea.)

Adler's characteristics as a psychologist can be at least sketched in by considering what certain of Freud's more famous formulations became in his hands.

> Adler was now proposing that sexuality be considered in its symbolic sense. According to his beliefs, women in our culture have a tendency to become neurotic, not because they covet the penis, but because they envy the pre-eminence of man in contemporary culture . . . . The Oedipal situation was understood not as the striving of the boy to achieve sexual pleasure with his mother, but as a symbolic battle. Feeling weak and defenseless, the son uses over-compensation to achieve superiority over father and dominance over mother.
>
> (Sheldon T. Selesnick)

Adler is the psychologist for people who don't much like psychology. Like Orwell, he was no genius.

INFERIORITY   One of Adler's ideas, however, has been successful enough to be routinely attributed to one or both of the geniuses, Freud and Jung: the inferiority complex.

Adler theorized that all human beings in infancy experience 'inferiority feelings' which are in fact vital to individual development. The basis for these feelings is physical, the child's helpless, puny being in a world of adults. Adler held this to be a universal infantile realization, and there is no need to search for particular evidence of it in Orwell's case, but some does offer itself.

> The enormous size of grown-ups, their ungainly, rigid bodies, their coarse, wrinkled skins, their great relaxed eyelids, their yellow teeth, and the whiffs of musty clothes and beer and sweat

and tobacco that disengage from them at every movement! Part of the reason for the ugliness of adults, in a child's eyes, is that the child is usually looking upwards, and few faces are at their best when seen from below. (4/86/vi)

That this, from 'Such, such were the joys', is an adult reminiscence and not directly a child's view seems to me to make it all the more remarkable as evidence of Orwell's unusual retention of his 'inferiority feeling'. He tells us, too, that *Gulliver's Travels* 'is a book which it seems impossible for me to get tired of'.

I read it first when I was eight—one day short of eight, to be exact, for I stole and furtively read the copy which was to be given to me next day on my eighth birthday—and I have certainly not read it less than half a dozen times since. Its fascination seems inexhaustible. (4/57)

That fascination certainly led to Orwell's political essay on Swift, but its roots seem to be in the child's experience in the Brobdingnagian world of adults. Inferiority feeling is, in the Adlerian view, universal and necessary. 'All human progress can be referred to the fact that the human being strives to overcome his inferiority' (Hertha Orgler). The infant develops its abilities, its power, so as to overcome the inferiority feeling, the inevitability of which explains Adler's maxim: 'To be a human being means to feel oneself inferior.'

Ida Blair's diary for 6 February 1905, reads: 'Baby [Eric] not at all well, so I sent for the doctor who said that he had bronchitis.' This records the beginning of the pulmonary weakness that was to kill Orwell at forty-six, but it was also the basis for the inferiority complex that dominated his mental life for many years, until he was able to overcome it.

The St Cyprian's school approach to a 'weak chest' was to combine the Erewhonian (illness is crime) with the Swiftian (disease is caused by repletion).

'Wheeziness,' or 'chestiness' as it was called, was either diagnosed as imagination or was looked on as essentially a moral disorder, caused by overeating. 'You wheeze like a concertina,' Sambo would say disapprovingly as he stood behind my chair: 'You're perpetually stuffing yourself with food, that's why.' My cough was referred to as a 'stomach cough,' which made it sound both disgusting and reprehensible. The cure for it was hard running, which, if you kept it up long enough, ultimately 'cleared your chest.' (4/86/iii)

Orwell's reaction in his adult life to his physical weakness was generally to ignore it. It would be wrong to say that he tried

physical overcompensation (it is hard to find positive compensations for pulmonary lesions), but it is certainly true that he often chose a way of life that a person with a non-compulsive attitude towards that particular weakness would have avoided. One has only to think of the books based on personal experiences—*Down and Out in Paris and London, The Road to Wigan Pier, Homage to Catalonia*—to see that he placed himself in situations very badly suited to his health. By denying that his lung condition made a real difference to the activities he ought to pursue, Orwell in fact adopted one aspect of the St Cyprian's code. He saw nothing reprehensible in being ill, but he did refuse to permit illness to himself as an excuse, and in fact chose activities as if following the line that physical incapacity or sickness could be referred to the will. There was much hard running in his life. The effect on Orwell's life expectancy was disastrous, but a rational assessment of, for example, the risks of going to Spain would have deprived him and us of *Homage to Catalonia*.

On the basis of this organ inferiority, there developed a striking case of inferiority complex. Orwell's own words and the pattern of his life from his schooldays until he published his first book reveal a failure to evolve a viable life-style, followed by a lengthy process of struggle and experiment from which a recognizably effective life-style did emerge.

'Life-style' as a term of Adlerian psychology means the organization of the individual psyche to serve a 'plan of life' (a term which was used before 'life-style'). The individual needs a goal, and the elements of the life-style are the means chosen to attain it. Both goal and means may be defined below the level of consciousness. Neurosis may be owed to an unattainable or irrational goal, producing a life-style to correspond, or it may be owed to the individual's failure to formulate any kind of goal that gives satisfaction. Orwell's seems to be the latter case. As he summed it up:

> The conviction that it was *not possible* for me to be a success went deep enough to influence my actions till far into adult life. Until I was about thirty I always planned my life on the assumption not only that any major undertaking was bound to fail, but that I could only expect to live a few years longer. (4/86/v)

As Orwell saw it, the school was a production line. Its 'sales' were made to parents who wanted to get their sons into 'good' public schools, and the examination successes of 'scholarship' boys like himself (the 'scholarships' at St Cyprian's were given in secret, unlike the public school scholarships which were public honours) were the advertising which proclaimed the school's efficiency. The scholarship boys were urged towards academic success by the image of a dreadful future if they failed.

> Either I won my scholarship, or I must leave school at fourteen and become, in Sambo's favourite phrase, 'a little office boy at forty pounds a year' . . . . it was universally taken for granted at St Cyprian's that unless you went to a 'good' public school . . . you were ruined for life. (4/86/ii)

A further spur for Orwell was the secret of his reduced fees at the school. This, in interviews with the Wilkeses, was 'a final, unanswerable argument, to be brought forth like an instrument of torture when my work became exceptionally bad'.

Orwell shows how he had to accept these arguments while rebelling inwardly against them. He got his scholarship but he never gave his emotional assent to the values those arguments upheld. Yet he had nothing—it is the child's plight to have nothing—to oppose the goal the school presented. The scholarships represented success, but Orwell was a failure in his own eyes.

THE POSITION OF POWER   As Freud is popularly the psychologist of sex, so Adler is popularly the psychologist of power. Popular estimation, as so often, is error on the base of truth. Just as inferiority feelings are the necessary stimulus to development, so the acquisition of power in one's environment is proper and beneficial. Orwell's childhood as he recalled it presents the spectacle of great inferiority feelings accompanied by powerlessness, since all demonstrations of power in his world were unacceptable to him. It took years of seeking for him to find acceptable ways to assert his own power in life. Yet that search equipped him to become the theorist of power we meet in the period of *1984*.

The schoolteacher is always more than an instructor in academic subjects, and in a boarding school system the teacher's rôle as surrogate parent can combine very forcefully with the teacher's rôle as a model for the exercise of power. Orwell's moral rebellion against the values he saw offered by his school was complete because he rejected both aspects. He withheld his consent to Mrs Wilkes as 'Mum', and every manifestation of the exercise of power he saw in the school repelled him. The physical and psychological weaponry of the proprietors, the value of wealth and upper-class connections, the ideology of bullying disguised as 'character', even the public school sporting code: he turned from all of them. (Football for Orwell is 'not really played for the pleasure of kicking a ball about, but is a species of fighting. The lovers of football are large, boisterous, nobbly boys who are good at knocking down and trampling on slightly smaller boys. That was the pattern of school life . . . .')

Eton College bathers on the beach near Athens. Eric is on the extreme right.

At Eton, where he could abdicate even apparent interest in the ways to power, Orwell was lazy by choice and relatively happy. He made, however, little progress in evolving a life-style to accommodate his slowly shaping personality. His decision to join the Burma Police satisfied many needs but all of them external, distant from the deepest needs of his psyche. His novel *Burmese Days* and his two famous Burma essays, 'A Hanging' and 'Shooting an Elephant', display an anguished self-loathing, the self-disgust of a man living a lie. Burma actually confirmed the experience of St Cyprian's, for in the East Orwell discovered that his real power would have to come from writing and that his necessary identification was not with the wielders of power presented to him as models, but with those upon whom they used their power. In Adlerian terms, he overcame his inferiority complex by a positive identification with those stamped inferior by society, and he realized his own power by devoting the weapon of his writing to the cause of the powerless.

The conventional rôles of power, as displayed at school and in Burma, for ever afterwards made Orwell uncomfortable. He was enormously relieved to find that 'revolutionary discipline' really did work in the Spanish militias, where no one saluted and no one said 'sir'. Another interesting example is Orwell as literary editor of *Tribune*. He confessed his inadequacy: 'The fact is I am no good at editing.' He could not cope with the routine of the job. But, most telling of all, 'I have a fatal tendency to accept manuscripts which I know very well are too bad to be printed'. He attributed this to his years as a freelance. 'It is like taking a convict out of his cell and making him governor of the prison.' But really Orwell could not cope with the traditionally authoritarian rôle of editor.

Orwell's own true power was the power of his voice. Emblematically, a Fascist bullet tried to destroy one of his vocal cords, but the other 'compensated', overcame the inferiority. In conversational gatherings, Orwell often said little because his voice had little power. But then his writing compensated.

There are two footnotes to this topic. Orwell never mentions Adler, so one assumes he knew nothing about Adler's ideas. Yet Eileen, his first wife, did a graduate degree in psychology at the University of London, working on child psychology (an Adlerian speciality) with Cyril Burt. Finally the *Supplement* to the *Oxford Dictionary* confirms that Orwell seems to have been the first English writer to use the term 'life-style', in 1944.

3 Repute

'Orwellian': a mythology

'Orwellian' is one of the words that define our age.

A university scientist designs a device to detect and record from a distance a patient's heartbeat, so that doctors may check the condition of a victim of burns without touching him. A student remarks, however, that the device 'sounds like something out of *1984*'. The scientist is shocked to be 'an inadvertent collaborator with Big Brother'.

An American newspaper, of a bizarre conservative stamp, is apt to evoke Orwell approvingly in its editorial pages. The paper one day proposes to obtain tape recordings of speeches made in the state legislature and to subject those speeches to 'voice stress analysis' so as to detect those speakers who will be 'scientifically proved' to be telling lies. The most Orwellian part of the episode is that the newspaper sees nothing Orwellian in the proposal.

Any application of technology which gives a government or a corporation a new advantage in its relations with the individual may be denounced as Orwellian, but not because Orwell's dystopian novel *1984* has much to say about technology, though the belief that it does is widespread. Rather the book gave the middle decades of the twentieth century an unforgettable image of man forced to renounce his human individuality by the power of the state. When we say 'Orwellian' we mean intimations of human life without individuality, privacy, or any activity, physical or mental, which the state may define as against the interests of the collective—itself. It was this relationship of the individual to the state that came to the mind of a *New York Times* writer the day after Solzhenitsyn was exiled in 1974.

> In Leningrad last April I met a Soviet systems analyst. He was a clever and supremely confident man, who saw himself as an engineer not only of computers but of human souls. He foresaw the day of a new Soviet man, with his psychological drives all channelled into 'socially useful' activity.
>
> What about Aleksandr Solzhenitsyn? he was asked. There will be no problem in the future, he replied. People will be conditioned so that there is no disruptive individualism in their make-up. There will be no more Solzhenitsyns.

Anthony Lewis did not name Orwell, but his repugnance towards the Soviet utopia is exactly that which runs through Orwell's later writings and which he had openly expressed in 1939.

> The terrifying thing about the modern dictatorships is that they are something entirely unprecedented .... In the past every tyranny was sooner or later overthrown, or at least resisted, because of 'human nature', which as a matter of course desired liberty. But we cannot be at all certain that 'human nature' is constant. It may be just as possible to produce a breed of men who do not wish for liberty as to produce a breed of hornless cows. (1/149)

'Orwellian', therefore, is the adjective derived from the name of the author of *1984*, and *1984* is one of the most recent and notable documents in the long tradition of British political philosophy and literature which has struggled, with success that might yet prove temporary, to modify if not overthrow the image of human nature and the theory of the state based upon it that were postulated by the most shunned of English geniuses, Thomas Hobbes.

However, those who find 'Orwellian' useful may never have read *1984*, for the book has by now achieved the peculiarly mythological status of books which are known without necessarily being read. Big Brother and doublethink and the Thought Police exist in the public consciousness in a strange company that includes Don Quixote and Robinson Crusoe and certain authors who have themselves become myths, such as Kafka.

His 'mythic' reputation is not confined to the image of *1984*. *Animal Farm* too is a myth. A passenger suffering the murderous tedium and confusion of a congested airline terminal sees 'VIPs' ushered effortlessly through and murmurs, 'All passengers are equal but some passengers are more equal then others'. The egalitarian promises of a hundred revolutions have become the reality of privilege not removed but simply moved, from one group to another, and the slogans are glossed and rewritten to fit the new reality. Orwell's fable of the shrivelling of revolutionary promise is brilliantly encapsulated in the one line everyone knows, the 'single Commandment' that eventually replaces the seven that were first inscribed on the wall of the barn at Animal Farm.

To the mythic existences of *1984* and *Animal Farm* may be added a third myth, particularly in America: the myth of style. In 1971, the American National Council of the Teachers of English (NCTE) held a convention, passed resolutions, and appointed committees. One resolution was on 'Dishonest and Inhumane Uses of Language' (that is, 'commercial propaganda', or advertising); another dealt with 'the Relation of Language and Public Policy' (especially 'semantic distortion' by politicians, bureaucrats, and broadcasters). The committee to act on these resolutions was called the Committee on Public Doublespeak, a term coined on the analogy of Orwell's Newspeak and doublethink and chosen for its 'rich Orwellian overtones'. Orwell, indeed, was co-opted to serve this enterprise in several ways. The 'background' to the second resolution began: 'Most English teachers accept Orwell's point, in "Politics and the English Language", that language is often used as an instrument of social control.' Moreover, the Committee was reported to have invented an award, named after Orwell, to be given each year for the worst example of public doublespeak.

Orwell's iconic rôle in all this was consistently maintained. The Doublespeak Committee was largely a reaction to the war in Vietnam. A couple of years later Watergate came along to add a mountain of material. The NCTE published a book of essays, *Language and Public Policy*, to share its findings on such topics as 'Watergate Lingo: A Language of Non-Responsibility' and 'Mendacious Messages from Madison Avenue' and 'Ethics in Public Discourse'. Orwell is invoked throughout to sanctify the undertaking: 'Following in George Orwell's tradition . . .'; 'quoted Orwell's point that . . .'; 'Orwell's grim prediction . . .'.

It might be argued that this is solely an American myth of Orwell, dependent for its existence on a large academic industry— the teaching of essay-writing in colleges—and on the presence in every anthology used in composition classes of one particular essay by Orwell, 'Politics and the English Language'. Because of its captive audience of college students, this essay must be the most widely read in America of all of Orwell's works. But though in Britain 'Politics and the English Language', and its six rules of composition, often more ambiguous than they seem, does not have totem status, style is still important as an Orwell myth. Just as one 'knows' Big Brother and Newspeak and doublethink and that all animals are equal, so one 'knows' that good prose is like a window-pane, and that 'the present political chaos is connected with the decay of language, and that one can probably bring about some improvement by starting at the verbal end'. Orwell has become the patron of those who measure the decline of the West by the impurity of prose style.

From 'patron' to 'patron saint' has been a short step for Orwell. The greatest of the Orwellian myths is the myth of George Orwell himself, but this is only in part his own creation. Eric Blair created a literary self and called it 'George Orwell'. Orwell wrote, and when the subject was autobiographical he wrote about a man called Orwell, who may be defined as those parts of Eric Blair's existence that fitted Orwell's literary sensibility. Eric Blair, for instance, went to St Cyprian's School, Eastbourne, and Eton. George Orwell went to St Cyprian's, but never really went to Eton: since he hardly mentions Eton in his writing, that school is not a part of Orwell's life.

In the Introduction he supplied for the American edition of *Homage to Catalonia*, Lionel Trilling recalls a remark by one of his students about Orwell: 'he said suddenly in a very simple and matter of fact way, "He was a virtuous man".' The pleasure they found in this remark, says Trilling, came from its odd, archaic quality.

> We were glad to be able to say it about anybody. One doesn't have the opportunity very often. Not that there are not many men who are good, but there are few men who, in addition to being good, have the simplicity and sturdiness which allow us to say it about them, for somehow to say that a man 'is good,' or even to speak of a man who is 'virtuous,' is not the same thing as saying, 'He is a virtuous man.' By some quirk of the spirit of the language, the form of that sentence brings out the primitive meaning of the work virtuous, which is not merely moral goodness, but fortitude and strength.

This characteristically subtle meditation moves gracefully around a pair of terms not named. One is 'hero', the other 'saint'. The saint in fact is the refinement of the moral hero who conforms closest to Trilling's definition of 'simplicity and sturdiness and activity', and a quality of saintliness is certainly one element in Orwell's reputation.

Orwell's 'sainthood' or 'virtuousness' is bestowed upon him by others. There is no element of self-consciousness in it. (If there were, he would, of course, be immediately disqualified.) Yet it is not a negligible part of the Orwell mythology. His standing in our culture is a function of our admiration for his virtue, chiefly, I believe, because he practised a polemical trade, political writing, with full awareness of its temptations and weaknesses, and without hatred. He has a reputation for prophecy, yet he almost enjoys the failure of his predictions. 'How could I write such things?' he asked in 1944, continuing with an analysis of his failure. A characteristic utterance in *Homage to Catalonia* is: 'I warn everyone against my bias, and I warn everyone against my mistakes. Still, I have done my best to be honest.' His failure to be a good hater covered both the largest groups and individuals. He wrote several articles at the end of the war against vengeance on Germany ('Revenge is Sour', 'The Politics of Starvation') and in 1938 replied to a question from Stephen Spender. 'You ask how it is that I attacked you not having met you, and on the other hand changed my mind after meeting you.' Orwell confessed to using Spender as 'a symbol of the parlour Bolshie' and as 'a sort of fashionable successful person'. Not having met Spender, 'I could regard you as a type and also an abstraction'.

Even if when I met you I had not happened to like you, I should still have been bound to change my attitude, because when you meet anyone in the flesh you realize immediately that he is a human being and not a sort of caricature embodying certain ideas. It is partly for this reason that I don't mix much in literary circles, because I know from experience that once I have met and spoken to anyone I shall never again be able to show any intellectual brutality towards him, even when I feel I ought to, like the Labour MPs who get patted on the back by dukes and are lost forever more. (1/123)

Orwell quite often performed the duty of intellectual brutality, but all his work gives credibility to his statement that it was a duty he could perform only *in absentia*, so to speak. This is not saintliness. The best word for it is Orwell's ideal, *decency*, a concept that his work is dedicated to defining.

The myths of *1984*, of *Animal Farm*, and the myth of style are all matters on which Orwell's writing can itself be brought to comment—as it will later in this book. On saintliness the comment should be made at once.

'Reflections on Gandhi' was written in 1949, and has a typical opening sentence: 'Saints should always be judged guilty until they are proved innocent.' Sainthood is one theme of the essay. Orwell defines it and rejects it.

Orwell opposes the 'humanistic' attitude to the 'religious' one. In his terms, the humanistic belief is that 'Man is the measure of all things, and that our job is to make life worth living on this earth, which is the only earth we have'. Gandhi's teachings make sense 'only on the assumption that God exists and that the world of solid objects is an illusion to be escaped from'. Gandhi's asceticism and other-worldliness deter Orwell, but not so much as his rejection of close friendships and exclusive loves. These rejections are justified in Gandhi's eyes because loyalty to individuals can lead one into trouble, and love of humanity as a whole precludes giving preference to an individual.

This is sainthood, and this is why 'sainthood is . . . a thing that human beings must avoid'

The essence of being human is that one does not seek perfection, that one *is* sometimes willing to commit sins for the sake of loyalty, that one does not push asceticism to the point where it makes friendly intercourse impossible, and that one is prepared in the end to be defeated and broken up by life, which is the inevitable price of fastening one's love upon other human individuals. (4/133)

Orwell's sincerity: Homage to Catalonia

Orwell's reputation depends a great deal on his efforts to tell the truth, particularly in situations where competing versions of the truth were being sold noisily. His attempts to meet his own criterion of 'sincerity'—'The first thing that we ask of a writer is that he shall not tell us lies, that he shall say what he really thinks, what he really feels'—are so distinctive a part of his literary personality that it becomes easy to caricature him as Mr Valiant-for-Truth, self-righteous, complacent, and dogmatic. But really he was none of those things; he was no hero in his own eyes. He knew that the willingness to tell the truth will not necessarily produce it, and that personal observation and individual memory—on which he had to rely—were fallible tools. Yet progress may be made though perfection is unattainable, and Orwell had to keep trying.

His efforts lead those who study his works into some ancient thickets of difficulty. Orwell knew that a writer is most truthful when his art is most successful, yet the evident presence of his artistry raises at once the problem of 'documentary'. In documentary, where truthfulness is presumably the supreme value, the work of the artist's shaping hand apparently conflicts with truthfulness. If it can be shown, for instance, that the author has fused two separate incidents into one for artistic effect—meaning an increase in one kind of truth—then another kind of truthfulness, the basic adherence to what really happened, the aim of documentary, is inevitably impaired. And the problem is complicated further in that memory, and perhaps a writer's memory most of all, itself makes these 'artistic adjustments'. Stories become better in the telling, not always by an act of the will. In trying to legislate for such eventualities, the critic drifts among absurdities and impossibilities. Every reminiscence is suspect, and the better written ones most of all. It is easy to gather criteria to disprove the truth-telling ability of all autobiography since it is easy to show that all writing dependent on memory—or in the service of conviction, or fulfilling a purpose of interpretation—is a form of fiction. Indeed, the American novelist, Wright Morris, has defined fiction as 'anything processed by memory'.

Concern for truth, then, is a main strand in his literary character, and one which it is instructive to follow if one wishes to appreciate the distinctiveness of his work. *Homage to Catalonia* (1938) is a pivotal book in Orwell's career, since what he learned in Spain determined much of his future. The book is explicitly an attempt to tell the truth about the war in Orwell's experience, and the attempt pervades all aspects of the book. Two such aspects are

Spanish Civil War posters supporting the Republican cause

DEFENSAR MADRID
ES
DEFENSAR CATALUNYA

P.O.U.M
OBREROS ¡A LA
VICTORIA!

those of form, of the kind of book this was going to be, and historical accuracy, of *Homage to Catalonia* as a source document for the
historian.

'A BAD COPY OF 1914–18'   War had a large share in Orwell's experience before ever he thought of going to Spain. His last years at
St Cyprian's and part of his time at Eton passed during the First
World War, 1914–18. His father, though too old to be a combatant,
was an officer during the war, and Eric Blair served in the Officers'
Training Corps at school. His very first publication, in the *Henley
and South Oxfordshire Standard* in 1914, was a patriotic poem. His
service in the Burma Police was quasi-military, and many of his
fellow-officers were veterans of the First World War. Listening to
their talk, Orwell learned of the horrors of that war, but also heard
the speakers' 'steadily growing nostalgia'. Too young himself for
the war, he felt himself 'a little less than a man' because he had
missed it.

The paradox here is vivid but not analysed by Orwell. To have
missed the war was a matter of regret, yet the war as Orwell
described it was an experience no one could rationally desire. He
said he had been

> toting a rifle ever since I was ten, in preparation not only for war
> but for a particular kind of war, a war in which the guns rise to
> a frantic orgasm of sound, and at the appointed moment you
> clamber out of the trench, breaking your nails on the sandbags,
> and stumble across mud and wire into the machine-gun barrage.

This stereotype of trench warfare seemed to be reproduced by the
Spanish War.

> I am convinced that part of the reason for the fascination that
> the Spanish civil war had for people of about my age was that
> it was so like the Great War. At certain moments Franco was
> able to scrape together enough aeroplanes to raise the war to a
> modern level, and these were the turning-points. But for the rest
> it was a bad copy of 1914–18, a positional war of trenches,
> artillery, raids, snipers, mud, barbed wire, lice and stagnation.
> In early 1937 the bit of the Aragon front that I was on must have
> been very like a quiet sector in France in 1915. (1/168)

'Fascination' is an ambiguous term, but it certainly seems to imply
attraction. In his recorded reminiscences, Orwell suggests that at
least part of his desire to get into the Spanish War was owing to
the chance it gave him to share an experience for which he had
been too young in 1914. The more the war in Spain resembled the
First World War, the better. A 'bad copy of 1914–18' was better
than a really up-to-date war.

Orwell's Spain, 1936–1937

But the image that Orwell gives of the First World War is in reality drawn far less from his own memories, which were all of the 'home front', than from his reading of the memoirs of soldiers of that war. The flood of war books in the 1920s and 1930s comprised every conceivable attitude towards the conflict, but one particular viewpoint became dominant. This is the attitude that Orwell defined as characterizing all such memoirs.

> The books about the Great War were written by common soldiers or junior officers who did not even pretend to understand what the whole thing was about. Books like *All Quiet on the Western Front, Le Feu, A Farewell to Arms, Death of a Hero, Good-Bye to All That, Memoirs of an Infantry Officer*, and *A Subaltern on the Somme* were written not by propagandists but by *victims*. They are saying in effect, 'What the hell is all this about? God knows. All we can do is to endure.' (1/164/i)

Such books make no propaganda *for* war, but, despite Orwell's assertion, they make very effective propaganda against it. The soldier as victim is an ideological product quite as much as the glory of war. The attitude advanced by such books was understood by Orwell. '1914–18 was written off as a meaningless slaughter, and even the men who had been slaughtered were held to be in some way to blame.' Orwell by 1940 had accepted that this was a myth, but he knew too its power as a literary theme. The books of personal reminiscence about the war 'are the records of something completely meaningless, a nightmare happening in a void. That was not actually the truth about the war, but it was the truth about the individual reaction. The soldier advancing into a machine-gun barrage knew only that here was an appalling experience in which he was all but helpless.

The physical circumstances of the Spanish War seemed to reproduce those of 1914–18, and Orwell had his psychological reasons for wanting an experience as close as possible to that of the 1914–18 infantryman. He had absorbed the classic memoirs of that war, and when he came to write his own the stylistic, structural, and ideological patterns of the 'war book' were paradoxically those he expected to employ. As the book was written, however, it revealed to the reader and perhaps to Orwell himself a wide and startling divergence from the model in his mind's eye.

Homage to Catalonia begins, as so many of Orwell's writings do, with striking effectiveness. Orwell gives us one of his icons, an emblem that captures the great and essential meaning of an experience. He recalls meeting an Italian militiaman at the Lenin Barracks in Barcelona and taking an immediate liking to him. They exchanged a couple of words and the Italian, on leaving, 'gripped my hand very hard. Queer, the affection you can feel for a stranger! It was as though his spirit and mine had momentarily succeeded in bridging the gulf of language and tradition and meeting in utter intimacy.' He comments, to make the general point, 'One was always making contacts of that kind in Spain'. Orwell adds one sentence that seems to threaten disillusionment: 'But I also knew that to retain my first impression of him I must not see him again. . . .'

'War, to me', he writes from his reading in an older war, 'meant roaring projectiles and skipping shards of steel; above all it meant mud, lice, hunger, and cold.' Given that tuberculosis was in fact his deadly enemy, Orwell's dread of the cold was well founded, but the dread is formed in the style of the war memoir: 'the stand-to's in the grisly dawns, the long hours of sentry-go with a frosted rifle, the icy mud that would slop over my boot tops'. From this he turns to another 'horror', the quality of the troops with whom he marched. 'You cannot possibly conceive what a rabble we looked.' They had 'less cohesion than a flock of sheep', (the image was familiar after 1914) and many of the troops were boys of sixteen or less. Their shouts, 'meant to be war-like and menacing', were in fact 'as pathetic as the cries of kittens'.

This paragraph seems to prepare for a sequel in which these helpless troops will fulfil their destiny as victims, but no such sequel comes. Orwell has developed his pattern of incompetence and help-lessness as far as he can take it without damaging the truth, and the truth is that these troops were not victims at all.

Orwell's narrative at this point modulates into another key, and one which the predominance of 'helpless victim' motifs has not introduced. Orwell asks, 'Where are the enemy?' Someone points vaguely and Orwell gazes in vain through the spectacles of war books. 'According to my ideas of trench warfare the Fascists would be fifty or a hundred yards away. I could see nothing—seemingly their trenches were very well concealed.' Then, 'with a shock of dismay', he sees the enemy position on a hilltop seven hundred metres away. 'I was indescribably disappointed. We were nowhere near them! At that range our rifles were completely useless.' This is the disillusionment of the volunteer who finds that the war is not war enough, or perhaps that the literary image is inadequate to 'real life'.

The irony has turned upon the narrator himself, and his comic indignation at the war's failure to live up to its literary reputation is then deflated by a reminder that this is a real war nevertheless. Orwell despises the war. 'I made no attempt to keep my head below the level of the trench.' But a bullet flies past his ear and he ducks. 'All my life I had sworn that I would not duck the first time a bullet passed over me; but the movement appears to be instinctive, and almost everybody does it at least once.' It is virtually an apology. He has in effect planned this moment; he expects to be able to control his reactions; he has read the books. Yet still he ducks, for his literary preparation is inadequate. His body betrays him and eventually he is to learn, and is to make one of the big truths of his book, that the body is right.

In the war books, too, the comradeship and mutual love of the soldiers had been presented as the universal palliative for the horrors of the trenches. They soon discovered that they were fighting, not for the large abstractions—nation or liberty or glory—but for each other, those with whom they experienced the horrors. The war books rejected politics since politics had failed to justify the horrors, and found a smaller, compensatory meaning in love for fellow soldiers. Orwell quite deliberately places his vignette of the Italian militiaman at the very beginning of *Homage to Catalonia* to emphasize the importance for him of this element of loving friendship, but the emphasis is there for a still more important reason. Orwell departs from the model of the war book most of all in finding that comradeship has true political meaning.

Students of the war memoir as a genre classify such books as 'liberal' if they emphasize above everything else the horrors of war, and as 'conservative' if they place the human relationships fostered by the war above the horrors. By this criterion, *Homage to Catalonia* is clearly 'conservative'. (Just as surprisingly, it is finally a very happy book.) The community which the war opened to Orwell was perhaps the most cherished thing in his life. Such a friendship, in other words, was Socialism in action, and where the war memoir stressed friendship to make sense of experience when politics could not, Orwell's memoir makes friendship into politics. The cause for which he fought was the society, the *polis*, that he found in the trenches and which represented the new form of society he had found in Barcelona on his arrival there from England. That encounter—'I was breathing the air of equality'—was Orwell's experience of conversion, and in writing to Cyril Connolly he uses the language of the convert: 'I have seen wonderful things and at last really believe in Socialism. . . .'

Orwell's discovery of his political faith in the comradeship of the battlefield is somewhat disguised in *Homage to Catalonia* by the constant detestation with which he speaks there of 'politics'. This detestation goes so far as to suggest to Orwell that he can separate his account of the fighting from political matters by putting them into separate chapters. (It is a reflection of his own preferences that leads him to suggest that the reader, nauseated as Orwell is by politics, should 'skip' these chapters. The reader following the suggestion would read solely of the lesser horrors of war.) In effect, what Orwell really means by politics in *Homage to Catalonia* is betrayal. He meant that the society of the soldiers at the front, the Socialism of the trenches, was betrayed by the quarrels among the various parties that made up the Republican coalition. He felt obliged to give an account of these quarrels, but he did not enjoy writing it, and although he came to think that *Homage to Catalonia* was 'about the best book I have written', he believed to the end that the political chapters blemished the book. Actually, the political chapters were some of the best writing he ever did.

Setting out to put his memories of war into literary form, Orwell had believed that truth could be served by an adherence to what he considered some of the most truthful books of his time, the memoirs of the First World War. But the basic attitude of such memoirs—that the war was tragic, absurd, futile—did not fit his own experience, and so the form of his own book had to diverge from his model. In particular, the apoliticism of the First World War memoirs could not be sustained, since all the truths Orwell got from Spain were political ones, including the comradeship of the soldiers.

The genre to which *Homage to Catalonia* truly belongs was later defined by Orwell as the 'political book . . . a sort of enlarged pamphlet combining history with political criticism'. It had emerged during the last ten years (since 1913) and had become an important literary form. Orwell's list of authors of 'political books' includes Trotsky, Silone, Borkenau, and Koestler, but no English writer. There is no way of knowing whether Orwell realized that he had earned a place in the list.

Unofficial history

Victor Gollancz, who until then had published all of Orwell's books in Britain, refused *Homage to Catalonia* even before it was written because he did not agree with its politics. Secker and Warburg published the book, but most of the reviews that treated it at any length denounced it as a defence of Trotskyite and anarchist traitors to the cause of the Spanish Republic. It sold 'damm all'. In 1938, therefore, Orwell's readers were few and mostly hostile, but it is a paradox of a familiar kind in Orwell's career that *Homage to Catalonia* is now, in the English-speaking world at least, the only memoir of the Spanish War widely popular and still read. It is the single book people are most likely to have read on the subject, giving Orwell surprising prominence as an authority on the war. It is a prominence, however, that does not imperil his reputation, for *Homage to Catalonia* in great measure attains Orwell's ambition for it. He said of the group of authors he named as writing the 'political book' that they were trying to write 'contemporary history, but *unofficial* history, the kind that is ignored in the text-books and lied about in the newspapers'. Such history waits for the later historian, what Orwell called the 'liberal historian . . . one who believes that the past cannot be altered and that a correct knowledge of history is valuable as a matter of course'.

The judgement of liberal historians on *Homage to Catalonia* does not, of course, give us absolute truth. No such truth is finally attainable, and in any case the Spanish War is still a divisive and emotional event. Most of the contemporary books about the war are distorted by propaganda. After his de-conversion from Communism, for instance, Arthur Koestler rejected the first half of *Spanish Testament* (retaining the account of his imprisonment, *Dialogue with Death*) because he could then admit that it was propaganda. Orwell was particularly sensitive to the weaknesses of his subjective point of view and warns against it all through his book. In the event, however, *Homage to Catalonia* emerges as one of the least distorted of the Spanish War books, and the historians' reliance on it is extensive.

Orwell's account of life in the Republican militias is universally accepted as accurate and is often drawn upon by the historians of the fighting. Here Orwell's style, with its awareness of the First World War memoirs, assures the historian that Orwell is seeing with his own eyes, that there is no romantic haze distorting things. His account of the night raid on the Fascist trenches, for instance, would have been less convincing had it been written in the style actually employed in a dispatch to the *New Leader*: '"Charge" shouted Blair . . . . In front of the parapet was Eric Blair's tall figure, coolly strolling forward through the storm of fire. He leapt at the parapet, then stumbled. Hell, had they got him? No, he was over . . .' (Stansky and Abrahams).

The skilful realism Orwell himself employed conforms to modern attitudes to war. It is impossible to doubt, given this style, that Orwell is reporting accurately. Sober realism, however, is not sufficient when the investigation moves from life in the militias to the political meaning of events, and especially the events of the 'May days' in Barcelona in which Orwell was caught up. Raymond Carr calls this 'that treacherous frontier where direct observation borders on political analysis', and the historians agree that on this territory Orwell shows some weakness, largely because for this task direct observation needed supplementing by something like academic study. This difference in effectiveness in moving from direct observation to political analysis is, I take it, why Hugh Thomas calls *Homage to Catalonia* 'a better book about war itself than about the Spanish war'.

Thomas and Raymond Carr are two 'liberal historians' who have examined Orwell's 'unofficial history' and have passed judgement on it. Both identify certain failings of Orwell.

Thomas, in a footnote to Orwell's 'Notes on the Spanish Militias' (1/126), lists a number of errors Orwell made about the composition and alliances of the alphabet soup of parties and unions in Republican Spain. Thomas's chapter in *The Spanish Civil War* on the Barcelona troubles occasionally shows that Orwell relied too much on his own observation. He insisted, for instance, that no artillery was used during the fighting, but Thomas records an occasion when it was. These failings are all attributable to what is generally the strength of Orwell's book, its individualism. The memoir can contribute invaluably to the history, but a historian needs more eyes than his own; no memoirist can see the whole picture and becomes untrustworthy when he forgets that fact.

Raymond Carr's critique of *Homage to Catalonia* as history concentrates on Orwell's failures of judgement rather than on his errors of fact.

However, errors of judgement are not exactly untruths, and what historians' critiques of *Homage to Catalonia* show is the limitation of sincerity. Orwell in his book tells us what he truly believed, and we see that he was sometimes wrong, albeit for the best of reasons—loyalty to the POUM militia and the desire to right the injustice they suffered. After he had finished the book, Orwell continued to think about the Spanish War, and subsequently wrote several articles about it. These show that he found himself in a half-articulated dilemma over the POUM 'line'. His emotions pulled him one way and reason tugged against them. Thus, in a letter to Frank Jellinek, who had written a book on the Spanish War from a Communist angle, he was able to admit that sympathy for the POUM had led him into distortion:

> Actually I have given a more sympathetic account of the POUM 'line' than I actually felt, because I always told them they were wrong and refused to join the party. But I had to put it as sympathetically as possible, because it has had no hearing in the capitalist press and nothing but libels in the left-wing press. Actually, considering the way things have gone in Spain, I think there was something in what they said, though no doubt their way of saying it was tiresome and provocative in the extreme. (1/145)

This statement is Orwell's admission of some insincerity in the writing of *Homage to Catalonia*. Later reflection had allowed him to remember his differences with the POUM which his anger at injustice had buried while he was writing the book.

The statement to Jellinek cannot apply, however, to the POUM belief that effective opposition to Fascism could be mounted only by Socialist militancy, and (as a corollary) that 'capitalist' or 'bourgeois' democracy was essentially the same thing as Fascism. Orwell committed himself to belief in these POUMist ideas for quite a while longer, until after the outbreak of the Second World War.

The Spanish Civil War was the supreme test for the truth-telling power of any political writer of the 1930s. *Homage to Catalonia* satisfies Orwell's demand for sincerity but reveals as it does so that sincerity was not quite enough. The truth included the measurement of desire against actuality, of 'ought' against 'is', and that aspect of Orwell's book shows some weakness. He knew it himself, but the realization took a long time to emerge. If one supplements *Homage to Catalonia* with the essays and letters Orwell wrote a little later about the war, particularly 'Looking Back on the Spanish War', then one can award him the title of 'liberal historian'. The accent is unmistakable.

> The Trotskyist thesis that the war could have been won if the revolution had not been sabotaged was probably false. To nationalise factories, demolish churches, and issue revolutionary manifestos would not have made the armies more efficient. The Fascists won because they were stronger; they had modern arms and the others hadn't. No political strategy could offset that. (2/41/vi)

4 Attitudes, beliefs, and ideas

'. . . a writer's political and religious beliefs are not excrescences to be laughed away, but something that will leave their mark even on the smallest detail of his work' (2/43).

Cyril Connolly once said that Orwell 'could not blow his nose without moralising about conditions in the handkerchief industry'. This offers us an obsessive bore, and no doubt to anyone only intermittently on his wave-length, Orwell could and can be a bore. Yet Connolly's sneer also points to a most characteristic truth about Orwell: his ability to perceive the politics of everyday life, the political aspects of conditions usually thought apolitical. He had a remarkable ability to see how the varied manifestations of a culture took part in the evolution of political ideas, how they were part of a political debate, and his best writing investigates the form and extent of this interplay.

He was not, however, an *a priori* theorist. His friends have reported that he could be expected to state abruptly odd generalizations of a political sort: 'All tobacconists are Fascists', or some such poser. But these were the green fruit of his habit of pondering his experience—of tobacconists, in this case—for the laws to explain what he had seen. Orwell was not the kind of dogmatist who undertakes in advance to prove that anything—from the design of buses to the Albigensian heresy—is the product of Communist conspiracy or capitalist exploitation. But it is true that political thinking was his basic method, and the account of his attitudes, beliefs, and ideas that follows is organized to reflect that fact. What should emerge is indicated by Paul Fussell Jr, in introducing a volume of his own essays: 'I am persuaded by the performance of George Orwell that literary, cultural, social, ethical and political commentary can be virtually the same thing . . . .'

Human relationships

If one thinks of *1984* in terms of its literary kinships, not its 'sources' but those works it resembles in its basic events, one discovers that it begins like *Romeo and Juliet* and ends like the Grand Inquisitor episode from Dostoevsky's *The Brothers Karamazov*. (In the middle, of course, there is a brilliant parody in essay form: Goldstein's book.) Romeo and Juliet, to focus on the basic relationship of the book, fall in love with the wrong people—each other—violating certain arrangements society has made and which, as a quite inci-

61

dental effect, make their love unacceptable to society. Winston and Julia also provoke the hostility of their society by loving each other, but they are not punished for choosing the wrong persons, as are Romeo and Juliet. In Oceania, love itself is the crime. Love is the greatest private experience, 'a world of its own', and therefore the Party, dedicated to controlling the lives of its subjects, must control it—and consequently eliminate it. A further and more important reason is that the Party has a use for the thwarted sex instinct: 'sexual privation induced hysteria, which was desirable because it could be transformed into war fever and leader worship.' The embrace of Winston and Julia is therefore 'a political act'.

Orwell's thinking about politics is the main intellectual strand of his life. He belongs undoubtedly to the very group he most frequently attacked, the left-wing intelligentsia. Yet 'political thinker' as it applies to Orwell is a problematical term, demanding definition. He came from, and never questioned, the British empirical tradition. In the philosophical sense, he was no idealist. Political theory interested him for its actual or potential effect on people's lives, meaning that for Orwell political theory had to have dramatic potential. He said once that he was not really a novelist, but even if we agree with that, it is still impossible to deny that he saw the ideas of politics as human arrangements, setting out the relationships between people and that he wrote only about real people. He pointed out in the English a 'lack of philosophical faculty', defined as 'the absence in nearly all Englishmen of any need for an ordered system of thought or even for the use of logic'. (2/17/iii) This is nearly a good description of Orwell himself. He was no systematizer and certainly not one who would go wherever logic led, since human life to him was not supremely logical. When he performs the type of task that is routine for a political intellectual, such as differentiating patriotism from nationalism, he is always efficient but often conveys an air of uneasiness until he can refer the concepts he is discussing to the lives of people.

Orwell as a 'political thinker', therefore, has more in common with a reporter than with a professor. In Alex Zwerdling's words, 'His distrust of ideology motivated him to test all theories against his own feelings, and against the reality of other people's lives.' Politics for him took human form. Winston and Julia's 'political act' is rendered political by the structure of their society. It is the proper function of politics, in fact, to refrain from 'politicizing' such a relationship, for politics must have limits, since the state in which no such limits exist is totalitarian. On the other hand, some of the limits set for politics in Orwell's day and ours had to be brushed aside, for to accept them signified complicity in human degradation. Orwell's picture of the woman struggling to unblock the wastepipe in *The Road to Wigan Pier* is a call to political action.

She knew well enough what was happening to her—understood as well as I did how dreadful a destiny it was to be kneeling there in the bitter cold, on the slimy stones of a slum backyard, poking a stick up a foul drain-pipe. (I)

The political theory that has nothing to say about this existence is wasting Orwell's time.

Colonialism

His more than four years' service as a policeman in Burma was enormously useful to Orwell. If he had written, like Maxim Gorky, a book called *My Universities*, the Imperial Indian Police would have had a large part in it. The experience taught Orwell about himself, gave him the subjects for a full-length novel and two of his most impressive essays, and shaped one of the permanent strands of his personal belief.

The developments of the Burma years were highly complex ones. Orwell's writings record the problems, amounting at times to anguish, of a young man who increasingly finds himself in an impossible situation, doing a job he cannot believe in, everywhere pressured to conform while growing steadily more non-conformist in his own mind.

Orwell used the terms 'imperialism' and 'colonialism' interchangeably. For him the motive of empire was simply greed. Colonies existed for the material advantage of the colonial power, and the ideological and institutional superstructure of colonialism rested on that sole foundation. He described the British and French empires as 'in essence nothing but mechanisms for exploiting cheap coloured labour' (1/155). The British despotism in Burma 'clothes itself in a mask of democracy' which (in 1929) seemed to achieve its purpose, since the British were not then unpopular. 'The English have constructed roads and canals—in their own interests, sure enough, but the Burmese have profited from them—they have built hospitals, opened schools, and maintained national order and security.' Ultimately, however, the British are in Burma to rob the Burmese: 'if the English have rendered any service to Burma, it has had to pay for it very dear.'

The brutal economic facts of empire remained an important element in Orwell's thinking when he became a Socialist. The peculiar satisfaction, almost glee, that he derived from the rôle of loyal opponent of the Left was stimulated by his reminders to his fellow Socialists of the imperial facts he claimed they forgot all too easily. 'What we always forget is that the overwhelming bulk of the British proletariat does not live in Britain, but in Asia and Africa.' In fact, there are two classes of proletariat.

The European peoples, and especially the British, have long owed their high standard of life to direct or indirect exploitation of the coloured peoples. This relationship has never been made clear by official Socialist propaganda, and the British worker, instead of being told that, by world standards, he has been living above his income, has been taught to think of himself as an overworked, downtrodden slave. (4/88)

Quite largely, indeed, the workers were won over to Socialism by being told that they were exploited, whereas the brute truth was that, in world terms, they were exploiters. (4/108)

The paradox of the British proletariat on the backs of the proletariat of the empire was what Orwell called 'the essential hypocrisy of the British labour movement'.

The attitude of the so-called left-wing in England and France over this imperialism business simply sickens me . . . the working class in England and France have absolutely no feeling of solidarity with the coloured working class. (1/46)

The issue of the empire, in fact, helped determine Orwell's original allegiance to the Left and simultaneously established him as the critic inside the movement.

The reductive definition of empires as 'mechanisms for exploiting cheap coloured labour' is projected into *1984*. Orwell united his view of empire with his observation of conditions in Europe in 1942.

The forced-labour camps all over Europe and North Africa where Poles, Russians, Jews and political prisoners of every race toil at road-making or swamp-draining for their bare rations, are simple chattel slavery. The most one can say is that the buying and selling of slaves by individuals is not yet permitted. (2/41)

Goldstein's book depicts the three superstates contesting by war the possession of

a rough quadrilateral with its corners at Tangier, Brazzaville, Darwin and Hong Kong, containing within it about a fifth of the population of the earth . . . . a bottomless reserve of cheap labour . . . . The inhabitants of these areas, reduced more or less openly to the status of slaves, pass continually from conqueror to conquerer, and are expended like so much coal or oil . . . .

This is totalitarian imperialism, the monster offspring of ugly parents.

In correspondence with F. Tennyson Jesse, whose book on Burma ('written from the angle of . . . benevolent imperialism') he had reviewed, Orwell pointed out her two great omissions, which were in fact his two great criticisms of imperialism. 'Nothing about the economic milching of the country ... nor about the disgusting social behaviour of the British till very recently.' (4/32) 'Disgusting social behaviour' may sound nannyish, but to understand Orwell it is important to see how vital this was to him. By social behaviour he meant—in the broadest and most elevated meaning of the term—manners, the system of signals by which the members of a culture claim and award status, signify acceptance or rejection, esteem themselves and others. Orwell found that he believed in a code of manners that was essentially democratic and egalitarian. The very fabric of imperialism, however, enforced unmannerly acts.

Orwell's *Burmese Days* is a novel of the bad manners of empire. The British class system has been modified by grafting onto it systematic racial discrimination. As Jeffrey Meyers has observed, *Burmese Days* is Forster's *A Passage to India* with all the possibilities of decency and niceness squeezed out, for Orwell saw nothing to redeem British conduct in Burma. The imperial arrangement works to heighten every possibility of abrasion and nastiness. All parties are affected. Orwell recalled an incident when his ship docked at Colombo:

> One of the coolies had got hold of a long tin uniform-case and was carrying it so clumsily as to endanger people's heads. Someone cursed at him for his carelessness. The [white] police sergeant looked round, saw what the man was doing, and caught him a terrific kick on the bottom that sent him staggering across the deck. Several passengers, including women, murmured their approval. (Crick, p. 79)

To Orwell this was a symptomatic occurrence. Force and brutality were in his view the basis of all political and social relationships under imperialism (a diagnosis, incidentally, as violently repudiated by his fellow colonial servants as his account of his schooldays was by some of his schoolfellows). He discovered that a policeman saw the essentials of the imperial system up close and undistorted by cant. And what the policeman saw was ugly indeed.

> The wretched prisoners squatting in the reeking cages of the lock-ups, the grey cowed faces of the long term convicts, the scarred buttocks of the men who had been flogged with bamboos, the women and children howling when their menfolk were led away under arrest—things like these are beyond bearing when you are in any way directly responsible for them. (*Road to Wigan Pier*, IX)

This is the repudiation of the exercise of power whose origins we examined earlier. Orwell for a while even believed that all government was evil and that the policeman is not a necessary element ('sentimental nonsense'). But he could not continue to be a policeman himself because he always identified himself with those arrested. 'I never went into a jail without feeling (most visitors to jails feel the same) that my place was on the other side of the bars.' (Most visitors, I suspect, don't feel the same, but Orwell's assumption is highly characteristic.)

'Disgusting social behaviour' moreover, enveloped all who lived under the system. The Burmese reflected British attitudes. 'No one had the guts to raise a riot, but if a European woman went through the bazaars alone, somebody would probably spit betel juice all over her dress.' As Bernard Crick has remarked, 'Orwell's way of championing the Burmese was not to idealize them but to say, like Mark Twain, 'God damn the Jews, they are as bad as the rest of us!'

Orwell knew in 1936 that the British empire was dying; he knew, too, that it was 'a great deal better than the younger empires that are going to supplant it', but having seen it from the inside, so that it pressed agonizingly on his own deep repugnance towards power, he never had a good word to say for it. In fact his attitude grew harder. In 1938 and 1939, Orwell was in Marrakech in French Morocco for his health. His essay 'Marrakech' is a series of vignettes of colonialism, with the prominent theme of dehumanization. All colonial empires, he declared, were built on the difficulty of seeing the black or brown masses as human beings.

> Are they really the same flesh as yourself? Do they even have names? Or are they merely a kind of undifferentiated brown stuff? . . . They rise out of the earth, they sweat and starve for a few years, and then they sink back into the nameless mounds of the graveyard and nobody notices that they are gone. And even the graves themselves soon fade back into the soil. Sometimes, out for a walk, . . . you notice that it is rather bumpy underfoot, and only a certain regularity in the bumps tells you that you are walking over skeletons. (1/153)

'When the white man turns tyrant it is his own freedom that he destroys.' That is the lesson of 'Shooting an Elephant'. The destruction of colonialism will restore to the white man the freedom not to walk on skeletons.

'The terribly difficult issue of class'

The single most important element in the formation of Orwell's political character is his reaction to the class system. Nothing else approaches its power over his emotions, in strength or in duration. Had his reaction to class differences been even slightly less intense or of some other formation, he would have been a markedly

Orwell in Marrakech, 1938

different person and writer. Orwell's Burma writings show colonialism as the class system sharply modified—worsened—by racism. *The Road to Wigan Pier* discusses class extensively. *Homage to Catalonia* gives Orwell's reactions to discovering a classless society and to witnessing its erosion. Class was always on his mind; it led him to Socialism, basically because he believed that Socialism would produce 'a world of free and equal human beings', where no one would call another his master. There was never a moment of conversion to this view; Orwell believed it throughout his life as a writer.

Obviously, so passionately held a belief had to have powerful psychological propulsion, but it seems now impossible to recover it. It is clear that Orwell followed the pattern of those social rebels who attack the class system, in whatever form they encounter it, not because they are its victims but because they are its beneficiaries. Orwell was not born to any great social advantage, except that his middle-class parents were determined that he should do as well as he could out of the system. Had he shared their ambition, there is no reason why he should not have gone from his Eton scholarship, which gave him very good social connections, to Oxford or Cambridge and then to some position of establishment power. At Eton he began to rebel, simply by being somewhat lazy, against the regimen of the scholarship boy, and began looking with interest at those who stood much lower than him in the social caste system. The very first letter in *The Collected Essays, Journalism and Letters*, when he was a schoolboy of seventeen, describes 'my *first* adventure as an amateur tramp' (my italics). On leaving school, he took the rather unusual road into the Burma Police, and on returning to Europe he bore no trace of any socially conventional ambition. His great preoccupation at this stage seems to have been to 'reclassify' himself by plunging from time to time into the world of tramps, doss-houses, and casual labour. Orwell tells us that this plunge was as much a physical compulsion as a moral one. He had to overcome resistance imposed on him by his own class background to physical proximity with lower-class people. This 'reclassifying' preceded by some time a political understanding of the class system. His Socialism was a response—quite a lagging response—to his class-consciousness, and class-consciousness underlies his whole political development. He called it 'this perpetual uneasiness between man and man', a curse and a nuisance, and for him it was the great motive force.

In the last decade of his life, the obsession with the 'Russian myth' and totalitarianism dominated Orwell's mind and it is true, too, that he had by then achieved a condition of stability and confidence for himself on the issue of class. His writings no longer present it as a primary concern. But its underlying importance is unchanged. In *Animal Farm*, revolution to overthrow a class system leads to the creation of a new one. In *1984*, class distinctions, especially between Party and proles, are institutionalized as never before. These books dramatize in their own ways what was for Orwell the single most revealing and most condemnatory fact about Soviet society:

> the so-called collectivist systems now existing only try to wipe out the individual because they are *not* really collectivist and certainly not egalitarian—because, in fact, they are a sham covering a new form of class privilege.

In *1984*, one of the shoots of hope for Winston and Julia is the moment, on their introduction to the Inner Party quarters of O'Brien (Part Two, VIII) when he reveals that his manservant, Martin, is one of the conspiracy. He sits down with them, and that too is a 'political act'.

'I have no talent for acting. I cannot, for instance, disguise may accent.'

One surprising aspect of Orwell's reclassification of himself is its relation to his prose style, for it shows that the famous Orwell style was not an invariable possession, and that his earliest attempts to write about his plunge into the sub-world of tramps and the underclass produced a style which seems to indicate some acute problems of self-presentation and social discomfort.

Two pieces published in the *Adelphi* in 1931 (both over the name of Eric A. Blair) were 'The Spike' (April) and 'A Hanging' (August). Orwell's account of the execution he attended in Burma is much anthologized, generally accepted as an example of the characteristic virtues of his prose, in particular clarity, directness, and a total freedom from mannerism. 'The Spike', however, is quite another thing. Its subject matter—an overnight stay in a workhouse—is mainstream Orwell, but the style differs radically from that of 'A Hanging'. The tramps have to strip for a medical inspection.

> No one can imagine, unless he has seen such a thing, what pot-bellied, degenerate curs we looked. Shock heads, hairy, crumpled faces, hollow chests, flat feet, sagging muscles—every kind of malformation and physical rottenness were [sic] there. All were flabby and discoloured, as all tramps are under their deceptive sunburn. Two or three figures seen there stay ineradicably in my mind. Old 'Daddy' aged seventy-four, with his truss, and his red, watering eyes: a herring-gutted starveling, with sparse beard and sunken cheeks, looking like the corpse of Lazarus in some primitive picture: an imbecile, wandering hither and thither with vague giggles, coyly pleased because his trousers constantly

Down and out in Paris (above) and in London (below)

slipped down and left him nude. But few of us were greatly better than these; there were not ten decently built men among us, and half, I believe, should have been in hospital. (1/11)

What jars most in this is the word 'we'. Orwell puts himself into the picture but every other feature of the style distances him from the tramps. The style, in fact, unites Orwell (or Blair) over the heads of the tramps with a reader who can appreciate the cultivated allusions. Terms such as 'degenerate curs' and 'decently built men' create exactly the *de haut en bas* attitude that Orwell inveighs against in *The Road to Wigan Pier* when discussing Socialist literature: 'always completely removed from the working class in idiom and manner of thought'. It is not that the style here should be 'proletarian', whatever that means, but that it should not connote rejection and separation by the author, since he seems really to want acceptance and union. The style, in fact, carries a political message quite against the thematic current of the piece. It produces a strong impression of insincerity, 'the worst thing we can say about a work of art'.

The difference between 'The Spike' and 'A Hanging' is not that in four months or so Orwell got better as a stylist. His attitudes in 'A Hanging' indicate a confidence in his analysis of his Burma experience which is not present in his relations with the tramps. He explains in *The Road to Wigan Pier* (IX) how his association with the tramps was a necessary assuaging of the guilt he brought back from Burma and from all his past, but he also says, 'I was still half afraid of the working class. I wanted to get in touch with them, I even wanted to become one of them, but I still thought of them as alien and dangerous.' That fear produced the style of 'The Spike'. Anyone who thinks Orwell was incapable of really bad prose should read it.

Orwell used much of 'The Spike' in *Down and Out in Paris and London*, but made changes. Here is the later version of the passage quoted above.

You cannot conceive what ruinous, degenerate curs we looked, standing there in the merciless morning light. A tramp's clothes are bad, but they conceal far worse things; to see him as he really is, unmitigated, you must see him naked. Flat feet, pot bellies, hollow chests, sagging muscles—every kind of physical rottenness was there. Nearly everyone was undernourished, and some clearly diseased; two men were wearing trusses, and as for the old mummy-like creature of seventy-five, one wondered how he could possibly make his daily march. Looking at our faces, unshaven and creased from the sleepless night, you would have thought that all of us were recovering from a week on the drink.

These stylistic changes represent shifts of attitude. Orwell is less fastidious; he has moved closer to the tramps, and—paradoxically—he has done it by eliminating 'I' and by generality, focusing not on named individuals but on classes and categories: 'Nearly everyone was undernourished.' The closing of the gap between narrator and tramps permits compassion. The mercilessness of the earlier description moves from the narrator himself and is now a quality of the light. What it reveals, the narrator must report. Greater intimacy with the reader—'you'—softens the attitude to the tramps. 'Daddy', a year older, is still rather repulsive, 'a mummy-like creature', but now 'one wondered' how he managed the walking. Most strikingly, the 'herring-gutted starveling', Lazarus's corpse, and the imbecile have all gone. The new conclusion, 'a week on the drink', is feeble, perhaps misplaced humour. Generally, however, the shift in style is a reduction of the class defensiveness displayed by Orwell's earlier prose on this topic. The changes help us to see that the really characteristic 'Orwell style' embodies an important attitude to life. This is not yet 'windowpane prose' but it is moving that way, and as Orwell later said about political change, 'It is always the *direction* that counts'.

Socialism

'To the vast majority of people Socialism means a classless society, or it means nothing at all.'

'I belong to the Left and must work inside it', he wrote in 1945. The statement sounds firm and obvious, but in fact it demands extensive qualification. The only political party that Orwell ever actually belonged to was the symptomatically named Independent Labour Party (from June 1938 until early in the war). He did march with the Left, but he was usually out of step and often headed in a different direction. As a Socialist he renounced Marx, Lenin, Trotsky and Stalin. (Clement Attlee reminded him of 'a recently dead fish'.) Yet he was quite sincere in his loyalty to the Left, and it is impossible to believe that, if he had lived long enough, he would have become a Conservative. He was a genuine radical, an opponent of orthodoxy (from the Greek, 'right thinking') but he included in his opposition the orthodoxy of the Left. He was, as so many have perceived, the Left's loyal opposition.

A familiar sequence in political lives is the transformation of the youth of middle-class conservative origins into a leftist firebrand. The political change is often followed by a cultural reformation, 'proletarianization', whereby James becomes Jim and lunch dinner. In Orwell's case, as we have seen, the cultural change took pre-eminence. He adopted Socialism as a programme to bring about for society as a whole the kind of change in human relationships that he had made for himself in his own life. His Socialist proposals are 'necessary safeguards against the reappearance of a class system'. It is important to note this reversal of the usual order of events. Orwell's emotions were most deeply invested, not in ideas or in dogma, but in the relations between people.

The Road to Wigan Pier (1937) and *Homage to Catalonia* (1938) incorporate the stages of Orwell's commitment to Socialism. Besides its description of working-class life in the North, *The Road to Wigan Pier* is a political autobiography, and a pained enquiry into the cultural failure of British Socialism in the thirties, by which is meant the failure of Socialist intellectuals to cross the cultural barriers that separated them from the working classes. Orwell himself could be nothing but a Socialist intellectual. The style of Socialist intellectuals, however, disgusted him, since it seemed to heighten the class barriers that the policies of Socialism were designed to destroy. If you argued for Socialism but showed—by your speech, your amusements, your dress, your diet, by every cultural manifestation—that you were not of those with whom you claimed alliance, then to Orwell you were undermining the cause. There is a tone of hysteria and anguish in the book because Orwell knew that, despite the sympathy with which he went and was received, he could never be of the working class, yet he fully understood and shared the 'temperamental conservatism' that recoiled from representatives of Socialism, the intellectuals, his own group, who seemed, in working class eyes, to be cranks and prigs, the fruit-juice drinkers, nudists, sandal-wearers, sex-maniacs, Quakers, Nature cure quacks, pacifists, and feminists against whom he rants in the book. In *The Road to Wigan Pier*, Orwell is a Socialist without a home (and Wigan Pier itself turns out not to exist). His vigorous assertions that Socialism is 'a way out' and 'elementary common sense' sound a little hollow when he raises his voice in frustration at Socialism's self-imposed handicaps, its awful image.

Hysteria and hollowness disappeared in Spain. 'I have seen wonderful things and at last really believe in Socialism, which I never did before.' (1/99) His involvement in the Spanish Civil War provided exactly the experiences he had failed to find on the road to Wigan Pier, the experiences he needed to be able to rest confidently on his belief in Socialism. Revolutionary Barcelona was the city of his dreams. 'It was the first time that I had ever been in a town where the working class was in the saddle .... Above all, there was a belief in the revolution and the future, a feeling of having suddenly emerged into an era of equality and freedom. Human beings were trying to behave as human beings and not as cogs in the capitalist machine.' (1) He was overwhelmed by the style and manners of the revolution. The discovery that a lot of it was pretence—the middle classes posing as proletarian revolutionaries—did not disillusion him. What he first saw was how a truly egalitarian society would work. His time in the trenches, fighting with the POUM militia, only confirmed that belief, and here there was no pretence. 'The Spanish militias, while they lasted, were a sort of microcosm of a classless society.' Those months 'formed a kind of interregnum in my life, quite different from anything that had gone before and perhaps from anything that is to come, and they taught me things that I could not have learned in any other way . . . . one was experiencing a foretaste of Socialism, by which I mean that the prevailing mental atmosphere was that of Socialism'.

In the development of his ideas, Orwell's Spanish experience is the single greatest formative influence. Ideas important in *1984* and *Animal Farm*, for instance, have their origins there. But the most important effect of the Spanish engagement was confidence that Socialism could work, that it would produce 'a world of free and equal human beings', and that Orwell himself had a place in it. In the dozen or so years of life that remained to him, he asked a lot of hard questions about Socialism, particularly about the record of institutions calling themselves Socialist. Such criticism was part of the rôle he gave himself. But however painfully he probed, he never moved from the Left. Spain gave him the assurance to stay, the picture of the future to hope for.

Socialist measures will realize for Orwell the great ends of liberty, equality, and fraternity, or in Orwell's own formulation, 'political democracy, social equality, and internationalism' (4/46). Such a world would be that of democratic Socialism. This was Orwell's dream, his ideal picture of the future, his political ambition. Yet he was firmly unutopian, never believing that his ideal would be quickly or easily achieved—and, I suspect, aware that it might never be achieved.

The measures Orwell advocated as possible means to his end of democratic Socialism apply basically, of course, to British conditions. Democratic Socialism in one country is the subject of *The Lion and the Unicorn: Socialism and the English Genius* (1941), a typically individual and—insofar as its predictions are concerned—often erroneous pamphlet which later gave Orwell the opportunity for some rather gleeful self-correction. Part of the pamphlet is a list of Orwell's suggestions for 'the people's war aims', a programme that would turn the Second World War into a 'people's war'. The six items include three relating to overseas affairs (freedom for India, the creation of what came to be called the Commonwealth, and a rather vague or symbolic 'Declaration of formal alliance with

China, Abyssinia and all other victims of the Fascist powers'). The three referring to England are fascinating in relation to the actual accomplishments of the post-war Labour Government.

Orwell wanted:

1 nationalization of land, mines, railways, banks, and major industries;

2 limitation of incomes on such a scale that the highest taxfree [presumably he meant gross or pre-tax] income in Britain does not exceed the lowest by more than ten to one;

3 reform of the educational system along democratic lines.

Nationalization was less thoroughgoing after the war than Orwell had proposed, and certainly was insufficient to bring about his desired end. He wanted enough nationalization to do away with 'the class of mere owners. . . . State-ownership implies, therefore, that nobody shall live without working'. Land should be nationalized, though some land ownership (limited at the most to fifteen acres, outside cities) would be allowed. Orwell believed that agriculture could continue with the farmers, when competent, continuing as salaried managers. The optimism of these projections is not their point. Orwell advocated them as a means to an end. 'From the moment that all productive goods have been declared the property of the State, the common people will feel, as they cannot feel now, that the State *is themselves* . . . the dominance of a single class will have been broken.'

The limitation of incomes was proposed to serve the same end. A maximum normal variation of ten to one would set limits within which 'some sense of equality is possible. A man with £3 a week and a man with £1500 a year *can feel themselves fellow creatures*, which the Duke of Westminster and the sleepers on the Embankment benches cannot' (my italics). (Bernard Crick points out that if Orwell really meant his ten to one differential to be one of tax-free income, then 'his amateur economics did not match his amateur sociology—this would have been a far more stratified society than the one he lived in'.)

Educational reform was to be principally an attack on public schools, 'festering centres of snobbery', and, most emphatically (shades of St Cyprian's) on 'private' schools: 'the vast majority of them deserve nothing except suppression.' Orwell wanted 'a democratic educational system', and his proposal for getting it was to abolish those aspects which his own experience had shown to be undemocratic. Apart from a suggestion of 'flooding' the older universities and public schools 'with State-aided pupils chosen simply on grounds of ability', there is no evidence of real thinking about educational reform. He saw the educational system as a manifestation of class divisiveness, and that was what he wanted to change.

The means Orwell offered, then, to his end of Socialism concentrate on destroying the hierarchical aspects of British society. Orwell quite openly intended some of them as gestures—'We need gestures as well as actions'—and he says nothing about the measures that in fact combined to produce the post-war Labour Government's principal achievement: the Welfare State. That this was a conscious choice and not merely inadvertence or naiveté is shown by a recollection of T. R. Fyvel's. In 1946, Fyvel had to talk Orwell out of writing a column in *Tribune* attacking the Labour Government and Orwell's friend, Aneurin Bevan.

> If they as socialists had really wanted to change British society, they should have done three things: abolish the public schools, abolish all titles and abolish the House of Lords. He wanted to say that instead Bevan had let himself be diverted into enlarging the National Health Service and the public housing sector and into measures of nationalization—all well and good but these were administrative reforms and so largely bureaucratic and not tackling the basic inequalities of British society.

Inequality, one sees, had a lot to do with manners. Until Orwell could see no symbols of class divisiveness in the society around him, he could see no real progress towards Socialism. The political aim that Goldstein's book in *1984* attributes to 'the Low' is 'to abolish all distinctions and create a society in which all men shall be equal'. Orwell was with the Low. His particular animosity towards the Soviet Union is fueled by his knowledge that the one society on earth that proclaimed his own ideals was in fact a hideous travesty of them, 'a sham covering a new form of class privilege'.

Power: 'a boot stamping on the human face'

> 'The great serpent to destroy is the Will to Power: the desire for one man to have some dominion over his fellow man.'
>
> D. H. Lawrence

When he reviewed Zamyatin's *We* in 1946—the reading was part of the preparation for *1984*—Orwell commented, too, on Huxley's *Brave New World*.

> . . . no clear reason is given why society should be stratified in the elaborate way that is described. The aim is not economic exploitation, but the desire to bully and dominate does not seem to be a motive either. There is no power hunger, no sadism, no hardness of any kind. Those at the top have no strong motive for staying at the top . . . . (4/17)

If the economic motive is not present, Orwell would expect the alternative to be love of power. Without either to motivate the ruling class, life would become pointless and the society would crumble.

In *1984*, Orwell took care to see that his ruling élite was well motivated. 'Why should we want power?' O'Brien demands of Winston. Winston's answer is unsatisfactory, and O'Brien supplies the true one.

> The Party seeks power entirely for its own sake. We are not interested in the good of others; we are interested solely in power. Not wealth or luxury or long life or happiness; only power, pure power .... Power is not a means; it is an end. One does not establish a dictatorship in order to safeguard a revolution; one makes the revolution in order to establish the dictatorship. The object of persecution is persecution. The object of torture is torture. The object of power is power. Now do you begin to understand me?'

Orwell said that in *1984* he intended 'to indicate by parodying them the intellectual implications of totalitarianism', and the passage given above shows what he meant. The belief described here is, of course, one to which no politician or political theorist would admit. It is a parody by exaggeration—the idea expanded to absurdity— of Orwell's own explanation for some obvious and painful facts of politics and life.

We saw earlier how Orwell rejected the basic simplicity he saw in Marxism, its belief in the dominant economic motive for human behaviour. As his critics, both friendly and hostile, have seen, however, Orwell replaced the Marxist simplification, the single economic motive, with his own simplification, the desire for power. O'Brien expresses it in the form of the 'worst possible case'.

In his own person, Orwell accepted that the desire for power was the root of many manifestations in politics, but he could find no explanation for it. He had subjected the economic motive to some trenchant analysis; with the power drive he got nowhere. The following paragraph states his case perfectly.

> It is not easy to find a direct economic explanation of the behaviour of the people who now rule the world. The desire for pure power seems to be much more dominant than the desire for wealth ... the desire for power seems to be taken for granted as a natural instinct, equally prevalent in all ages, like the desire for food. Actually, it is no more natural, in the sense of being biologically necessary, than drunkenness or gambling. And if it has reached new levels of lunacy in our own age, as I think it has, then the question becomes: What is the special quality in modern life that makes a major human motive out of the impulse

to bully others? If we could answer that question—seldom asked, never followed up—there might occasionally be a bit of good news on the front page of your morning paper. (4/64)

By defining 'natural instinct' as equivalent to the desire for food, Orwell shows a reluctant awareness that the power drive might actually be a psychic compulsion, as his invoking of addictive practices—drunkenness and gambling—shows. These are not in his sense 'biologically necessary' yet they are undeniably human motive forces. But in his thinking about power, Orwell got no further than this. It seemed to be a fact, yet it was a mystery.

Once Orwell had formed the idea of power or 'bully-worship'— and the earliest reference I can find is January 1939—he went back to it repeatedly, with the culmination in *1984*. He found the idea attractive, I believe, for the psychological reasons set out earlier. The desire for power was bound to appeal to him as an explanation for all kinds of behaviour of which he disapproved, for the reasons were basic to his own psyche.

Alex Zwerdling suggests, however, that in evolving a determinism of power, Orwell was simply following the fashion of his century. Economic determinism was a nineteenth-century simplification. Orwell chose to replace it with twentieth-century psychology: his 'exaggerated dependence on the formula must be understood as a dialectical response to the complete rejection of all psychological explanations in Marxist theory.'

It is certainly true that Orwell criticized Marxism for that failing. 'The basic trouble with all orthodox Marxists is that, possessing a system that seems to explain everything, they never bother to discover what is going on inside other people's heads.' But the existence of lust for power never seems to have drawn him to psychological explanations. In fact, there is psychological significance in Orwell's almost careful refusal to investigate it. As an explanation, it was most useful to him as long as it was itself unexplained.

When one considers the nature of the phenomena caused by the mystery of power hunger, then one can clarify the form of the explanation. Orwell looked at the history of mankind and saw failure in the very places where success had been most likely, where intentions had been most benevolent. The history of revolutions, for instance, was particularly bitter, since so often the replacement for tyranny was tyranny. He totally recoiled from the hedonistic futures promised by so many revolutionary programmes; the promise of earthly paradise was false. Hunger for power could arise anywhere in any person, and it alone was a consistent motive in the undeniable tendency of human institutions to fail of their promises, to fall as if through a newly-invented myth of Original Sin.

History: predicting the past

A basic supporting principle of democracy is that the people must have access to documents, those 'public records' that are sometimes so far from being public. The most important of all such documents is the record of the past—history—and Orwell's own experience impressed on him that in the twentieth century governments and parties had begun manipulating history in a new and ominous way. When he decided on a job for Winston Smith, he made him a re-writer of history in the Ministry of Truth.

Orwell's experience in the Spanish Civil War governed his attitude in this matter. As the structure of *Homage to Catalonia* shows, with its division into military and political chapters, Orwell in fact found that there were two conflicts in Spain. There was the shooting war against Franco and there was the struggle on the Government side which Orwell presents as a conflict between the leftist parties, 'Trotskyites' to their enemies (this was the era of the great Soviet purges) who believed that the war could only be won if the social revolution went forward simultaneously, and the rest, dominated by the Communists, who were effectively anti-revolutionary in that they believed the revolution should wait until after victory, since to prosecute it during the war would antagonize the 'bourgeois democracies' whose aid the Republic needed. (Orwell's belief came to be that the Communists had no desire for a genuine revolution at any time; they simply wished to establish their own absolute power.)

The Communists dominated the Republican Government during Orwell's time in Spain. He was in Barcelona when the contest between the Government and its leftist opponents broke into the open. He was committed to the leftist, revolutionary, or 'Trotskyist' side, and thus experienced as one of the hunted the actions of a would-be totalitarian power suppressing its opponents. The greatest horror of all was that the Communists were quite systematic in the lies they told, in their rewriting of history, to justify the purge of such leftist parties as the POUM to whose militia Orwell belonged. Orwell had been wounded by a Fascist bullet, yet he found that he and all his fellow militiamen of the POUM were being described by government propaganda as Trotskyite traitors in active collaboration with the forces of Franco. Worse still—and it was the basis of Orwell's black suspicion of the English leftist intelligentsia—the publications of the Left in England tended to follow the government line and to repeat this fictional history, though there were plenty of participants, like Orwell himself, who tried to tell the truth about the Communists' anti-revolutionary stance and totalitarian ambition.

'I remember once saying to Arthur Koestler, "History stopped in 1936," at which he nodded in immediate understanding. We were both thinking of totalitarianism in general, but more particularly of the Spanish civil war.' (2/41) History, as opposed to the simple occurrence of events, exists only when the events are recorded, and much of what was written about the Spanish War was not history but fiction, 'history . . . written not in terms of what happened but of what ought to have happened according to various "party lines"'. So widespread and systematic had the abuse of history become in the thirties that Orwell could feel genuine alarm about two possibilities: that 'the very concept of objective truth is fading out of the world', and that there might come 'a nightmare world in which the Leader, or some ruling clique, controls not only the future but the past'.

That 'nightmare world', incorporating both possibilities, is, of course, *1984*. As a measure of the completeness of Orwell's preparation for his novel, a measure, that is, of the basic empiricism of his prophecy, there exists a revealing passage in his essay 'The Prevention of Literature' (1946). 'Organized lying', he states, is not incidental but integral to totalitarian regimes, 'something that would still continue even if concentration camps and secret police forces had ceased to be necessary.'

> From the totalitarian point of view history is something to be created rather than learned. A totalitarian state is in effect a theocracy, and its ruling caste, in order to keep its position, has to be thought of as infallible. But since, in practice, no one is infallible, it is frequently necessary to rearrange past events in order to show that this or that mistake was not made, or that this or that imaginary triumph actually happened. Then, again, every major change in policy demands a corresponding change of doctrine and a revaluation of prominent historical figures. This kind of thing happens everywhere, but it is clearly likelier to lead to outright falsification in societies where only one opinion is permissible at any given moment. Totalitarianism demands, in fact, the continuous alteration of the past, and in the long run probably demands a disbelief in the very existence of objective truth. The friends of totalitarianism in this country usually tend to argue that since absolute truth is not attainable, a big lie is no worse than a little lie. It is pointed out that all historical records are biased and inaccurate, or, on the other hand, that modern physics has proved that what seems to us the real world is an illusion, so that to believe in the evidence of one's senses is simply vulgar philistinism. A totalitarian society which succeeded in perpetuating itself would probably set up a schizophrenic system of thought, in which the laws of common sense held good in everyday life and in certain exact sciences, but could

be disregarded by the politician, the historian, and the sociologist. (4/16)

The writing of *1984* was a dramatizing of ideas of this type. For the 'schizophrenic system of thought', for instance, Orwell found the name 'doublethink' and shows us Winston struggling to master it under O'Brien's tuition. And since Orwell derived his ideas from history and from thinking about history, his dramatization was much aided by historical events.

The most striking of these was the Nazi-Soviet pact of August 1939, and its subsequent violation when Hitler attacked Russia in June 1941. In *The English People*, contrasting a British government, which 'may be unjust but . . . cannot be quite arbitrary', with a totalitarian government, Orwell cites this instance.

> The significant thing is not that [the German attack] was made without a declaration of war—that was natural enough—but that it was made without any propaganda build-up beforehand. The German people woke up to find themselves at war with a country that they had been ostensibly on friendly terms with on the previous evening. (3/1)

In Part Two, Chapter IX of *1984* occurs the scene during Hate Week in which it becomes known that Oceania is at war, not with Eurasia but with Eastasia. The speaker is in the middle of his speech when he is handed a slip of paper. He makes no pause but goes on, reversing the names of ally and enemy, and 'The Hate continued exactly as before, except that the target had been changed'. This is what Orwell meant by saying that in *1984* he employed parody. The German treachery towards Russia occurred overnight as far as the public was concerned; Orwell simply turns up the absurdity one notch and has the shift occur in the middle of a speech.

The emphasis on the importance of real history as the antagonist of totalitarianism is complemented by Orwell's own frequent recourse to history to help explain current events. He saw in totalitarianism, for example, 'a tendency to return to an earlier form of civilization', pointing out that in the past societies based on slavery had been massively stable—to counteract the optimism of those who argued that such societies would be inherently unstable. One of his most acute observations concerned a performance of Shakespeare's *King John*.

> When I had read it as a boy it had seemed to me archaic, something dug out of a history book and not having anything to do with our own time. Well, when I saw it acted, what with its intrigues and doublecrossings, non-aggression pacts, quislings,

people changing sides in the middle of a battle, and what not, it seemed to me extraordinarily up to date. (2/31)

Orwell resisted the view that history is cyclical but he grasped that the very ability to say, 'Creatures from the Dark Ages have come marching into the present' gave perspective and power to the observer in the political wars. The obverse is Winston Smith's helplessness as he tries to circumvent the account of the past given him by the Party. Winston is employed as an 'anti-historian', one who reshapes the past to bring it into conformity with the 'reality' of the present moment. But, as part of his rebellion, he tries to be a true historian, to find out what the past was really like. Meaningless fragments from the proles and some of the words—the ominous words—of 'Oranges and Lemons' from Mr Charrington are all he gets. His helplessness and isolation from the past are beautifully symbolized by his name. In 1948 'Winston' could refer to only one person. It still does. Yet in the book no one mentions that Winston is named after Churchill, because Churchill is part of the obliterated past. Winston does not know who Winston was.

Language and style

Orwell recorded that in adolescence he had discovered 'the joy of mere words, i.e. the sounds and associations of words' and he included among 'the four great motives for writing . . . Aesthetic enthusiasm', which covered beauty 'in words and their right arrangement' (1/1). But this pleasure in language, natural enough in a writer, was not to remain the only dimension of Orwell's interest in the subject. He came to see language as a most important element of reality, capable both of encouraging human community and of enforcing the isolation of the individual. Language had enormous power for both good and evil, and by means of two of his most widely diffused writings, 1984 and 'Politics and the English Language', Orwell made known his fear of the power for evil that the twentieth century had realized in language. Linguists concede that Orwell thus affected the general consciousness about language (in the English-speaking world) in a way that no linguist before Chomsky was able to do. As in certain others of his areas of interest, Orwell has proved to be the harbinger of a growing procession of later specialists, many of whom look askance at him—as he would at them.

For the premise of much late twentieth-century investigation of the 'human sciences'—that language is the foundation, the matrix of consciousness and the transmitter of the structures of social existence—gives language an importance that Orwell would have endorsed but does so to serve ideological ends he would have found very dubious. Moreover, the doctrinally demanded obscurity of style that envelops the writing of late twentieth-century theoreticians of theory would have been harshly judged by the criteria Orwell established for the meaning of style. Most of all, the rejection of empiricism, the denial of truth's attainability, and disbelief in any verifiable relationship between the word and the world are tenets that would have outraged Orwell's fundamental beliefs. Starting from the shared basic premise of the epistemological importance of language, Orwell travelled to very different conclusions.

He did not do so, it must be quickly admitted, by the fast, straight roads of logical rigour and absolute self-consistency. His thinking about language evolved along a number of lines that occasionally crossed and even entangled themselves. Professional linguists now looking back at his work can find it amateurish, but it is amateurish in the very best sense. Orwell's passionate interest uncovered and widely publicized, before many of the professionals arrived on the scene, a number of new ways of thinking about language. He was far from systematic, but his willingness to plunge into large problems compensates easily for any mistakes caused by his impetuosity. He got things moving. But an understanding of his ideas on this topic will require the steady separation of the principal strands.

Orwell's greatest single perception was the rôle of language as a political tool. He saw that language could be manipulated by a group holding power to help maintain its position over other groups, and in *1984* he imaginatively elaborated the ways in which language might be used to that end. But before looking at the elaborated results of Orwell's observations and thinking, we should accept the opportunity he gave us of understanding the origins in his own mind of his language obsession. This we can recover from an essay, 'New Words', which was published only after Orwell's death and to which his editors assign the tentative date of 1940.

'New Words' is a call for the wholesale creation of new words. This is the remedy for a condition that strikes Orwell as calamitous: 'our language is practically useless for describing anything that goes on inside the brain' (2/1). He has ventured into psycholinguistics, generalizing from his own experience, and what he tells us about the mind is fascinating (particularly insofar as he assumes the general application of features that may be unique to him).

Orwell describes the existence of two kinds of thoughts. To one of these he significantly attaches the label 'verbal'; it is a thinking *in* words.

It is true that most of our waking thoughts are 'reasonable'—that is, there exists in our minds a kind of chessboard upon which thoughts move logically and verbally; we use this part of our minds for any straightforward intellectual problem, and we get into the habit of thinking (i.e., thinking in our chessboard moments) that it is the whole of the mind. But obviously it is not the whole.

A large part of mental activity consists of the 'disordered, un-verbal world belonging to dreams'. This 'stream of nameless things', by virtue of the non-existence of words to make it communicable, reinforces human isolation, since the 'unverbal part' of the mind is the most important; from it come all motives: likes, dislikes, aesthetic feelings, ideas of right and wrong. Yet no words exist to make this activity communicable. The individual with an inner life 'is aware of the practical impossibility of understanding others or being understood—in general, of the star-like isolation in which human beings live'.

Orwell's motive for defining this problem and his solution are characteristic of him. The 'star-like isolation' of humans is the condition underlying his actions in politics, his aesthetic ideas, and his views on language. The purpose of language is communication, yet language is woefully inadequate. The solution proposed—'to invent a vocabulary . . . which would deal with parts of our experience now practically unamenable to language' so that expressing one's meaning would be simply 'a matter of taking the right words and putting them in place, like working out an equation in algebra'—this solution is typical of Orwell's language views since it concentrates almost entirely on lexicon, on the vocabulary available to speakers. Realistically, this is a great practical weakness in both the proposal of 'New Words' and in the system of Newspeak, but it is typical that Orwell should see individual words as the basic reality of language. Almost all his language proposals, whether genuine on his own behalf or parodistic on behalf of the Party in *1984*, are concerned with vocabulary.

'New Words' displays Orwell's fear that language's inadequacy will mean no progress in overcoming human isolation. One of his basic assumptions is the separability of thought and language. 'New Words' postulates the existence of thought-with-language and thought-without-language, the second kind being the predominant species. The relationship of thought to language is a fundamental problem of psycholinguistics. It has found no generally accepted solution, but in 'New Words' Orwell simply assumes that thought can exist without language, and makes that a postulate for his arguments. In much of his thinking about language, Orwell assumed—to employ a formulation of George Steiner's—that language conveys 'a pre-established or separately extant content, as a cable conveys telegraphic messages'. At later stages of his thought he imagined this inadequacy of language as a medium of transmission for 'separately extant content' being systematically extended as a means of reinforcing the isolation of individuals, an isolation required for the efficiency of totalitarianism. Again focusing on vocabulary, he shows us Syme in *1984* describing the destruction of words, the shrinking of the dictionary, as orthodoxy of thought is progressively attained by the elimination of the possible thought represented by every word that is destroyed.

In 'New Words' Orwell's fear concentrates upon the incommunicability of that part of the mind not covered by the logical-verbal 'chessboard'. To arrive at the situation presented in *1984*—mind-control by control of language—he had to take one more step; he had to show how both the 'chessboard' and the incommunicable 'dream thoughts' could be brought under political control. He created doublethink to ensure that the mind could rest comfortably among contradictions. But the most important development was Orwell's acceptance—a tactical acceptance, perhaps, to ensure the effectiveness of parody—of the dependence of thinking upon words. In 'New Words', the logical-verbal part of the mind seems easily communicable and unproblematic; in *1984* even logical-verbal communication will only be easy, in the Party's plans, for the reason that in its ideal manifestation language will 'issue from the larynx without involving the higher brain centres at all'. Orwell named this 'duckspeak', language quite independent of thought, the thoughtless utterance of the 'correct' opinions. Normal logical-verbal thinking will have to operate with a drastically reduced and redefined set of words. The effect will be to make independent, rational thought simply impossible, since it will depend on words that are no longer available. In *1984* the condition of namelessness systematically expands to cover all areas of the mind the Party deems dangerous. The shrinking of vocabulary gives the Party control of the thoughts of individuals, or will do so when the language has been redesigned. The words wherewith to 'think wrong' will not be available.

That this method of thought-control would work must be highly doubtful. The nature of speech as an inherently creative faculty, for example, would supply a 'recombinant' power enabling people to find ways of using the controlled stock of words for new meanings. Moreover, Orwell pays too little attention to syntax; his Newspeak syntactical model seems to be journalistic 'cable-ese'—'Oldthinkers unbellyfeel Ingsoc', and so on—which involves a suppression of syntax so drastic as to render many 'sentences' undirectional, with ambiguity everywhere. Possible weaknesses can be listed at length. But they are irrelevant. Newspeak is a parody, in Orwell's sense of the term, of the desire for thought control realized by means of linguistic manipulation. From these two realities of the world he knew he produced an imaginatively enhanced 'ideal'—a language that canalizes all thought, thus shaping reality to a chosen pattern.

In the 1930s and 1940s, the view that individual languages might order reality in ways that differed markedly from one language to another was very much 'in the air'. It was, in fact, an old idea given apparently new support by empirical evidence. In the early nineteenth century, the great German *savant*, Wilhelm von Humboldt, had—and again I follow George Steiner—'posited language as the centre of man'. In his work *On the Differentiation of the Structure of Human Language, and its Influence on the Spiritual Evolution of the Human Race*, Humboldt argued that language and human experience could be correlated.

> He would lay bare the concordance between the *Weltanschauung* [world view] of a given language and the history and culture of those who speak it. Essential to this analysis is the belief that language is the only true and only verifiable *a priori* framework of cognition. Perception is organized by the imposition of that framework on the total flux of sensations . . . . Different linguistic frameworks will divide and channel the sensory flux differently . . . . Language is a universal. But so far as each human tongue differs from every other, the resulting shape of the world is subtly and drastically altered.

In the twentieth century, some linguists have attempted to provide for these intuitions of Humboldt's a basis of semantic and anthropological fact. Humboldt had supposed in every language a deterministic, world-shaping power, and by the study of North American Indian languages, chosen because of their linguistic and cultural distance from European ones, the ethnolinguist Benjamin Lee Whorf tried to demonstrate the differing shapes of the world as 'seen' though the language of the Hopi and the Shawnee. In the period from 1936–39, Whorf published several papers on 'an American Indian model of the universe' which, to his own satisfaction and that of a large school of disciples, provided 'unimpeachable evidence' for the thesis descended from Humboldt and expressed again in 1929 by Edward Sapir:

> The 'real world' is to a large extent unconsciously built up on the language habits of the group. No two languages are sufficiently similar to be considered as representing the same social reality. The worlds in which different societies live are distinct worlds, not merely the same world with different labels attached.

Chronologically, it is possible that Orwell knew of this twentieth-century adoption of Humboldt's thesis, now called the Sapir-Whorf hypothesis, but it is much more likely that he 'breathed in' an idea that was in the air at the time, or that he developed it unaided. His own starting point was probably the experience of the Spanish War, where he had first encountered systematic political lying and had observed the power of words to shape a political world-view that went counter to the reality he could see. He was, however, temperamentally incapable of falling back into total relativism. Truth there was, and it was knowable. But truth had powerful enemies, and language could be perverted to help them. What we see happening in *1984* is a sardonic extension of the Whorf-Sapir hypothesis. Orwell shows what his political experience had taught him, that within what is called one language, here English, it is possible for words to convey violently differing world-views. He then shows the power of the totalitarian state pushing forward one of those world-views so as to crush the others. 'The purpose of Newspeak was not only to provide a medium of expression for the world-view and mental habits proper to the devotees of Ingsoc, but to make all other modes of thought impossible.'

Newspeak is a parody, an observation of fact extended absurdly for dramatic effect. The truth on which the parody is built is Orwell's view that in his century language had been employed against humanity, particularly in politics. The concern Orwell felt about this made him a critic, and a very famous one, of current language use. His main utterance on the subject is an essay, 'Politics and the English Language' (1946), which—as stated earlier—has acquired canonical status as the credo of those who hold that the English language is in a state of decay and that to shore up its ruins is to support civilized values. Since this group seems to include almost everyone who earns a living by teaching or writing English, 'Politics and the English Language' has a home in every textbook of composition, and Orwell's name can be involved as a final authority in matters of style and usage.

Readers always seem to remember best Orwell's account of political euphemism. Political events are often so foul that they can be defended 'only by arguments which are too brutal for most people to face, and which do not square with the professed aims of political parties'. Hence language is chosen that permits defence of the indefensible by clouding over the cruel reality. 'Defenceless villages are bombarded from the air, the inhabitants driven out into the countryside, the cattle machine-gunned, the huts set on fire with incendiary bullets: this is called *pacification*.' One side's *freedom fighter* is the other side's *bandit*. Orwell spears and displays this aspect of political language so effectively that his account has become definitive. When the Official Voice speaks of *revenue enhancement* or *fraternal assistance* or *protective reaction strikes*, the chorus of protest that arises claims the sanction of Orwell. He it was who made us aware that a *people's democratic republic*, despite the double tautology, is a place where the will of the people is usually the creation of an oligarchy. His analysis of the motives for political euphemism is correct in stressing its ability to protect the user from too much reality, but he never switches his perspective so as to perceive that euphemism of this kind at least conforms to Oscar Wilde's definition of hypocrisy: it is vice paying tribute to virtue. Someone who speaks of genocide as a 'final solution' at least supposes an audience that might not be able to endure the brutal fact. For Orwell, euphemism is an element in his view of political language as a nefarious process of mind-numbing, with 'Duckspeak' as its ultimate form.

His indignation at the use of language to conceal rather than to reveal is the basis of the programme of reform set out in 'Politics and the English Language'. To counter the politics that employs *language-as-concealment*, Orwell proposes *language-as-revelation*. What emerges from the essay is, as one might expect, a programme to accomplish ends exactly opposite those desired by the proponents of Newspeak. The Party wants a language that will *be* truth, since it will be impossible to see through the language. Orwell proposes a language so completely transparent as to be unable to conceal or distort truth, a language in which lies can only appear as lies. Both of these theories propose beginning, as Orwell put it, 'at the verbal end'. To reform language, for good or evil, is to acquire control of thought. The absurd tyranny of Newspeak is self-evident, but the programme proposed in the essay—a benevolent tyranny—is the accepted aim of the 'composition establishment'. Orwell has furnished it with a theory of what writing should be and how it should be attained. Or, to come closer to historical accuracy, Orwell has given his endorsement to a traditional argument about the relationship between language and reality that goes back at least as far as Aristotle. And for obvious reasons, Orwell as patron of this theory is more acceptable than Aristotle, but his modernity should not conceal the theory's classical roots. In taking it over as his own, Orwell was retailing most unexpectedly what he had been taught about language, style, and reality at Eton. English as a subject, English literature, that is, was not taught at Eton until some time after Orwell had left, but the study of languages, particularly Latin and Greek, had its theoretical basis, and the writing of English prose needed its own academically approved models.

The decay of language is an unqueried premise drawn from that source. Orwell assumes that a language can decay, and that

English in 1946 was 'in a bad way'. The analogy is organic, that a language, like a living organism, will go through stages of immaturity, maturity, and decay. The idea was powerfully supported in classical culture by the 'myth of decline', that the world in all its aspects was decaying, and in the study of classical languages it was reinforced by the authority of the language, or rather the style, of certain periods and authors held up as models for the learner. Cicero's Latin differs markedly from that centuries later of St Jerome, but in the humanist tradition of stylistic formation, these authors were not simply two stylists of different periods, using a language that had naturally and inevitably changed; Cicero wrote good Latin and Jerome wrote an inferior, decayed version. Cardinal Bembo in the Renaissance advised against reading the New Testament in Greek, since its *koine* Greek was an inferior brand compared with the uncorrupted Hellenic style.

Much of Orwell's schooling upheld this view, but at the opening of 'Politics and the English Language', while stressing the modern decadence of English, he denies that the language is an organic entity, 'a natural growth', subject to natural processes of maturing and decaying. Orwell sees determinism in that analogy, and he believes the language—'an instrument which we shape for our own purposes'—can be saved by the efforts of its users.

Orwell follows this proclamation with his famous 'catalogue of swindles and perversions'—a significant choice of terms to indicate aspects of modern style he does not like; his distaste is given moral and natural authority. The 'swindles and perversions' are a short anthology of passages chosen to illustrate bad modern prose, followed by Orwell's analysis of the characteristic 'vices' of modern English, dying metaphors, pretentious diction, and so on. His general conclusion is that modern English prose 'lacks concreteness' and is 'prefabricated'. The modern writer prefers the abstractly vague to the concretely specific (this is the point of Orwell's rendering Ecclesiastes 11:9 into a parody of the modern) and he allows language to do his thinking for him by accepting ready-made portions of sentences 'tacked together like the sections of a prefabricated hen house'.

The result is that language completes the circle by corrupting the thought of the writer. Lack of concreteness moves the writer away from reality; the 'invasion of the mind by ready-made phrases . . . anaesthetizes a portion of one's brain'. And politics—no one can stay out of politics—takes advantage of this corruption. Politics—'a mass of lies, evasions, folly, hatred, and schizophrenia'—will require a writer to be insincere, and 'the great enemy of clear language is insincerity'. This circular motion—language corrupting thought corrupting language—can go on forever, and the decline of the English language will be irreversible.

But the cycle can be interrupted, and Orwell's prescribed method for interrupting it is vigilance. The writer of expository prose must be alert at all times. He must be perpetually critical of every word, phrase and sentence that he writes, having in mind always certain principles of exclusion and rectification that will keep his prose from deviating from the desired model. The single dominating principle is 'to let the meaning choose the word, and not the other way about. In prose, the worst thing one can do with words is surrender to them.' Since Orwell conceived of thought occurring before language, of language as a container of thought, he could prescribe a wordless shaping of ideas followed by a process of choice, as the writer looks for the appropriate dress for his completed thought. 'Afterwards one can choose—not simply *accept*— the phrases that will best cover the meaning, and then switch round and decide what impression one's words are likely to make on another person. This last effort of the mind cuts out all stale or mixed images, all prefabricated phrases, needless repetitions, and humbug and vagueness generally.' Orwell then gives his famous six rules for the writing of prose ('If it is possible to cut a word out, always cut it out')—rules derived, it should be noted, from *The King's English* by the brothers Fowler (1906), a manual of style and usage that had, I suspect, great authority among those who taught Orwell his letters. He ends by reaffirming that 'the present political chaos is connected with the decay of language' and that vigilance in the use of language can contribute to political improvement.

As a way of teaching writing, Orwell's scheme is so widely accepted that its actual weirdness is hard to see. Its premises, however, are plainly set out: language is separate from thought; meaning should choose the word, and never *vice versa*; prefabricated sections of language are unacceptable; eternal vigilance is the price of clarity; and language can be a perfectly transparent medium ('Good prose is like a window-pane', as he said elsewhere) whose transparency will reveal, to his readers and to himself, any insincerity on the part of the writer, specifically, of course, political insincerity. To all of which one may say, using some words of Fielding's, there can be but one objection; namely, that it is not true.

Every one of these premises is, at the least, problematical. Language's relationship to thought is a highly vexed question, but it is safe to say that Orwell's premise of separateness is not true. The person who asks 'How do I know what I think until I see what I write?' is not proposing an utterly absurd theory of the relation of thought and language. All syntactical language construction draws on 'prefabricated' phrases. (Orwell was uneasily aware of this: 'Look back again through this essay, and for certain you will find that I have again and again committed the very faults I am protesting against.') Vigilance is rightly employed in avoiding absurd combinations and 'prefabs' that are hackneyed, but the utter rejection of 'prefabrication' is impossible. Language, even expository prose (Orwell omits 'creative' writing) can never be an utterly transparent medium, merely revealing facts 'out there'. Further, the kind of vigilance Orwell proposes is exalted to a paralysing degree. Such absolute self-consciousness in 'prose construction' will really only bring writing to a stop.

'Politics and the English Language' shows Orwell betrayed into extremism. His positive model of language use, to counter the parody model of Newspeak, is a counsel of perfection, so remote from attainment as to present another, though inadvertent, parody. Orwell's basic fear seems to be of rhetoric, of any element in prose that indicates the attempt to persuade, that smudges the transparent pane. In this, he is faithful to a tradition that runs back through Mill and Locke to Aristotle, who anticipated Orwell by a couple of thousand years in setting out a method of rhetoric that paradoxically accommodates the fact that its author distrusted rhetoric. Aristotle, too, believed that language ideally ought to be a transparent medium, with no effect on the facts that it transmitted. Therefore, when he thought of what rhetoric did he was in a distrustful quandary. As Richard Lanham describes Aristotle's dilemma: 'to teach someone about rhetoric, how to use words self-consciously, means teaching him how to be insincere, how to lie, how to sin.' Orwell completely endorses the need for sincerity, and hence also the suspicion of rhetoric, but instead of following Aristotle's self-contradictory recipe ('a writer must hide his art and seem to write naturally') his belief in the attainability of a prose without artifice lets him advise a complete self-consciousness in the writer, self-consciousness to stifle rhetoric, to do away with any feature of language that could compromise language's transparency.

Orwell too, by advocating total transparency, assumed the existence and desirability of a language without the distortions of style. The paradox of that effort harmonizes with the paradox of George Orwell, one of the great masters of English prose, abjuring his art, and George Orwell, a self artfully created as a literary and social persona, claiming to be a pre-existent self with nothing to hide.

I believe it was his schooling at Eton that taught him the theory of language decay, that there should be a closeness of words and things and that rhetoric was essentially deception. He seems to have believed firmly that language was separate from thought, and that there existed an integral self, not a performative self defined by its interactions with its surroundings. His fundamental and instinctive empiricism supported many of these views. His experience in Spain and in politics generally had confirmed his view that the arts of language could be employed for vilely deceptive purposes, and he held the arts just as responsible as their users. Politics did most of its business by means of words; the business was usually foul; language and rhetoric were accomplices both before and after the fact. The supporting principles for this view of language were Orwell's basic beliefs, but that does not alter the impossible extremism of what he advocates.

The advocacy puts him in strange company, since he is in effect giving his support to a class system, a thing he always detested. The educated do in some circumstances behave as a class, and one large manifestation of such behaviour is the defence of their own dialect against variation and change. All such alteration—be it neologism, elegant variation, mistaking one word for another, adding new sense, jargonizing—is bad, and people who can be caught at it are sappers at the foundations of civilization. With the aid of Fowler's *Modern English Usage*, letters to *The Times*, and the columns of those journalists in the classy papers who work as 'language critics', the polluters of the dialect are exposed to ridicule.

Now Orwell was a sensitive reader of manners, but to reduce his criticisms of style, meant to protect people against the political abuse of language, to this kind of oneupmanship is a sad mockery. But he brought it upon himself. When he turns in his essay from the 'swindles and perversions' to their ideal replacement, he lays out a set of rules adopted uncritically from men such as the Fowler brothers and Sir Arthur Quiller-Couch. Along with the rules, he adopts their underlying premises: that 'standard English' is not a dialect, but variations from it are; that language can be transparent; that change in language is always bad—not, maybe, in principle, but always in practice. And unfortunately it is not really possible to dissociate Orwell from the great corollary of all this: by their words shall ye know them, or, unacceptable language is the mark of unacceptable people.

This is snobbery, but snobbery to be enjoyed has to be disguised, in this case as the desire to keep language rational and communication unimpeded by error. This pretence makes easy the co-opting of Orwell, who finds his rules used as a sheep-from-goats detector. If he had not got worked up about the baseness of the 'not un-' construction ('not unimportant') or 'the disgusting verb "to contact"' or lamented that 'plane sailing' had become 'plain sailing', one could acquit him of enjoying these usage games. But he did enjoy them, without seeing where they came from or where they led. His great concern with the language abuse of politics dwindles to a concern for particular usages as markers of social differentiation.

Yet to use Orwell in this way means ignoring one or two remarks he makes in 'Politics and the English Language'. He says, for instance, that the defence of the English language does not imply 'the setting up of a "standard English" which never must be departed from'. Since differentiation on the basis of language always deals in such departures, the language critics ignore this, as they equally assiduously ignore the remark that the defence of the language 'has nothing to do with correct grammar and syntax, which are of no importance so long as one makes one's meaning clear'. It is true that Orwell's own prose hardly embodies these principles, but at least he utters them and thus distances himself from those who want him as an authority.

Orwell's ideas about language are a very important element in his thought, but on this topic, more perhaps than on any other, the reader has to retain critical perspective. Whenever Orwell projected satirical exaggerations from observed realities he set problems for himself and for his reader, problems of truly fertile complexity as he stretches the bounds of his own art and ideology. His thinking about language and his use of that thought in his works are an example of this complexity. The critic may have to decide that Newspeak is not a real possibility, while accepting enthusiastically that, as a satirical manifestation of what might be called the totalitarian will—the will to modify the most basic human behaviour—Newspeak is a brilliantly effective invention.

An account of Orwell on language ought to end positively, since—for all his fear and confusions—his work gives greatly encouraging evidence of the force of language for good. The whole body of his writing, obviously, underlines this truth, but a more particular instance of it is the writing of Winston Smith. Winston's first act of rebellion (he assumes it means death if he is caught) is to begin to keep a diary. This has obvious narrative advantages for Orwell, but it is more important as a way of indicating language's effectiveness in defining and opposing the inhumanly oppressive elements in the world of Oceania. The diary, first of all, sets memory free. It gives the intellect matter to work with other than that permitted by the Party, and counters the official doctrine of the mutable past. Writing is also a weapon against the solitude imposed by the Party. Although Winston can expect no reader of his diary, the act of writing is an act of hope. 'He was a lonely ghost uttering a truth that nobody would ever hear. But so long as he uttered it, in some obscure way the continuity was broken. It was not by making yourself heard but by staying sane that you carried on the human heritage.' Despite its futility, Winston is writing 'for the future, for the unborn', and in so doing he breaks out of 'the locked loneliness in which one had to live'. Syme, that devoted but too intelligent servant of the Party, later remarks that 'Orthodoxy is unconsciousness'. And writing, Orwell shows, is—in the world of *speakwrite*—the action of resistant consciousness.

The religious sense of life

In a notebook he kept in the last year of his life, Orwell described a seventeenth-century crucifix he had recently read about. This *objet d'art* concealed within itself a stiletto. 'What a perfect symbol of the Christian religion.' (4/167) In January of 1950, Orwell made his will, directing that 'my body shall be buried (not cremated) according to the rites of the Church of England'. Once again, the reconciliation of apparent contradictions that we call paradox comes into play. The remark about the crucifix-cum-stiletto is more than a sneer, and the desire for Christian burial is more than an unbeliever's way out. There was a great deal about Christianity, including certain of its fundamentals—such as belief in God and an after-life!—that Orwell rejected. Yet he saw religion, particularly Protestantism, as having been the great modernizing and liberating force in Western civilization, the agency that had brought into being what Orwell called 'the autonomous individual', in whose defence he had enlisted as the forces of totalitarian collectivism closed in—or rather returned.

Orwell was thus, and very characteristically, a man who rejected as irrelevant most elements of Christian belief and a passionate believer in 'the religious sense of life' and in the form of human individuality that Protestantism had nurtured. The detailed elements of this paradox are worth examining.

Orwell is often called an 'agnostic', but if by that is meant that he 'did not know' whether there was a God, then 'atheist' would be more accurate. Yet one sees at once how much Orwell would have disliked those labels, particularly 'atheist', which suggests a proselytizing sort of commitment—Bernard Shaw giving a lecture—utterly alien to Orwell's style. (His request for Church of England burial was testimony to his 'Protestantism', but a stronger element was his allegiance, not to Church—though he loved its liturgy—but to England.) But it is not the existence of God—still less the figure of Jesus—that Orwell uses to define his own attitude. For him the test is the belief in personal immortality and in the existence of an afterlife. Moreover, defining his own attitude is not as important as defining the general state of mind on this subject, since from there he can proceed to the political implications of the matter.

If everything ends for the individual in death, which is quite the opposite of what men have believed strongly for centuries, then the foundations of the individual's moral sense are undermined. 'The real problem of our time is to restore the sense of absolute right and wrong when the belief that it used to rest on—that is, the belief in personal immortality—has been destroyed.' (3/23) If one assumes 'that no sanction can ever be effective except the supernatural one, it is clear what follows. There is no wisdom except in the fear of God; but nobody fears God; therefore there is no wisdom.' (2/3). The supernatural sanction had upheld the whole system of morality, of reason employed in choice, and since political choice extends from moral choice, politics was a matter of right and wrong, and it, too, depended on belief in the supernatural.

In looking at the events of the 1920s and 1930s, Orwell summed up 'our present predicament' so as to display the link between politics and morality. Capitalism had failed, but so had collectivism (presumably in Nazi and Soviet forms). 'There is no way out of this unless a planned economy can be somehow combined with the freedom of the intellect, which can only happen if the concept of right and wrong is restored to politics.' (3/30) There must be true Socialism and individualism; politics must be acknowledged to be moral choice—but matters of right and wrong were still to be judged by mankind's moral sense, and that must rest on something other than the 'supernatural sanction'.

What was that foundation to be? The answer is in one way disappointing since Orwell died before he could get very far with the problem, but in another way the asking of the question proved to be a great intellectual event in his life, and a productive event. *1984* works out the dilemma posed by the disappearance of the supernatural sanction, focusing on negative or pessimistic possibilities. From the mid-1930s onwards, Orwell's novels handle the theme he saw as the great modern dilemma and which he identified as central to the work of James Joyce:

> the whole of this modern world which he is describing has no meaning in it now that the teachings of the Church are no longer credible. He is yearning after the religious faith which the two or three generations preceding him had to fight against in the name of religious liberty. (2/31)

Orwell sees his own writing as pondering and attempting to answer the questions raised by the disappearance of religious belief. He does far more pondering than answering. He found the importance of the question so great as to preclude all other questionings: 'One cannot have any worthwhile picture of the future unless one realizes how much we have lost by the decay of Christianity.' (3/24)

First, Orwell has rejected the personal immortality offered by traditional religious orthodoxy. 'The Kingdom of Heaven, old style, has definitely failed' but more recent orthodoxies are no more successful. '"Marxist realism" has also failed, whatever it may achieve materially.' Even more emphatically, Orwell rejects the 'picture of the future' and the purpose for living offered by much Socialist propaganda in its 'Utopian' or 'hedonistic' forms:

'that human beings desire nothing beyond ease, security and avoidance of pain' (212). This misbelief has led to the failure to understand the success of the great dictators.

> Hitler . . . knows that human beings *don't* only want comfort,
> safety, short working-hours, hygiene, birth-control and, in
> general, common sense; they also, at least intermittently, want
> struggle and self-sacrifice, not to mention drums, flags and
> loyalty-parades. However they may be as economic theories,
> Fascism and Nazism are psychologically far sounder than any
> hedonistic conception of life. (2/2)

What these ideologies possess, in however degenerate a form, is
spiritual values, some explanation of 'man's destiny and the reason
for his existence' (3/24), and it is for those that Orwell is searching
in a world from which a deity and the concept of personal immortality have vanished. In *A Clergyman's Daughter* he gave the thought
to his protagonist, Dorothy Hare: 'Faith vanishes, but the need for
faith remains the same as before.'

One striking feature of Orwell's attempt to fill the need for faith
is its vocabulary. If 'the Kingdom of Heaven, old style', has failed,
the vocabulary of the search for faith needs no revision. Orwell
speaks repeatedly of man's 'soul', for instance, and though he has
rejected Heaven's existence and material Utopias he can still say
that 'the Kingdom of Heaven has somehow got to be brought on
to the surface of the earth. We have got to be the children of God,
even though the God of the Prayer Book no longer exists' (2/3).
This reliance on traditional language is more than instinctive
conservatism. Religion has fulfilled humanity's basic need, and the
continuity of the language stresses the unwavering nature of that
need and the rejection of the alternatives usually offered. The
answer was not hedonism and could not be religion, but it must
fulfil a spiritual need.

Orwell named his answer 'brotherhood'—the name he also gave
to the conspiracy Winston Smith seeks to join. Death is final; the
individual has no personal immortality. Yet 'the religious attitude'
whereby men live neither for bread alone nor for themselves
alone—'Men can only be happy when they do not assume that the
object of life is happiness' (3/68)—is valid. Men *can* find meaning
in their individually brief and finite existences.

The basic components of Orwell's faith—as he worked it out in
the last years of his life—were that each person is, or is capable
of being, an autonomous individual on what one might call the
Protestant model and is, at the same time, 'a cell in an everlasting
body', the human race. The vocabulary gets confused, but one can
keep it clear if one realizes that in this spiritual matter, as in
politics, Orwell wanted both a form of collectivism (the 'everlasting

body' or a democratic Socialist state) and an almost absolutely high value for the individual.

Orwell reaches his conclusion that human beings have a sense of community, of brotherhood, simply by pondering general human behaviour, especially behaviour the opposite of 'hedonistic'.

> Men die in battle—not gladly, of course, but at any rate voluntarily—because of abstractions called 'honour', 'duty', 'patriotism', and so forth.
>
> All that this really means is that they are aware of some organism greater than themselves, stretching into the future and into the past, *within which they feel themselves to be immortal* . . . . People sacrifice themselves for the sake of fragmentary communities nation, race, creed, class and only become aware that they are not individuals in the very moment when they are facing bullets |my italics|.

Then, with a millenarian touch,

> A very slight increase of consciousness, and their sense of loyalty could be transferred to humanity itself, which is not an abstraction. (2/3)

Orwell cannot be said to have 'come to rest' in this union of opposites, the individual cell in the collective body. The two ideas pulled against each other persistently in the thinking of his later years. He had, in fact, created another paradox, and one which refused to accept a peaceful reconciliation. In *1984* the terms of conflict are the same. Winston Smith struggles to be the autonomous individual, and is not only tortured but—more insidiously— tempted to submerge his asserted individuality in a collective that claims to be—but is not—the everlasting body. Winston's rebellion begins and ends in the insistence that two and two make four, that there is an objective reality, and Orwell's own belief is similarly founded. Empiricism meant everything to Orwell. The universe was real, not an illusion, not 'all in the mind'. The objective existence of nature, reported by the senses, allowed the senses to define a personal self, possessing the power of judgement and embodying the freedom of the individual conscience. In fact it is reasonable to say that empiricism was a religious belief for Orwell; it gave meaning to the universe, the only meaning it could have after the failure of religion. It is typical of Orwell's alignment that he should have known and appreciated the real meaning of Marx's famous remark about 'the opium of the people'.

> Marx did not say, at any rate in that place, that religion is merely a dope handed out from above; he said it is something

that people create for themselves to supply a need that he recognized to be a real one. (2/3)

Orwell, an unbeliever with a religious temperament, included Marx's solution among the systems he rejected, but he conceded the need that Marx recognized, and sought his own solution.

Part Two
The Literary Character of Orwell

5 Novels, essays and criticism

1 'Writer' as 'novelist'

It is usual to assume that someone called a 'writer' is a novelist. Likewise, a 'book' is often assumed to be a novel. When Orwell stated, in 'Why I Write', that he knew, from the age of five to six, that he would be a writer, he thereby implied, and later openly stated, that he meant to be a novelist: 'I wanted to write enormous naturalistic novels with unhappy endings, full of detailed descriptions and arresting similes, and also full of purple passages . . .' Orwell achieved his height of success, however, when the novels he wrote had acquired, as a result of the pressures and influences that this book has investigated, a hybrid character, crossing the 'pure' realistic novel with concerns Orwell attributed to himself when he said he had become 'a sort of pamphleteer'. When he told Julian Symons 'I am not a real novelist' he spoke with accuracy if 'real' is taken to mean 'pure'. *Animal Farm* and *1984* are adulterated novels; that is their strength.

Orwell's critical writing is dominated by the novel (his success with the hybrid forms came too late for him to do much thinking about that development). To learn and to ponder his views on the novel allows one to see the important connection between his literary and political ideologies, and to define his literary engagement with the world which he could not let alone, since the times in which he lived would not allow it.

Orwell's theory of the novel

'The written word loses its power if it departs too far, or rather if it stays away too long, from the ordinary world where two and two make four.'

He was an untheoretical literary theoretician, for he held to a commonsense concept of realism in the novel which deprecated elaborate discussion. 'There is no need to get bogged up in metaphysical discussions about the meaning of *reality*.' All of Orwell's interesting theoretical pronouncements occur with reference to specific authors. A piece with an apparently promising title, 'In Defence of the Novel', turns out to be about reviewing, not very interesting, but on Henry Miller or Smollett or Gissing he is capable of a very useful theoretical pronouncement.

His essay on Smollett, for instance, carries a large implication in its title: 'Scotland's Best Novelist'. Orwell is defying the literary establishment in not ceding that title to Sir Walter Scott. (I suspect, in fact, that he is defying the literary establishment embodied in his prep school headmistress, 'Mum' Wilkes, with her 'cult of Scotland' and her absurd teaching of history.) The defiance involves a theory of realism, partly technical but also moral and eventually political.

Technique first: ' "Realism" ... when applied to novels ... normally means a photographic imitation of everyday life. A "realistic" novel is one in which the dialogue is colloquial and physical objects are described in such a way that you can visualize them.' Orwell's encounters with Henry Miller and his work were the most important in his literary career, and from Orwell's reviews of Miller's books, and his letters to Miller, we can assemble a fuller account of realistic technique. In 1935 Orwell reviewed *Tropic of Cancer* and greatly admired it, chiefly for its *moral* realism. He and Miller corresponded, and Miller sent Orwell *Black Spring*, a book that caused Orwell some doubts: '*Tropic of Cancer*, dealing with events that happened or might have happened in the ordinary three-dimensional world, is more in your line.' He observed Miller's fantasy (though I think he underestimated the extent of it): 'the way in which you would wander off into a kind of reverie where the laws of ordinary reality were slipped just a little but not too much'. In *Black Spring*, however, the slippage was often too great for Orwell.

> I think on the whole you have moved too much away from the
> ordinary world into a sort of Mickey Mouse universe where
> things and people don't have to obey the rules of space and time
> .... I have a sort of belly-to-earth attitude and always feel
> uneasy when I get away from the ordinary world where grass is
> green, stones hard, etc.

Orwell is rejecting 'the squashy universe of the Surrealists', an essential component of Miller's literary make-up, and asserting his own belief in the value of quotidian reality in literature and of the technique to reproduce that reality.

The novel in English in the modern era has been mainly fed by two streams, the naturalistic and the symbolic, and James Joyce's *Ulysses* is the great result of that confluence. Orwell is wary of the symbolic method, but he does revere Joyce. For him, therefore, *Ulysses* is a great naturalistic novel embellished with a variety of rather suspect symbolic properties and techniques. This is exactly the pattern of his qualified praise of Henry Miller. When those men employ techniques that allow Orwell to feel that his belly is to the earth, then he is their admirer. When they abandon 'the ordinary three-dimensional world', he cannot go with them.

This inability has deep roots and profound implications. In his praise for Smollett's realism, Orwell moves rapidly from the matter of technique to that of moral realism. Smollett has 'outstanding intellectual honesty' in his attitude towards human motives. He and other eighteenth-century novelists 'may be weak at describing scenery, but they are extraordinarily good at describing scoundrelism'. Human nature in Smollett is not masked in sentimentality or romanticized, and Orwell finds this realistic. In the novels that Orwell significantly prefers to *Humphry Clinker*—'no longer worth reading'—neither Roderick Random nor Peregrine Pickle 'is ever shown acting from an unselfish motive, nor is it admitted that such things as religious belief, political conviction or even ordinary honesty are serious factors in human affairs'. Orwell is not, however, endorsing this hard-nosed view of human nature. In adopting it,

> by simply ruling out 'good' motives and showing no respect whatever for human dignity, Smollett often attains a truthfulness that more serious novelists have missed. He is willing to mention things which do happen in real life but are almost invariably kept out of fiction.

(He gives, as an instance, Roderick's getting VD—'the only English novel hero, I believe, to whom this has happened'.) The virtue, even heroism, of the novelist who struggles to 'get into' his work more reality than has hitherto been achieved is a recurrent motif in Orwell's criticism. The realistic novelist who is advancing the art of fiction is one who succeeds in making the novel's imitation of reality ever more comprehensive.

Given the period of history in which Orwell lived, it was inevitable that his investment in literary realism would mean a continuing interest in censorship. The heroic realist, trying to encompass more and more of reality, soon collides with the barriers of law designed to keep certain aspects of existence out of literature. Orwell's very first article as a professional writer was (in French) on censorship in England. The word 'unprintable' occurs frequently in his criticism as an indication of his awareness of the barriers, and it is certainly no accident that 'unwholesome' writers like Smollett and Gissing, or often prosecuted ones, like Joyce and Miller, stimulated his acts of critical decision. (This interest actually brought Orwell into contact with the law. 'While I was writing my last book two detectives suddenly arrived at my house with orders from the public prosecutor to seize all books which I had "received through the post".' Thus he lost his copy of *Tropic of Cancer*.) Censorship sets its own legal limits and Orwell was generally hostile to those, but he is more interested, and more interesting, on the limitations that literature itself imposes. The objective desired is a better imitation of reality, but the occasion for the desire is the inadequate imitation found in earlier literature. Thus we can see Joyce's originality most easily when we recall what fiction was like before he came along:

> instead of taking as his material the conventional and highly simplified version of life *presented in most novels*, Joyce attempts to present life more or less as it is lived . . . . Joyce is attempting to select and represent events and thoughts as they occur in life and *not as they occur in fiction* [My italics].

Realism of this stature begins, then, as an implicit act of literary criticism. The novelist decides that previous attempts have not come close enough to reality; fiction can do better.

As a novelist, Orwell wanted to do better himself. To bring fiction closer to reality was a worthy ambition. But it is not self-evident why that should be so. Why did 'ordinary reality' attract him so much?

The answer is found once more among Orwell's remarks on Joyce and Miller:

> . . . now and again there appears a novel which opens up a new world not by revealing what is strange, but by revealing what is familiar. The truly remarkable thing about *Ulysses*, for instance, is the commonplaceness of its material. Of course there is much more in *Ulysses* than this, because Joyce is a kind of poet and also an elephantine pedant, but his real achievement has been to get the familiar on to paper. He dared—for it is a matter of *daring* just as much of technique—to expose the imbecilities of the inner mind, and in doing so he discovered an America which was under everybody's nose. Here is a whole world of stuff which you have lived with since childhood, stuff which you supposed to be of its nature incommunicable, and somebody has managed to communicate it. The effect is to break down, at any rate momentarily, the solitude in which the human being lives (1/164/i)

Realism of this order, essentially a realism of the mind's operations, puts human beings in touch with each other, and for Orwell that is its supreme value. In the voice of Henry Miller, too, 'a friendly American voice with no humbug in it', he detects 'an implicit assumption that we are all alike . . . . Read him for five pages, ten pages, and you feel the peculiar relief that comes not so much from understanding as from *being understood*'. Nothing is more valuable to Orwell than this effect, and since it is the product of literary realism, Orwell is a committed realist.

Theories of fiction other than the realistic seem to him to separate people rather than to bring them together. Even subject-matter can have an alienating effect. Orwell regrets that Henry Miller's work depicts an 'expatriate life',

> people drinking, talking, meditating and fornicating, not . . . people working, marrying, and bringing up children; a pity, because he would have described one set of activities as well as the other.

Closer to home, deeper run the roots. Reviewing Cyril Connolly's *The Rock Pool* at roughly the same time as his critique of Miller, Orwell again emphasized the moral value of 'everyday reality'. The subject-matter (expatriates once more) distresses him: 'I think he would write a better novel if he would concern himself with more ordinary people.' Connolly seems to have a distaste for 'normal life and common decency' and to Orwell that is a saddening weakness; it limits his humanity and his achievement as a writer, two inseparables.

In Orwell's prescription of realism for the novel, an aspect that involves some poignancy is his repeated insistence that a 'true novel . . . will contain at least two characters, probably more, who are described from the inside and on the same level of probability—which, in effect, rules out novels written in the first person'. In some notes he made 'for and against novels in the first person' he states: 'in general an "I" novel is simply the story of one person—a three-dimensional figure among caricatures—and therefore cannot be a true novel.' No real human contact can be made. Orwell wrote only one novel in the first person, but all his novels, aside from *Animal Farm*, present essentially solitary figures. In each book only one character is described 'from the inside' with any success. Orwell's late realization of what he undoubtedly saw as a weakness contributed to his judgement of himself as 'not a real novelist'.

In studying Orwell's work, one repeatedly turns up ideas that seem to apply so well to events that have occurred since his death, and on which one longs to read his comments. The relationship of literary realism to human community which so attracted Orwell is also, however grotesque the discrepancy, the idealistic basis for the doctrine of Socialist Realism which was invoked as the justification for the cultural purge of Stalin's last years, when 'modernism', 'formalism', and 'cosmopolitanism' became deadly heresies. Orwell set out what he thought a novel 'should' be, but the prescription was based on the choice of procedures Orwell made from the works of authors themselves free to choose their techniques and to develop their theories. His comments on his humane realism transformed into the iron law of Socialist Realism would have been worth reading.

In his seminal essay on Henry Miller and political quietism,

'Inside the Whale' (1940), Orwell calls the novel 'practically a Protestant form of art; it is a product of the free mind, of the autonomous individual'. A writer, therefore, to perform the writer's basic function, to tell the truth, must sustain his or her autonomous individuality. The writer must be a Protestant, in the sense of being responsible for his own salvation, his own truth. The writer's conscience can be given into the keeping of no one else, and certainly not into the keeping of the state or the party. In 'Inside the Whale', Orwell picks his way carefully between the political possibilities for the artist. He cannot be the 'good party man' or subscribe to a religious orthodoxy since thus he ceases to be the autonomous individual. Miller's attitude—observing the chaos and self-destruction of society but with 'no impulse to alter or control the process that he is undergoing', passive, non-cooperative—is justified, since it reflects what people actually feel, whether or not they ought to feel it. Miller is therefore a realist, and Orwell ends the essay with a cry of despair for the future of the writer in an increasingly totalitarian world where Miller's is the only viable literary approach. 'Progress and reaction have both turned out to be swindles. Seemingly there is nothing left but quietism.'

Orwell's conclusions of despair, however, are always deceptive, since he never accepts them himself. His enduring belief, certainly the one on which he continued to act, was that quietism really meant acceptance, and to say '"I accept" in an age like our own is to say that you accept concentration camps, rubber truncheons, Hitler, Stalin', and a lot more. He continued to write so as to endeavour 'to influence the future' and to believe that 'a novelist who simply disregards the major public events of the moment is generally either a footler or a plain idiot'. Political involvement was an aspect of realism for Orwell, and he at least proves for his own work the maxim that 'no book is ever truly neutral'.

The Orwell novel: Coming Up for Air

Orwell's work as a novelist is in one way unfairly represented by *Coming Up for Air* (1939) since the book is so clearly his best novel, leaving aside *Animal Farm* and *1984*. Yet it does so plainly share the same matrix with Orwell's other novels that one can use it to represent the character of his fiction as a whole. Its relative success means that it displays most openly of all the books what Orwell tried to do as a novelist.

George Bowling, representative of the Flying Salamander insurance company, wins a little money on a horse and decides to sneak himself a holiday by revisiting Lower Binfield, the little town in the Thames valley where he was born. The visit has to be surreptitious because Hilda, George's wife, would never approve of money spent for such a purpose. So George tells her some lies and drives off to Lower Binfield, full of memories of the place as it was in his boyhood, before the First World War. What he finds is that the place of memory has, like his own life in the London suburbs, been swamped by the modern world. Every nostalgic locale is dreadfully altered. To cap George's visit, the RAF accidentally drops a bomb on the town, a practical demonstration of the warfare George knows to be coming. He returns to his job and family. Hilda will believe for ever that he has been with a woman, but the love affair George has attempted is with his boyhood past, and it has proved impossible to realize.

As a novel, the book seems to display two obvious weaknesses. Like his other novels, this too deals with a solitary character, but Orwell has compounded this fact with the greater failing—as he himself was soon to pronounce it—of making it a first-person narrative. The book is George's monologue and he is the only developed character. To an extent this is certainly a weakness. Hilda, for example, comes across as little more than the caricature shrew on a Donald McGill postcard, and Orwell's own inherent fairness makes the reader rebel against George's refusal of sympathy towards her.

But there is something to be said for the first-person narrative, too. Orwell is writing about one of his obsessive themes, the difference between the mental, moral atmosphere of the present and that of the not very distant past. George Bowling is convincingly enough of an intellectual to be shown, like his creator, worrying at this theme. And the dramatization of a shift of consciousness like this is most efficiently presented in the clash of memory and actuality in one person's mind. Lower Binfield in the past may not have been a paradise, but for George Bowling it had one paradisal quality he hopes to find again: peace.

> I dare say it was a dull, sluggish, vegetable kind of life. You can say we were like turnips, if you like. But turnips don't live in terror of the boss, they don't lie awake at night thinking about the next slump and the next war. We had peace inside us.

To find a plot or fable to dramatize the conflict of memory and the present would probably have been beyond Orwell. The simplest solution was to present George Bowling's memories and his shock directly.

The book's second obvious weakness, though, relates to the first. Since George's memories and reactions *are* the book, it is inevitably rather plotless, an elaborate description of a situation rather than a developing series of events. So intensely dramatic an event as the accidental bombing comes, in fact, to look like an attempt by Orwell to inject some drama of incident into the book (but even so, this particular incident looks far too much like a symbol enacted). Orwell's tendency as a novelist was always towards the description of situations. For plots he had to force himself; *1984* has the very minimum of incident, compared to its elaboration of the conditions of life in Oceania. *Coming Up for Air*, in fact, is rather essayistic. One can quite easily imagine Orwell using this material for an essay. (A. E. Housman's description of Ruskin lecturing on Leicester past—represented in a framed and glassed Turner water-colour—and Leicester present— Ruskin overpainted the pollution and ugliness on the glass—would be analogous.)

To say so, however, immediately indicates one of the novel's great strengths: the consciousness, the voice, of George Bowling. This is a great imaginative feat on Orwell's part. He saw that one weakness of the first-person novel was that 'The narrator is never really separable from the author'. George Bowling's opinions co-incide with Orwell's own for much of the time, but he never has ideas beyond his station, so to speak. Orwell did not make the mistake— he saw it in other novelists—of making all his characters intellec-tuals. Orwell wanted George to be 'rather thoughtful and fairly well-educated, even slightly bookish', but not a mouthpiece for Orwell. He just about makes Bowling credible as such a person. The consciousness we encounter, moreover, the voice we hear, is very attractive, particularly in its humour, while being convincing as that of a suburban insurance representative. To a less impressive extent, that is true in all of Orwell's earlier novels. He could create good characters, vivid consciousnesses, or at least one in each book; Flory, Dorothy Hare, Gordon Comstock: they all have vitality and presence, individual voices.

Another aspect of Orwell's imaginative power in the book is the successful and detailed evocation of George Bowling's childhood as the son of the seed-merchant in Lower Binfield. The estimate of this success has to take into account the fact that Orwell is not really describing his own childhood. The setting and atmosphere were part of Orwell's experience, but he places George Bowling's birth ten years before his own, and the details of the life of the child of a slowly failing petty tradesman had to be acquired rather than simply remembered. (He is equally careful to give Bowling a very different physique from his own, and uses fatness as a recurrent motif in the novel.) Orwell confessed the book's similarity to the work of H. G. Wells (not, of course, to the Wells of science fiction) and George Bowling himself pays tribute to the influence of *The History of Mr Polly*. But literary sources don't account for Orwell's wonderful grasp of the actualities of Bowling as a boy and young man, when people still seemed to be breathing real air.

The Bowling of 1938 is a fine achievement of a different order. Following his own prescription of realism, Orwell tries to provide

Wigan in 1939

a voice for the man in the street. George Bowling is a statistic come to life, not 'typical', for no individual can be that, but representative. Orwell took care to get the details of Bowling's life correct, using the experience of his friend John Sceats, an insurance man. The novel is soundly 'researched'. But the greatest realism is involved in the ideas and attitudes of Bowling. Orwell presents a political theme through his book, but it is political in a way typical of Orwell's thinking, and evolves from the political writing of *The Road to Wigan Pier*.

That book opens with a spectacular—it is tempting to say 'baroque'—description of domestic squalor: the famous Brookers' tripe shop. The disintegration of all domestic relations presented there is a political theme for Orwell. He begins in this way to dramatize the specific effects on people of the large and usually abstract issues of politics. Something larger than the quirks of individuality have produced this dreadful demoralization; the rest of the book looks for the causes.

George Bowling likewise describes for us what it is not too grandiose to call his alienation. He exists in an atmosphere in which he cannot breathe. Some drastic change has taken place since his childhood. Life's sweetness has been replaced by awful modernity, and the world seems bent on war. Bowling wants answers, and an important part of what Orwell wants to say is the simple fact that Bowling is not a Socialist. When he attends a Left Book Club meeting he is repelled by fanaticism and by manners, the style of the committed participants. Bowling looks at Socialists as Orwell looked at them in *The Road to Wigan Pier*. They ought to have the answer, but everything about them drives ordinary, decent people away. *Coming Up for Air* is a documentary report to the Labour movement about its failure with the ordinary people who ought to be its popular support. In reporting in this manner, Orwell is demonstrating his own version of the political commitment of the artist, but as usual it was a form of commitment that would bring him small thanks from the Left.

Essays

There was, once upon a time, a literary genre called the essay, started by Montaigne, misused by Bacon, over-solidified by Johnson, at its local perfection in Hazlitt, and run into the ground by Belloc and practitioners of booksy frivolity in the first half of this century.

A. Quinton

Orwell is one of the greatest of English essayists, and the only problem about saying so is the term *essayist* itself. Because the essay is the least well-defined of the literary genres and the one whose territory is most easily infiltrated from the nearby low-rent districts of journalism (and also, perhaps, because it is the most widely practised of literary forms, ubiquitous in schools and examinations), it confers the least standing on its practitioners. *Essayist* seems properly applicable only to writers locked away in literary history; by modern writers the term *essay* is conspicuously avoided. The essay has a number of names, but *essay* is not one of them. Articles, reviews, leaders, editorials, columns, pieces, critiques: all are essays, but not by name.

Orwell, however, used the term a lot for his own writing, and gave one of the two volumes of his essays published in his lifetime the firmly uncompromising title *Critical Essays* (1946). (In America, however, and symptomatically, it received a jazzier title: *Dickens, Dali and Others*.) But the use of the term did not stimulate Orwell to critical enquiry about the form or to introspection about his practice. He never mentions Hazlitt or Lamb, the classic essayists his own writing brings most strikingly to mind. He seems to have adopted the essay as the form of journalism he was best qualified to write, and in effect reinvented it for himself.

Orwell's acceptance of *writer* as *novelist* had considerable attitudinal effect on his early career, and to an extent concealed from him his own best abilities. His novel *Burmese Days* (1934) indicates what he wanted his early career to look like, but it was *Down and Out in Paris and London* (1933)—quite unpolitical and less accomplished than *Burmese Days*—that foretold what his greatest achievements as a writer would be. Essentially, *Down and Out* is a long autobiographical essay, describing the period in 1929 when Orwell lived in Paris and worked for a time as a hotel dishwasher, followed by descriptions of his experiences among the underclass of London and southeast England. It established a pattern for Orwell's non-fictional writings by taking experiences not very distant from the everyday—'in front of your nose' was his favourite phrase—and showing what they were like from the inside. Eating in a restaurant, encountering the homeless or the unemployed, putting coal on the fire, or reading in the papers about a war in Spain: with Orwell as a guide one gets the unaccustomed view. He has been on the other side. It is his own variation on the universal theme of appearance and reality, and it extends, too, to Orwell's literary essays. These are preponderantly about the authors 'everyone knows', but who are shown from unexpected angles: Dickens, Kipling, Swift, Tolstoy, Jack London. Or they are *names* everyone knows (Gissing, Smollett) who are shown to be worth reading, or writers utterly forgotten, who deserve resurrection (Leonard Merrick, Winwood Reade), or modern authors, moving against the currents of fashion, who meet Orwell's great criterion—they are 'grown up' (Koestler).

The essay as Orwell wrote it thus reflected his own basic radicalism, and his political radicalism finds a counterpart in the general attitude of the essays. The topics and authors he chooses to write about are surprising, generally in the very positive sense of causing the reader to perceive that his experiences are super-structures built on unexpected, even shocking foundations, or that the experiences have surprising meanings. The reader who dines in a restaurant discovers that his meal is the product of a crude and extensive industrial system. The vaguely remembered Smollett wrote novels possessing the virtues of realism. The shooting of an elephant, the culminating experience of the sporting sahib, lays bare the hollowness of imperialism. In front of your nose, if you will only look, everyday reality is very different from what you think. The radical habit of mind resists accepting surface truths, and the essay was Orwell's preferred means for getting at the truths beneath the surface.

Radicalism, in its political sense and in broader attitudes, is obviously one link between Orwell and his predecessors in the essay tradition, notably Hazlitt and Lamb. Hazlitt seems closest to Orwell, in politics, style, and life-style. His interest in power, his general 'Protestantism' of attitude, and his position as a radical critic of radicalism all remind one of Orwell. There is an isolation about Hazlitt very similar to that which Orwell had to accept as the price of his independence. Yet it is the more unlikely Lamb who provides the most fascinating—because insoluble—puzzle in Orwell's relationship with his literary forebears. It is not possible to present the evidence here, so I can only invite readers to make the comparison for themselves. Lamb's second essay about his schooldays, 'Christ's Hospital Five- and Thirty Years Ago', is in many ways so close to Orwell's 'Such, such were the joys' that students of mine who read both works always assume Orwell's debt to Lamb. Yet there is no proof at all that Orwell read Lamb or knew that essay; all the evidence is coincidence. Yet if coincidence is the final answer, it underlines the affinity of Orwell to that early nineteenth-century tradition. Lamb is in effect undermining himself, since seven years earlier he had written 'Recollections of Christ's Hospital', extolling the school. Orwell sees only one side to the case, and his method is to attack all the mythology that supports the private school. But, exactly in Lamb's manner, he relies for his basic data on memory and reflection; this is autobio-graphy organized for polemic. And, again like Lamb and Hazlitt, Orwell needed only one other support for memory and reflection: his reading.

At the beginning of his career as a non-fiction writer, Orwell showed some signs of being attracted to one very typical manifes-tation of the 1930s' spirit, the documentary movement, the 'creative treatment of actuality', as one of its pioneers, the film-maker John

Grierson, called it. *The Road to Wigan Pier* and *Homage to Catalonia* are sometimes called 'documentaries', but any definable documentary impulse was fast disappearing when Orwell finished *Wigan Pier*. That book has its share of *cinéma verité* effects, and its share of statistics, too, but a comparison of the final text with the diary (1/74) Orwell kept while researching the book shows that he employed selectivity and rearrangement, the basic artistic tools, to give his material its most effective shape. Once 'actuality' has received its 'creative treatment' the implicit claim of documentary to be the unvarnished truth is gone. The artist is creating a picture, and pictures look better, and are therefore more truthful, when varnished. After *The Road to Wigan Pier*, which contains a large element of autobiography, Orwell's basic research tools were his observations, his memories and reflections, and his reading. His subject matter is strikingly original, but his methods are those of the classic essayist.

'How The Poor Die'

To see Orwell's characteristic employment of the essay, and his methods, we can look at one of his late triumphs in the form, 'How The Poor Die', first published in a magazine in 1946. It is a reminiscent account of an episode of sickness during Orwell's stay in Paris in 1929, the period described much earlier in *Down and Out in Paris and London*. The essay does not mention the book, and Orwell does not explain why the book gave no account of his stay in hospital. As we read, however, we discover that Orwell's explanation of his memories has uncovered meanings in the experience that were probably not accessible when he was writing *Down and Out*. Memory and reflection over time have unearthed its significance, though Orwell pretends that the meaning was there when the events took place.

The title seems gratuitously melodramatic, but one learns to trust Orwell's titles. 'Die' is the shocking element, and one's first impression of the whole essay is likely to be the shocking effect of the grisly conditions Orwell reports. (In retrospect, it is surprising that only one patient's death is actually described in the essay.) Longer experience, however, will show that the title points out to us one of Orwell's discoveries, that the deaths of the poor are qualitatively different from those of everyone else simply because of the poverty. That is not all he discovers, but the title does point to a central truth.

This essay does not begin with one of Orwell's epigrams, but with a simple statement of his stay at the 'Hôpital X' in 1929. (It was in fact the Hôpital Cochin.) Technical adroitness in this essay occurs in the form of artful delays, and this opening provides one such instance. He describes the bureaucracy of the reception desk, his high temperature, and the compulsory bath—'just as in prison or the workhouse'—and his change into hospital clothes, nightshirt and bathrobe. Only then does he mention that it was a February night and that he had pneumonia. In this condition he was led two hundred yards through the open air to the hospital ward. The motif, to be consolidated throughout the essay, of the patient, the *impoverished* patient, as an insentient object is thus inaugurated by Orwell's own admission to the hospital.

Self-pity is quite absent and there is a note of wry humour, but before developing it, Orwell uses again his delaying technique. 'When we got into the ward I was aware of a strange feeling of familiarity whose origin I did not succeed in pinning down until later in the night.' But he does not tell us what it is, and for the effect of his essay it is best if, having been told, we forget. (And in my experience that is exactly what happens for most readers.) Forgetting is aided by the subsequent stages of the admissions routine. Orwell is subjected, by a doctor and student who take no human notice of him, to the process of cupping, 'a treatment you can read about in old medical text-books but which till then I had vaguely thought of as one of those things they do to horses.' Orwell has watched 'this barbarous remedy' employed on another patient 'with detachment and a certain amount of amusement' but then they do it to him, leaving him 'humiliated, disgusted and frightened'. But the cupping is not all. There follows the mustard poultice, 'seemingly a matter of routine like the hot bath'. But whereas the 'hot bath' was tepid, the poultice is hot. Other patients gather around with 'half-sympathetic grins'.

> I learned later that watching a patient have a mustard poultice was a favourite pastime in the ward. These things are applied for a quarter of an hour and certainly they are funny enough if you don't happen to be the person inside. For the first five minutes the pain is severe, but you believe you can bear it. During the second five minutes this belief evaporates, but the poultice is buckled at the back and you can't get it off. This is the period the onlookers most enjoy.

After this torture, Orwell is left to sleep but instead passes 'the only night of my life—I mean the only night spent in bed—in which I have not slept at all, not even a minute'.

The mastery Orwell displays in this opening deserves a little emphasis. He has established the attitudes and atmosphere of the hospital, the antiquated nature of the place and the treatment it gives. He has dramatized the impersonality of it, the attitude implicit everywhere that the patient, by virtue of his poverty, is something less than a fellow human being. He has put himself in the picture as the participant-observer, slightly distanced from the events by his ironical attitude. (The irony has a paradoxical effect. It works to allow Orwell his nearly clinical and exact descriptions of human degradation and suffering, and this permits the reader a clear view, since the exclamations of horror that would—without the presence of the ironical attitude—normally accompany the descriptions are suppressed by the irony. The total effect is to increase the impact of those scenes.) Finally, Orwell has slipped into and out of the reader's consciousness his 'strange feeling of familiarity', which can now await its reappearance.

After getting himself admitted to the hospital, undergoing his painful rites of passage, Orwell turns to the daily routine. He describes the progress through the crowded wards of the teaching physician, accompanied by a troupe of students and 'sometimes followed by imploring cries' from patients whose illnesses were not sufficiently interesting to attract attention. Orwell, however, 'with an exceptionally fine specimen of bronchial rattle', had students queueing to listen to his chest, sometimes tremblingly eager to get their hands on him, but 'not from any one of them did you get a word of conversation or a look direct in your face'. The non-paying patient was primarily a specimen.

Orwell's account of the patients crowded around his own bed begins with his right-hand neighbour, 'a little red-haired cobbler with one leg shorter than the other', who used to announce to Orwell the death of a patient by calling out his number and flinging his arms above his head. 'This man had not much wrong with him, but in most of the other beds within my angle of vision some squalid tragedy or some plain horror was being enacted.' The four cases that he then describes are certainly squalid tragedies or plain horrors, but the descriptions amount to a brief, allusive anthology of nineteenth-century French fiction. Balzac, Zola, and perhaps chiefly Maupassant have provided Orwell with this vision. A scene that Balzac did not live long enough to write ('In the bed beyond that a veteran of the war of 1870 was dying, a handsome old man with a white imperial, round whose bed, at all hours when visiting was allowed, four elderly female relatives dressed all in black sat exactly like crows, obviously scheming for some pitiful legacy') is followed by a vignette in Maupassant's manner (an old man 'was suffering from some disease that made him urinate almost constantly. A huge glass receptacle stood always beside his bed. One day his wife and daughter came to visit him. At the sight of them the old man's bloated face lit up with a smile of surprising sweetness, and as his daughter, a pretty girl of about twenty, approached the bed I saw that his hand was working its way from under the bed-clothes. I seemed to see in advance the gesture that was coming—the girl kneeling beside the bed, the old man's hand laid on her head in his dying blessing. But no, he merely handed her the bed-bottle, which she promptly took from him and emptied into the receptacle'). The memories of French fiction that enable Orwell to organize his scenes like this will become an open, rather than an allusive, form of reference later in the essay. It is clear that he regards such memories of his reading as reliable documentary evidence for an understanding of the past, a kind of information that, for the individual, parallels the folklore beliefs of classes and communities. The stay in the Hôpital X yields its greatest meaning by making such beliefs accessible to Orwell, and he puts his reading to work to form a context for those beliefs.

The mode of the essay now shifts from memories of incident to reflection, corresponding to Orwell's own remembered movement from the hospital (he 'fled ... without waiting for a medical discharge'). The last incident of his stay is the death of numéro 57, a demonstration-worthy case of cirrhosis of the liver. 'I had had time for a good look at numéro 57. Indeed I lay on my side to look at him.' It has been—and will be—the fate of numéro 57 to be gazed at, a living and now a dead specimen. But under Orwell's eyes he is the occasion for an essayist's reflection that suddenly turns on the reader with a sting of ironical recognition.

> As I gazed at the tiny, screwed-up face it struck me that this disgusting piece of refuse, waiting to be carted away and dumped on a slab in the dissecting room, was an example of 'natural' death, one of the things you pray for in the Litany. There you are then, I thought, that's what's waiting for you, twenty, thirty, forty years hence: that is how the lucky ones die, the ones who live to be old.

The prayer in the Litany has slightly less ironical point than Orwell gives it (one prays to be delivered 'from battle and murder, and from sudden death'—religiously unprepared death, that is), but the startling applicability of all the horrors and tragedies to one's normal wish to live a long life brings one to endorse if only for a moment—Orwell's verdict': 'it's better to die violently and not too old.' The horrors of a 'natural' death—'something slow, smelly, and painful'—are, however, only increased by the surroundings of a public institution, and with these thoughts Orwell moves to the last stage of his essay.

He concedes that the French hospital was worse than anything he could have encountered in England. British nursing has the Florence Nightingale tradition to professionalize it. 'The nurses at the Hôpital X still had a tinge of Mrs Gamp about them', a typical recourse to Dickens to provide the 'documentary' comparison. Even amongst French hospitals, this one was abnormally bad. A pause at this point might allow one to suppose that Orwell's experience has been in fact without general value, but not so. The value of it is now shown to be historical. Orwell's stay in the hospital has given him access to a living remnant of the past, and a particularly elusive form of the past at that. He has been able to explore the popular mind, to travel back in time, since the awful Hôpital X belonged in effect to an earlier period: 'something of the atmosphere of the nineteenth century had managed to survive, and therein lay its peculiar interest.'

The patients whom Orwell met were effectively nineteenth-century paupers in the charity wards of a nineteenth-century hospital, '*popularly regarded* as much the same thing as a prison, and an old-fashioned, dungeon-like prison at that' when 'the whole business of doctoring was looked on with dread *by ordinary people*'. The words I have put into italics indicate the form of attitude Orwell is uncovering. Among the patients, he found 'a lingering belief in the old stories that have now almost faded from memory in England—stories for instance about doctors cutting you open out of sheer curiosity or thinking it funny to start operating before you were properly "under"'. Because it dealt with poor patients in a pre-modern manner, the hospital has kept alive the folklore of a time before antiseptics and before anaesthetics, the 'anti-surgery tradition' as Orwell calls it. And he turns to literature to document it.

> Think of the conversations of Bob Sawyer and Benjamin Allen [in *The Pickwick Papers*], which no doubt are hardly parodies, or the field hospitals in *La Débâcle* [by Zola] and *War and Peace*, or that shocking description of an amputation in Melville's *White-jacket*! Even the names given to doctors in nineteenth-century English fiction, Slasher, Carver, Sawyer, Fillgrave and so on, and the generic nickname 'sawbones', are about as grim as they are comic.

And then he mentions Tennyson's poem 'The Children's Hospital' as best representing the anti-surgery point of view. When he weighs up the popular traditions and their embodiment in literature, Orwell finds much to be said for them. Pre-anaesthetic and pre-antisepsis surgery was brutal and often fatal. In the eyes of the poor a hospital was reasonably seen as a place of desperate last resort, and may in fact still be so. 'The dread of hospitals probably still survives among the very poor and in all of us it has only recently disappeared. It is a dark patch not far beneath the surface of our minds.'

Orwell's stay in the Hôpital X, the talk of the patients, and his own reading—popular rather than esoteric: Orwell assumes his reader will have knowledge of the books he mentions—have uncovered the 'dark patch' for him. In his last paragraph he finally returns to the 'strange feeling of familiarity' he mentioned much earlier. It was familiarity with the nineteenth-century hospital, 'which I had never seen but of which I had a *traditional knowledge*' (my italics). Entering the hospital had 'unearthed from my memory that poem of Tennyson's, which I had not thought of for twenty years'. (If Orwell's 'twenty years' is accurate, he would than have been about six years old. The poem is properly titled 'In the Children's Hospital'.) He had been sick and his nurse had read the poem aloud to him.

> We had shuddered over the poem together, and then seemingly I had forgotten it. Even its name would probably have recalled nothing to me. But the first glimpse of the ill-lit, murmurous room, with the beds so close together, suddenly roused the train of thought to which it belonged, and in the night that followed I found myself remembering the whole story and atmosphere of the poem, with many of its lines complete.

Orwell presents all the reminiscent reflection of the essay as something that occurred at the time, though that seems highly unlikely. By claiming so, however, he makes involuntary memory a vital part of the experience, and so the literary figure who comes to preside over the essay finally emerges as Marcel Proust, the last and greatest of those French realists to whom Orwell has been referring or alluding throughout. There is an almost ironical contrast, of course, between the social milieu of *A la Recherche du Temps Perdu* and that of the Hôpital X, but Proust and Orwell share, nevertheless, a tradition of realism, particularly the reality of mental events and of literature—reading—as part of that reality. Orwell's memories of the hospital and his reflections on it are steeped in literature, yet this fact seems to move him closer to the mind of the largely unlettered people whose folk memories he is enabled to reveal. Forty years later, however, one may fairly wonder if that would still be true, if folk memory and literature still fit so well together in the electronic age.

Orwell's best known essays are those which, in his own lifetime or afterwards, were collected into books. It is chiefly upon them that his reputation as an essayist stands. But the existence of the *Collected Essays, Journalism and Letters* is a reminder that Orwell wrote far more essays than were ever formally collected, and that he did much good work in the form of short essays. His *As I Please* columns for *Tribune*, for instance, ran for two periods between 1943 and 1945. Seventy-two of these columns appeared, and any might contain three or four short essays, many of which explored ideas that were to be used in *Animal Farm* and *1984*. In fact there is little perceptible difference between the 'essays' and the 'journalism' in Orwell's work, since the essay was the basic form of all his writing, perceptible even in his forms of fiction.

Criticism

It would not be difficult to define 'critic' so as to make it scarcely applicable to Orwell, yet to do so would be ridiculously unjust. Criticism, in any but its most arcane manifestations, was Orwell's way of intellectual life. His relationship to twentieth-century literary criticism, particularly in its academic forms, was odd and oblique, but only until academic literary criticism found itself entering territory where the 'reading' was of new kinds of 'texts' and where the footprints of George Orwell were the only signs of earlier exploration. Orwell's oddness has had the effect of making him the precursor of some highly characteristic late twentieth-century criticism, for criticism is acceding to Orwell's own definition of it, a definition made implicit in his practice though never put into formal terms. Orwell's best criticism is the search for meaning in the life of society. He was one of life's critical examiners, and the meaning he found could bear a variety of names. 'Political' is, of course, one. 'Semi-sociological' is a term he used himself. In the 1980s 'semiological' would be a likely choice.

Literary criticism

Literature was Orwell's native element, the human enterprise to which he naturally turned first to make and find the meaning of life. He was almost exclusively literary. Of the other arts, he was interested only in drama—dramatic literature—with an occasional mention of folk song. (Orwell did write theatre criticism for a while, but none of it is included in the *Collected Essays, Journalism and Letters.*)

The concentration on literature had no mandarin aspect. Orwell took particular notice of popular literature, even of what he called 'good bad books', and in fact did his most original criticism with some of the least refined of literary works. That criticism, simply by being his best, seems to settle his position on one of the great theoretical controversies of our century: the issue of the instrumentality of literature. In writing about 'Raffles and Miss Blandish' or 'Boys' Weeklies', Orwell is finding what is strictly speaking a non-literary or non-aesthetic use for his texts. They are a means to an end, which is an understanding of ideologies and attitudes only implicit in them. The primary value of literature, according to this process, is documentary; it provides access to past consciousness, and is material for the history of the consciousness.

Such instrumentality was clearly of great value to Orwell, but it would be a mistake to assume that therefore he abandoned the aesthetic position, the view that literature has value in and of itself, and that criticism should judge and explain a work of art as a work of art only. These opposing positions, in fact, co-existed in Orwell's mind, much as opposing views of the writer's function did. The chief energies of his criticism went into demonstrating the instrumentality of literature, into showing its documentary value, but he never abandoned the non-instrumental view. Thus, of a memoir of the Spanish War, he could write: 'Seeing that the International Brigade is in some sense fighting for all of us—a thin line of suffering and often ill-armed human beings standing between barbarism and at least comparative decency—it may seem ungracious to say that this book is a piece of sentimental tripe; but so it is.' When asked for his views on the award of the Bollingen Prize to Ezra Pound in 1948, Orwell wrote a reply, in effect a capsule verion of his essay on Salvador Dali, including these words:

> since the judges have taken what amounts to the 'art for art's sake position', that is the position that aesthetic integrity and common decency are two separate things, then at least let us keep them separate and not excuse Pound's political career on the ground that he is a good writer.

This formulation, particularly with its reference to 'common decency', seems to indicate that really Orwell dismisses the 'art for art's sake' view, but that is not so. If he did, he could in no way have approved of Pound's prize, but he does not oppose it; he points out the contrasting views, shows his own inclination, and makes nothing of the inconsistency of *not* making a final choice.

Since Orwell never made a systematic examination of his own attitude towards this inconsistency, he was able to persist in it. He could choose either attitude. His early review of J. B. Priestley's *Angel Pavement*, for instance, says all that needs to be said about Priestley's claims to real achievement, and does so solely on aesthetic grounds. But it is significant that this is one of Orwell's earliest book reviews. Though he never abandoned the non-instrumental view of literature, it seems undeniably odd to hear Orwell saying so forthrightly, 'a novelist is not required to have good intentions but to convey beauty'. He always believed the function of a novel was to be a novel and not another thing, but granted this as the ultimate criterion, he found the instrumentality of literature more interesting and more in conformity with his own talents. He clearly loved poetry very much, and supported its right to be appreciated aesthetically, for its 'music' or its 'texture', but as a critic of poetry he found little of interest to say until he asked questions of an instrumental type, such as about the connection between Yeats's 'obscurantist opinions and his tendency towards "quaint-

119

ness" of style'—'he is an exception to the rule that poets do not use poetical language'—or about Eliot's 'escape from individuality' into the Church of England. These are important questions, but Orwell seems to know that he cannot get very close to the ultimate reality of Yeats or Eliot by asking them. In effect Orwell decided to specialize on what he did best as a critic.

'From an anthropological point of view'

In 1936 Orwell took up a suggestion of Geoffrey Gorer's:

> What you say about trying to study our own customs from an anthropological point of view opens up a lot of fields of thought, but one thing to notice about ourselves is that people's habits etc. are formed not only by their upbringing and so forth but also very largely by books. I have often thought it would be very interesting to study the conventions etc. of books from an anthropological point of view.

He made a specific suggestion, too.

> It would be interesting and I believe valuable to work out the underlying beliefs and general imaginative background of a writer like Edgar Wallace. But of course that's the kind of thing nobody will ever print.

But when Orwell began to write from this angle, he did find publishers, and he extended the field from literature ('Charles Dickens' and 'Raffles and Miss Blandish') to popular magazines ('Boys' Weeklies') and the comic postcard ('The Art of Donald McGill'). This group of essays is Orwell's greatest contribution to criticism.

The essay on Dickens, the longest of Orwell's essays, is the precursor of a whole academic industry, and moreover tells us a great deal about Orwell himself. (It is full of judgements that seem to apply as well to Orwell as to Dickens.) The basic assumption of all this criticism is that it throws light upon the readership and, in the broadest sense, the culture within which it exists. Orwell, therefore, evaluates Dickens as a political figure—again, taking 'political' in its broadest sense—and relates his judgements of Dickens's artistic successes and failures to the Dickens who was a 'figure' in his society and continues to be one in twentieth-century Britain, a figure, that is, associated with issues of reform and social criticism. 'Where exactly does he stand, socially, morally, and politically?' That is the line of the enquiry. Both Dickens and his public, past and present, see his novels as attempts to change society. Orwell's essay evaluates those views.

In 'Raffles and Miss Blandish', Orwell compares the novels of the late Victorian writer E. W. Hornung with a best seller of the Second World War, James Hadley Chase's *No Orchids for Miss Blandish*: the 1900 version of 'glamourized crime' and the 1939 version. 'For sociological purposes they can be compared', for Orwell's object is to contrast 'the immense difference in moral atmosphere between the two books, and the change in popular attitude that this probably implies'. The contrast, which Orwell dramatized in another form in *Coming Up for Air*, is between a hierarchical and snobbish world, but one which, with its gentlemanly and chivalric codes has a sort of pastoral peace, and the world of Chase's gangsters, which is the world of bully-worship and violent sex: 'a daydream appropriate to a totalitarian age', the kind of literature written by machines for the proles to read in *1984*.

'Raffles and Miss Blandish' is, in fact, a document in Orwell's myth of the fall of the modern world into power worship, and it is his use of 'sociological' that causes doubt. Orwell makes an impressionistic comparison of his two authors, and draws conclusions about the 'moral atmosphere' each one breathes. Sociology, however, would demand greater rigour of method. How can the representative nature of these two books be ascertained? What numerical foundation is there for the conclusions Orwell draws? The sales figures are Orwell's only evidence, but the figures in isolation are not very useful. If we accept Orwell's moral judgement, we accept his myth of past and present, which may or may not be a sociological truth.

Orwell's interpretation of the ideology of 'Boys' Weeklies' is better founded. He can make a sound assessment of numerical popularity to support his interpretation. The magazines and postcards are phenomena sufficiently widespread to support his conclusions. At a certain age, boys demand adventure stories. 'They get what they are looking for, but they get it wrapped up in the illusions which their future employers think suitable for them.' By analysing the politics and ideology found in these papers, despite their claim to be free of all such ideas, Orwell brilliantly vindicates his own claim, made in 'Why I Write', that 'The opinion that art should have nothing to do with politics is itself a political attitude'. In fact, the boys' weeklies sell their readers, and 'all the better because it is done indirectly . . . a set of beliefs which would be regarded as hopelessly out of date in the Central Office of the Conservative Party'. Most of the magazines discussed are owned by Amalgamated Press. 'The *Gem* and the *Magnet*, therefore, are closely linked up with the *Daily Telegraph* and *Financial Times*.' The parody form of this connection in *1984* is called 'prolefeed'.

The atmosphere of 'The Art of Donald McGill' is very different, for the comic postcard is not part of a scheme of mind-control. 'There is no sign in them of any attempt to induce an outlook acceptable to the ruling class.' These highly stylized drawings, with their elaborate conventions ('Drunkenness is something peculiar to middle-aged men. Drunken youths or women are never presented') are a genuine expression of working-class culture, and they reveal in Orwell's analysis a series of surprises. The McGill postcard 'only has meaning in relation to a fairly strict moral code'. The sex jokes all have a background of marriage, not promiscuity, with the implication, anathema to the sophisticated, that 'marriage is something profoundly exciting and important, the biggest event in the average human being's life'. Jokes about nagging wives and tyrannous mothers-in-law 'do at least imply a stable society in which marriage is indissoluble and family loyalty taken for granted'. The postcards never present good-looking people who are not young. Middle age is a sort of unavoidable blight, but this too is a reflection of working-class maturity. 'For to look young after, say thirty, is largely a matter of wanting to do so.' In accepting the loss of youth, working-class people are 'more traditional, more in accord with the Christian past' than those who cling desperately to youth. '"Youth's a stuff will not endure" expresses the normal, traditional attitude. It is this ancient wisdom that McGill and his colleagues are reflecting, no doubt unconsciously . . . .'

Orwell sees the vulgar comic postcards of Donald McGill as an expression of saturnalia, a licensed excess, carnival, 'a harmless rebellion against virtue' that helps reconcile people to the hard demands of routine and self-sacrifice that society has to make of them.

> When it comes to the pinch, human beings are heroic. Women face childbed and the scrubbing brush, revolutionaries keep their mouths shut in the torture chamber, battleships go down with their guns still firing when their decks are awash. It is only that the other element in man, the lazy, cowardly, debt-bilking adulterer who is inside all of us, can never be suppressed altogether and needs a hearing occasionally.

Orwell's use of the comic postcard as his 'text' for this interpretation implies that he had begun to see that, for his 'anthropological point of view', books could be supplemented by the 'reading' of other phenomena. He made that extension of his field of enquiry, and in doing so made himself, as Philip Thody has shown, a pioneer of the investigation into the meaning of signs now associated with name of Roland Barthes and dignified with the name of 'semiology'.

Orwell had always believed—*Homage to Catalonia* shows it very clearly—that manners, people's routine contacts and exchanges with each other, were signs giving reliable indicators of underlying political relationships. (*Homage to Catalonia* begins with an embrace of true fraternity.) Orwell was a perceptive reader of such signs. Clothing carried meaning, too, and in one of his commentaries on the subject his analysis anticipates the Barthes of both *Mythologies* and *Système de la Mode*. His subject was the sahib's pith helmet, the 'solar topi'. Reading about Wingate's campaign in Burma, Orwell noticed that the Chindits wore slouch hats, not the classical pith helmet. Ten or twenty years earlier, all the European troops would have been believed to be in danger of mortal sunstroke because they did not wear the pith helmet. Orwell recalled what he had been told about the danger—to Europeans only—of the deadly rays of the oriental sun. 'Take your topi off in the open for one moment, even for one moment, and you may be a dead man.' Yet one day, presumably during his police service, his helmet was blown away and carried down a stream. Despite a whole day bare-headed, he suffered no ill effects. Nor, he noticed, did sailors who worked bare-headed in the rigging of ships. Then he discovered that the pith helmet was a recent invention. 'The early Europeans in India knew nothing of it. In short, the whole thing was bunkum.'

> You can only rule over a subject race, especially when you are in a small minority, if you honestly believe yourself to be racially superior, and it helps towards this if you can believe that the subject race is *biologically* different . . . this nonsense about Europeans being subject to sunstroke and Orientals not, was the most cherished superstition of all. The thin skull was the mark of racial superiority, and the pith topi was a sort of emblem of imperialism. (3/73)

When Orwell was thinking about a school for his adopted son Richard, he inclined towards Westminster. Among its good points was that 'They have abandoned their top-hats'. Such a sign to Orwell was not a comic triviality. It meant something; it demanded critical enquiry.

6 The great fictions: *Animal Farm* and *1984*

Not really novels

With hindsight, one can see that Orwell's success as a novelist would come in 'impure' forms, novels that stand a long way from the ideal self-sufficient novel of Henry James, the great theoretician of the realistic novel. Orwell's two great fictions, a beast fable and a dystopia, are basically 'romances', though they keep to the realism of surface which Orwell accepted as the basis of the novel's power. Both have strong documentary elements, as a further manifestation of 'impurity', and both are novels of ideas, since they are dramatic embodiments of Orwell's views on twentieth-century political history. 'Allegorical romance' might seem more appropriate to Spenser's *Faerie Queene*, but the term defines very well what Orwell is after in these two books. *1984* avoids every romantic convention of science fiction or utopian speculation, and includes large chunks of documentary material. But *Animal Farm*, undeniably the fiction of Orwell's that comes closest to perfection, is the most impure of all, judged by the Jamesian criteria. It follows the conventions of the beast fable, and although it has a Jamesian self-sufficiency, Orwell certainly did not want to succeed there, since the meaning of *Animal Farm* depends on the reader's possession of 'outside information'. The allegory depends on his knowing the events of the Russian Revolution. The book is clearly propagandistic, since Orwell intended it for use in his campaign against the 'Russian myth'. And, in consequence of these objectives, it simplifies, as a novel must *not* do if it is to be true to the complexity of life. The simplicity and simplification are the prices the book pays for its perfection of shape. *Animal Farm* is as much and as little a novel as *Gulliver's Travels*, and if less mysterious than *Gulliver* in the final analysis, then attaining its more limited satirical objectives with greater impact. If to be 'not really a novelist' is a limitation, then *Animal Farm* and *1984* display the strength of that limitation.

Animal Farm: *artistry*

Animal Farm appears on many syllabuses, and teachers can often tell of readers whose first experience of the book has left them quite unaware of meanings other than those of the story itself. The alle-

GEORGE
ORWELL

FOLWARK
ZWIERZĘCY

NIEZALEŻNA
OFICYNA
WYDAWNICZA

Clandestine edition, Warsaw, 1979

gorical dimension has not appeared; the historical application is unmade. Such readers have failed with the book, but quite pardonably, for so self-contained and self-sustaining is Orwell's tale that it never insists on its applications. A skilled reader, absolutely ignorant of all twentieth-century history, could be expected to detect that *Animal Farm* is, at very least, a fable, but the skilled reader would understand the conventions of fable. But if one knows nothing about literary convention, the fact that animals don't talk except in art is not enough.

The self-sustaining and self-contained story of *Animal Farm* is enormously deft, and before turning to the meanings that surround the central narrative, we should acknowledge the artistry that Orwell commands there.

Most impressive of all his achievements is the atmosphere of genuine tragedy which gradually envelops the unfolding story. Orwell seems to have handicapped himself drastically for the attaining of such a mood. The beast fable simplifies radically, especially in the depiction of character, and normally its effects are comic, at most pathetic. The book is a short one, often printed in less than a hundred pages, which does not seem to give time for the cumulative effects of tragic feeling. And a pervasive, hilarious, though bitter irony runs through the whole thing.

Orwell meets each of these limiting factors head-on. Like Swift in *A Modest Proposal*, he rigorously controls his own presence in the story while everywhere the force, even violence, of his own feelings comes through. The success of the animals' revolution, for example, is really euphoric because Orwell invests the event with his own passionate detestation of tyranny.

> They had never seen animals behave like this before, and this sudden uprising of creatures whom they were used to thrashing and maltreating just as they chose, frightened them almost out of their wits.

The animal revolution is a real 'objective correlative' for all the deep emotion Orwell feels for the greatest and most necessary human action, the strike back against tyranny, the action which—in numerous forms—pervades all his writing. When the animals gallop in ecstasy round the farm from which Jones has fled, their joy is Orwell's pleasure in the attainment of freedom. Never, in any way, does he later imply that the revolution was a mistake, that a return to Manor Farm would be best. Benjamin the donkey is in many ways a sympathetic character, but his passive conservatism—'things never had been, nor ever could be much better or much worse'—is not Orwell's. The whole satiric point of his book is that Manor Farm *is* re-established, by the failure of the revolution. The whip in the trotter of the bi-pedal Napoleon is a sardonic irony, but a measure too of tragic loss. Late in the book, after the first 'purge', the animals—the 'lower animals'—gather again on the knoll from which they had first gazed on the liberated farm. On the day after the revolution 'they could hardly believe that it was all their own'. Now, 'with a kind of surprise they remembered that it was their own farm'. In the unarticulated thoughts of Clover, Orwell puts into words the tragedy of their loss.

> These scenes of terror and slaughter were not what they had looked forward to on that night when old Major first stirred them to rebellion. If she herself had had any picture of the future, it had been of a society of animals set free from hunger and the whip, all equal, each working according to his capacity, the strong protecting the weak . . . . Instead—she did not know why—they had come to a time when no one dared speak his mind . . . . (VII)

Clover's only expression of these feelings is to begin to sing *Beasts of England*. 'The other animals sitting round her took it up, and they sang it three times over—very tunefully, but slowly and mournfully, in a way they had never sung it before.' Orwell follows this brilliantly conceived lamentation with a fine stroke of bitter irony. Squealer announces the abolition of their anthem. 'In *Beasts of England* we expressed our longing for a better society in days to come. But that society has now been established. Clearly this song has no longer any purpose.' Such reasoning of the need, and the progress of tyranny by tiny steps, each inscrutable yet glossed with rationalization, is a method that is not absurd to compare to that of *King Lear*. And Orwell manages his simplified characters and the brevity of his narrative so as to strengthen the tragic impression.

The movement of history in the realistic novel—*War and Peace*, *The Quiet Don*, *Dr Zhivago*, or *August, 1914*—seems to demand great length of narrative and complex multiplicity of character. Something similar is found in those tragedies of Shakespeare where individuals' lives are most clearly projected against the background of public life: *Lear, Hamlet, Antony and Cleopatra, Coriolanus*. History is Orwell's subject in *Animal Farm*, and although individuals dramatize the story, the tragedy is not an individual's tragedy. The simplified individuality of the beast fable allows the story of history to be the tragedy, and allows that story to be told with great narrative economy. The convention of the beast fable will allow the animals to be individuals only as long as their representative nature is felt. The animals are convincingly a whole people, a nation. Thus the tragic 'emotion of multitude' which Yeats found in the paralleling of plots in *King Lear* is present in the simplicity, both of characterization and of narrative, in *Animal Farm*. The passage of time does not need the turning of many pages. We know the characters

127

completely very quickly; the changes in their existence are the movement of history itself. And the bitter irony of the book is that of an inevitability that mocks the inevitability of revolution. Once the 'new class' of Napoleon, Snowball, and the pigs begins to emerge, it is inevitable that all of the Seven Commandments of Animalism will be broken and hence rewritten. Indeed, in 'but some are more equal than others' Orwell found the perfect climax for the ironical advance of the narrative. When the last commandment is rewritten (and its rewriting becomes inevitable with the incident of the milk, at the end of Chapter II), the book's perfection of form and statement is complete.

Animal Farm: *propaganda*

> As an instrument of destructive propaganda it has no equal anywhere; its effect upon succeeding generations is unparalleled outside religious history; had its author written nothing else, it would have ensured his lasting fame.
>
> Isaiah Berlin, of *The Communist Manifesto*

Animal Farm is a weapon Orwell designed for the campaign he fought after the Spanish War in order to save Western Socialism from the 'Soviet myth'. He wanted it to be 'a story that could be easily understood by almost anyone and which could be easily translated into other languages' (3/110). The form of fable he chose and the brevity of the text are means to the essential end of universal access and unmistakability. Orwell is unrelentingly didactic, so firmly so, indeed, that the 'aesthetic' success of *Animal Farm* involves the book in some ideological tangles (see below).

The particular purpose of Orwell's fable brings to mind his interest in another form of writing, the pamphlet (he collected pamphlets and began publishing an anthology of them). The 'greatest of all socialist pamphlets', as Isaiah Berlin has called *The Communist Manifesto*, provides the ideas in Major's speech to the animals (I), but it also governs the basic form and strategy—the shape—of *Animal Farm*. *The Communist Manifesto* is simple and powerful; its rhetoric is sweeping, a bold picture—or poster—in primary colours; its irony is heavy but effective. In Marx's German and in translation, it is one of the most widely read books of all time. *Animal Farm* is planned to reproduce every one of these features, and does. Orwell was not only providing an alternative reading of Marxist history but also a formal alternative to the most influential Marxist book. *Animal Farm* is a spiritual parody of *The Communist Manifesto*.

Allegorical ingenuity

At the Moscow Book Fair some years ago, a copy of *1984* was allowed to remain on display at the stand of a Western publisher. A copy of *Animal Farm*, however was resolutely excluded by the authorities. When one studies the allegorical details of the book, it is not hard to see why. The events of *Animal Farm* are transformations of the events of the Russian Revolution, and the wit Orwell displays in finding farmyard parallels for the events of history is amazing, undeniably one of the great pleasures of reading it. This should be emphasized for, as in other aspects of the book, this success too poses ideological problems.

Orwell said that, in basing the book on the actual history of the Russian Revolution, he dealt with the episodes schematically and changed their chronological order: 'this was necessary for the symmetry of the story.' (3/110) Changes include the omission of a Lenin figure. Major is Marx, Napoleon Stalin, and Snowball Trotsky. Lenin, the combination of idealist and prototypical totalitarian, is a complex personality with a complex rôle. Since Orwell wished to emphasize idealism's collapse into tyranny, a figure combining both elements, rather than embodying one or the other, would demand the novel's resources of complexity and not the fable's simplifications. The omission greatly helps 'the symmetry of the story'.

On every page, in tiny details as well as in large elements, Orwell's ingenuity is manifest. Jones the Farmer, who represents the Czarist régime, has 'fallen on evil days. He had become much disheartened after losing money in a lawsuit, and had taken to drinking more than was good for him.' The demoralization and social collapse of Russia after the reverses of the First World War are embodied in perfectly natural details. The Nazi-Soviet non-aggression pact of 1939 is figured in Napoleon's sale of timber to Frederick (Frederick the Great as 'ancestor' of Hitler). The discovery that Frederick's banknotes are forgeries is followed by Frederick-Hitler's invasion (VIII). Jeffrey Meyers, who has made the most detailed list of Orwell's parallels, includes a spectacular item from the Great Purge trial of Bukharin in 1938.

> Gorky's secretary Kryuchkov confessed, 'I arranged long walks for Alexei Maximovich, I was always arranging bonfires. The smoke of the bonfire naturally affected Gorky's weak lungs.' During the purge in *Animal Farm*, 'Two other sheep confessed to having murdered an old ram, an especially devoted follower of Napoleon, by chasing him round and round a bonfire when he was suffering from a cough.'

Wonderful comedy, dripping blood.

Writing to one of his publishers, Orwell suggested a small change.

> In Chapter VIII ... when the windmill is blown up, I wrote 'all the animals including Napoleon flung themselves on their faces'. I would like to alter it to 'all the animals except Napoleon' ... I just thought the alteration would be fair to J. S. [Joseph Stalin], as he did stay in Moscow during the German advance. (3/98)

Both the desire to be fair and the attention to detail are typical.

Orwell's wit in transforming details in his allegory is perhaps excelled by his reproduction in new terms of the states of mind necessary for totalitarianism. He wonderfully conveys, for instance, the incessant rewriting of the past and the ever-abundant rationalizations necessary to adjust theory to reality.

> You have heard then, comrades ... that we pigs now sleep in the beds of the farmhouse? And why not? You did not suppose, surely, that there was ever a ruling against *beds*? A bed merely means a place to sleep in. A pile of straw in a stall is a bed, properly regarded. The rule was against *sheets*, which are a human invention. (VI)

The satire of Squealer, however, differs in an important way from the other details cited above. Those details refer specifically to Russian events, but Squealer, although the Soviet experience provides ample justification for his existence, represents a wider, general tendency. He might as easily be a Jesuit as a party-line Communist. A pair of hard questions about *Animal Farm* concern the extent to which it addresses general questions about the process of revolution in history, and the extent to which it is bound to the specific instance of the Russian Revolution. In a letter of 1947, Orwell said the book was 'intended as a satire on dictatorship in general', but it is reasonable to feel some doubt about the book's presentation of that intention. Does the book address general questions about the process of revolution in history, or is it too tightly bound to the specific instance of the Russian Revolution? Does Orwell's ingenuity in finding parallels for Russian events draw the eye away from wider applications? Is the general lesson of the book that all revolutions fail?

Hard questions

When he wrote *Animal Farm*, Orwell had several worrying questions about Socialism on his mind. His main objective, or at least the objective he started with, was—as we have seen—to separate democratic Socialism from what had happened in Russia: 'the destruction of the Soviet myth was essential if we wanted a revival of the Socialist movement.' But more fundamental questioning occurred too. Looking back at the history of revolutions, Orwell had to combat the doubt of their efficacy. Had revolutions really advanced the cause of liberty? Had they really brought Socialism closer? And—a still graver doubt—did the experience of Socialist revolutions, particularly the Russian one, indicate that Socialism, or the ambition for Socialism, leads inevitably to totalitarianism? Was the lust for power so ingrained in human nature that it would always thwart the ideal of liberty, equality, and fraternity?

These were not rhetorical questions for Orwell. He genuinely debated them, and voiced the debate in his journalism. In *Animal Farm*, however, decisions of literary form combine to endorse one point of view, with the result that the book is a brilliant rhetorical success while advancing an ideological position that was in fact gloomier and more certain than the one at which Orwell himself had arrived. Orwell was thinking through real doubts about Socialism, but the book he had written seems to confirm those doubts. He had made it easy for conservatives to use his book to attack democratic Socialism itself, to make up his mind for him.

The choice of beast fable was brilliant for the reductive simplicites of satire, but as a weapon it has two edges. Beast fable is a conservative aesthetic, presenting conservative estimates of human nature. It links outward shape unbreakably to predominating traits of character: sheep are silly, easily led, without individuality; donkeys are individualistically anarchic and stubborn; pigs are gross, greedy, and selfish. Orwell, it is true, modifies conventional links of this kind for his own purposes. The pigs have to be intelligent, for example, which does not seem to conform to farmyard experience. (Orwell kept a pig on Jura, and loathed it: 'disgusting brutes ... we are all longing for the day when he goes to the butcher.' (4/126)) But once established the characteristic is permanent. Seen through the lens of beast fable, human nature is split into separate components and is governed by a presumption of permanence.

Now the permanence, the unmodifiability, of human nature is an issue that separates conservatives from those who pointedly call themselves 'progressives'. When he was writing *Animal Farm*, Orwell was debating this issue for himself. The book alone, however, because it is a beast fable, seems to indicate that Orwell had come down on the conservative side.

Why, for instance, do the pigs become the new class? why, at the end, are they indistinguishable from humans in the eyes of the 'lower' animals? In the story, the only possible explanation is that they behave that way because of their 'nature'. They justify themselves by pointing to the facts of the animals' revolution, but such justifications all follow the form of Squealer's definition of a bed. The real motive is selfishness.

131

Trotsky, to explain the corruption of the Soviet Revolution, had written *The Revolution Betrayed*, which, as Alex Zwerdling shows, had greatly helped Orwell's thinking. Trotsky rejects all psychological, spiritual, or 'human nature' explanations for the re-establishment of class privilege in the Soviet Union. His reasons for it are historically, geographically, and economically specific to the case of the Russian Revolution. And he believes that the stage Russia has reached will lead to a further revolution which will realize the original goals. 'All indications agree that the further course of development must inevitably lead to a clash between the culturally developed forces of the people and bureaucratic oligarchy.'

Orwell was neither so optimistic nor so willing to rely solely on historical and case-specific explanations. It is true that at the end of *Animal Farm* the re-establishment of tyranny means that a second revolution will be needed to free the animals again, but the story gives no hint of optimism that such a revolution will come or be more successful than the first if it did come. A second revolution, moreover, would presumably have to get by without the pigs, who, having proved themselves naturally corrupt, could not be trusted with leadership. Their intelligence, however, would also be lost to the revolution. When one tries to translate this into human and social terms, awful complexities appear. The pigs of beast fable are one factor in the human mind and in human society. How can one such strand, no longer conveniently isolated within porcine form, be identified, never mind suppressed? The shape and conventions of Orwell's story combine to support the view that revolutions fail because of what a theologian would call original sin. Human nature is corrupt and cannot, in earthly existence, be perfected. The revolution in Orwell's fable can neither exist without its pigs (old Major, too, is a pig) nor triumph as long as they exist.

When Orwell debated these issues outside *Animal Farm*, his positions were more tentative and less pessimistic. Six months after finishing the book, he wrote an article about Arthur Koestler (3/68) which is fascinating, particularly as a commentary on *Animal Farm*. Orwell identifies the Moscow trials as the central subject of Koestler's work. 'His main theme is the decadence of revolutions owing to the corrupting effects of power, but the special nature of the Stalin dictatorship has driven him back into a position not far removed from pessimistic Conservatism.' Orwell reads Koestler's novel about Spartacus, *The Gladiators*, as an allegorical discussion of modern proletarian revolution. 'Revolutions always go wrong—that is the main theme', but on the question of *why*, Koestler falters. The freed slaves in his novel fail because of their hedonism, the expectation of being able to live in a post-revolutionary paradise. 'If Spartacus is the prototype of the modern revolutionary', says Orwell, 'he *should* have gone astray because of *the impossibility of combining power with righteousness.'* [my italics] Orwell does not immediately elaborate on this statement. Taken as an axiom, it seems to be as pessimistically conservative as any position found in Koestler; it indicts the lust for power as the fatal enemy of right-eousness, and the lust for power seems to be a constant in human nature.

Yet as he discusses Koestler's writings, Orwell is clearly far from totally accepting the pessimism he finds there. Koestler 'comes near to claiming that revolutions are of their nature bad . . . . Revol-ution, Koestler seems to say, is a corrupting process.' Orwell is stating this view without identifying himself with it, and when he comes to summarize Koestler's situation, he reveals a train of thought that significantly modifies the conclusion one draws from *Animal Farm*. Koestler has retained a belief in what Orwell calls 'hedonism'; this 'leads him to think of the Earthly Paradise as desirable'.

> Perhaps, however, whether desirable or not, it isn't possible. Perhaps some degree of suffering is ineradicable from human life, perhaps the choice before man is always a choice of evils, perhaps even the aim of Socialism is not to make the world perfect, but to make it better. All revolutions are failures, but they are not all the same failure.

Orwell has thought beyond *Animal Farm*. Major's speech at the beginning of that book offers a vision, in the words of *Beasts of England*, 'Of the golden future time'. The glad day will bring 'Riches more than mind can picture, / Wheat and barley, oats and hay', but this hedonistic image is more than balanced, in Major's speech and in the song, by the more important vision of freedom: 'Rings shall vanish from our noses, / And the harness from our back.' In his thoughts on Koestler, Orwell downplays hedonism still further. He seems prepared to accept lowered expectations, but not to align himself with pessimistic conservatism. The defeat of tyranny will not produce an earthly paradise, but it is still the purpose of revolution. To reshape his conclusion somewhat: all revolutions are failures, but some are less failures than others. Orwell continued to believe that the revolution was betrayed, yet *Animal Farm* shows failure as inherent in revolution.

In *Animal Farm* time is circular, another pessimistic and conservative image. From tyranny to revolution to tyranny is a figure of no progress, of cycles going nowhere. Yet outside his book, Orwell would not draw that conclusion. On the more difficult problem of combining power with righteousness, *Animal Farm* is again negative, but the problem continued to haunt Orwell, and is investigated at length in his last book and second great fic-tion, *1984*.

When Orwell himself tried to define the literary make-up of *1984*, in letters to his publisher and friends, he showed his awareness that his subject had demanded an unusual compression of literary types: 'this is a novel about the future—that is, it is in a sense a fantasy, but in the form of a naturalistic novel.' Elsewhere he called the book 'a satire'. (4/85, 158) The difficulty of getting these elements to combine was not presented by the elements of fantasy or satire, nor by the elements of prophecy or the methods of parody also seen in the book by Orwell and others. These elements have often combined, especially in the systematic disillusionment of literary dystopia ('hypothetical place, state, or situation in which conditions and the quality of life are dreadful'). The recalcitrant element is the naturalism, the almost scientific realism of circumstantial detail and character. Orwell's commitment to realism, his refusal—even in *Animal Farm*—to countenance a 'Mickey Mouse universe', is as strong in *1984* as it was when he was writing to Henry Miller, and it explains much of the individuality of the book.

To meet Orwell's own demands, *1984* had to fulfil its didactic purpose *and* to avoid leaving 'the ordinary three-dimensional world'. The method he chose is encapsulated in the opening words of the novel, for, as usual, Orwell here is a brilliant beginner.

> It was a bright cold day in April, and the clocks were striking thirteen. Winston Smith, his chin nuzzled into his breast in an effort to escape the vile wind, slipped quickly through the glass door of Victory Mansions, though not quickly enough to prevent a swirl of gritty dust from entering along with him.
>
> The hallway smelt of boiled cabbage and old rag mats.

The basic style is of realism in its 'disillusioned' form. The wind is vile, the dust (which is to acquire a symbolic rôle in the novel) swirls, and the Orwellian smells play their customary subversive rôle. But the first sentence combines realism ('a bright cold day in April'; it is clearly an English spring) with an element of fantasy: 'the clocks were striking thirteen'. This element, standing first in the passage, dominates all the rest. Everything else may seem drearily ordinary, even the name of the flats (for how many Victory Mansions have there been in England?). But a world in which all clocks strike an unlucky thirteen is not the world we know, whatever subsequent familiarities there may be. The clocks striking thirteen, along with the litres and dollars, are manifestations of revolutionary rationalism, the first sign we get that systematic ideology has great influence in this world.

On the first page of Orwell's book, we encounter other details like this that stand out as question marks in the recognizable flux of the all-too familiar world of 1948, the world of power-cuts and shortages. Winston has a varicose ulcer; why has it gone untreated? What is Hate Week? Who is Big Brother? Why cannot the telescreen, the 'oblong metal plaque like a dulled mirror', a glass darkly, be turned off? Orwell employs his realism basically to make the world of *1984* a world his readers will know, a close approximation of the privations and people of the years when the book was being written, thus establishing a base of human solidarity between his characters and his readers. But on this basis of recognized familiarity, the characters lead startlingly strange lives. They do weird things, either reluctantly or with enthusiasm—which is still weirder. The atmosphere is one of general fear, yet everyone proclaims happiness and fulfilment. The lives we are shown, particularly Winston's, of course, are full of absurdities designed to stand prominent against the ordinariness and drabness of the easily comprehended—because 'realistic'—fabric of those lives. The questions accumulte in the reader's mind as the book unfolds. The reader struggles to formulate general ˙ principles to answer the questions he becomes burdened with, until the book tilts and the questions are given their answers.

Let us see how this works by examining a small episode from near the beginning (Part One, V).

Winston's neighbours in Victory Mansions include the Parsons, husband and wife and two children, who are Orwell's representative family of Party members in the book. The nature and quality of family life stood for him for the nature and quality of all the life of the state, but this is a truth that the book does not assert but allows to emerge. Winston is asked by Mrs Parsons, 'a colourless, crushed-looking woman', to unblock the sink for her. Her appearance, her weariness, and the blocked sink indicate Mrs Parsons' ancestry. She is the woman Orwell saw kneeling on the cobblestones to unblock the drain-pipe in *The Road to Wigan Pier*, on her face 'the most desolate, hopeless expression I have ever seen'. Wigan, the 1930s unemployment and depression are to account for that woman. But Tom Parsons is a fellow worker of Winston's. Victory Mansions and the Parsons' flat are run-down but not slums. Life is pinched but not poverty-stricken. So why does Winston get the impression that there was dust in the creases of her face? She tells him why. '"It's the children," said Mrs Parsons, casting a half-apprehensive glance at the door.'

The Parsons' children are the classic awful children, but their awfulness has mystifying qualities. Their pretence that Winston is a Eurasian spy and a thought-criminal scares Winston, and not just because he *is* a thought-criminal (thought-crime has already been explained). These children are dangerous, 'tiger-cubs which will soon grow up into man-eaters'. The boy's desire to hit or kick him is evident, and eventually he shoots Winston with his catapult. '"Goldstein!" bellowed the boy as the door closed on him. But what struck Winston was the look of helpless fright on the woman's greyish face.'

After the encounter with the actuality of the Parsons kids—the question raised—Winston thinks about parents and the children in his society.

> Nearly all children nowadays were horrible. What was worst of all was that by means of such organizations as the Spies [the Party's youth movement] they were systematically turned into ungovernable little savages, and yet this produced in them no tendency whatever to rebel against the discipline of the Party . . . . hardly a week passed in which the *Times* did not carry a paragraph describing how some eavesdropping little sneak— 'child hero' was the phrase generally used—had overheard some compromising remark and denounced its parents to the Thought Police.

The Parsons children are thus placed in a familiar pattern of twentieth-century totalitarian organization, where a party engrosses the activities and loyalties formerly centred in the family. Thus Parsons, the living model of the good Party man, proudly tells how his daughter denounced a man because his shoes seemed 'funny', and later he recalls how his kids set fire to the skirt of an old woman at a market who was wrapping sausages in a newspaper portrait of Big Brother. The casual brutality is most horrible because of the official sanction it carries. Daydreaming, Winston sees the axe of denunciation falling on all who are in any degree remote from the standard of zeal set by Parsons. 'Within two years those children would be denouncing her to the Thought Police. Mrs Parsons would be vapourized. Syme would be vapourized. Winston would be vapourized. O'Brien would be vapourized. Parsons, on the other hand, would never be vapourized.' This prediction, which seems so reasonable, based on the characters and actions we have encountered so far, is much more inaccurate than correct. It is offered as an explanation of the conduct and attitudes we have been shown in these people. On that basis, Winston displays his understanding of the system by predicting how it will deal with these individuals. When Parsons is dumped into jail with Winston—denounced by his children for words uttered in his sleep, but still proud of those children—or when O'Brien appears as Winston's interrogator, we see the ways in which Winston's understanding is limited. Our understanding then equals his, so reader and protagonist are educated together over the last section of the book.

Orwell displays a realistic world invaded by what appear to be elements of fantasy (though every one of them, such as the parents scared of denunciation by their offspring, has already happened somewhere or can be certainly predicted—such as two-way television), and then, by highly varied means, explains them to us. It is a book of question and answer. The first half is, in the main, an accumulation of questions. The flood of answers starts to come when Winston and Julia have established their 'home' over Mr Charrington's shop, and Winston is able to read a couple of chapters from Goldstein's book before the Thought Police break in.

The device of the book, the most apparent and seemingly least dramatic of Orwell's expository methods, has often caused doubts. When the American firm Harcourt, Brace were considering publication of the novel, and could see the glint of a Book of the Month Club edition in the distance, they apparently relayed to Orwell a suggestion of the Club's judges that he abbreviate the 'book within the book'. He would not compromise.

> I can't possibly agree to the kind of alteration and abbreviation suggested. It would alter the whole colour of the book and leave out a good deal that is essential. I think it would also—though the judges, having read the parts that it is proposed to cut out, may not appreciate this—make the story unintelligible. (4/144)

Without Goldstein's book, the dramatic structure of the novel would be fatally impaired. The story would be unintelligible, not simply because the reader would be deprived of information about Winston Smith's world, but because there would be no experience of exhilaration for the protagonist to share with the reader as he seems to have knowledge within his grasp, giving him a special kind of power in his hitherto powerless world. 'The best books, he perceived, are those that tell you what you know already.' What he knows already are the individual pieces of a puzzle. He has stared at them for years without seeing how they are related, what big pictures they make. Goldstein's book provides the pattern. Things move into place. Winston understands, and we, who have experienced a bewilderment like his, understand too. The sense of triumph, of power, supplied by the wonderfully purposive prose in which Orwell casts Goldstein's explanation, is a very special and important fulfilment. This kind of knowledge, this access to the reasons underlying the often absurd, apparently meaningless barbarities and conventions of the day-to-day life of Oceania, is why Winston has rebelled. He wanted education. He is getting it, benevolently, from a book that understands him and his needs. Winston's search for understanding has brought him Julia. It seems to have brought him O'Brien. And—in what is one of the most hopeful human contacts he has—it has brought him this book. It allows him intellectual fulfilment as urgently craved as the fulfilment of Julia's love (significantly, he reads it aloud to Julia in their bed, adding the sexual element to the replication of two incidents from his boyhood recalled elsewhere in his writing, both surreptitious reading in bed, and of titles that resonate eerily with *1984*: *Gulliver's Travels* and H. G. Wells's *The Country of the Blind*.)

To gratify Winston's and the reader's craving to know, by inserting chapters from a book, is only superficially undramatic. The gratification when it comes is overpowering—again like the sexual relationship of the lovers—and the exhilaration of freedom carries the reader along, too. Such knowledge justifies the peril of the quest for it. Things are going well. The telescope—that cherished instrument of knowledge in *Homage to Catalonia*—is in our grasp. And then it is snatched away.

Winston becomes aware of silence and stops reading. The sentence at which he stops is one of enormous promise. It offers him the 'central secret' about the mad world in which he lives, 'the original motive, the never-questioned instinct that first led to the seizure of power and brought doublethink, the Thought Police, continuous warfare and all the other necessary paraphernalia into existence afterwards. This motive really consists . . . .' Here Winston stops, and soon after he falls asleep. When he wakens, he and Julia have only a few moments left before the Thought Police break in. The tantalizingly unfinished sentence is to be completed, in very different circumstances, by O'Brien.

The central secret, Winston will learn, is the lust for power, but his education under O'Brien's tutelage—the last stage of the book—will be quite devoid of the joy of knowing that Winston experiences as he reads Goldstein's book. Ironically, knowledge *of* power is to be knowledge *without* power for Winston, and the deprivation of joy will lead him to the love of Big Brother. O'Brien admits to having been one of the authors of Goldstein's book, but the application of doublethink shows how the book can be the work of the Thought Police and yet give so satisfactory an account of the underlying theory of the Ingsoc state. For O'Brien and company, the ability to hold simultaneously to two contradictory beliefs permits the production of an analysis explaining the state which, in their 'other' minds, they would denounce as a heretical lie.

Winston's catechetical sessions with O'Brien complete the expository structure and purpose of the book. Like Dostoevsky's Grand Inquisitor, O'Brien is there to explain, to answer, though he employs the methods of catechism—a truer analogy than the 'Socratic method'—to lead Winston towards the truth. Finally, Winston has to love Big Brother. To make this possible, he is brought, by methods of terrorism, to sacrifice Julia and the symbolizing nature of his love for her. In fact, however, 'Do it to Julia!' is the culminating explanation. To understand what it explains, we must look at Julia's place in the book.

The greatest and most influential work of fictional exposition in Western culture is a poem that Orwell began reading in his last illness, just before *1984* was published. He added a postscript to a letter to Anthony Powell: 'I'm reading Dante! (With a crib of course.)' (4/157) If we want to understand how character is conceived and how it functions in *1984*, Dante's *Divine Comedy* offers some analogies, though comparisons imply no suggestion that Dante's poem in any way contributed directly to the writing of Orwell's book, simply that the lens of Dante helps one to read Orwell's text.

Dante has two principal guides through the Inferno, Purgatory and Paradise. Vergil guides him most of the way through the first two books, and Beatrice is his guide through the last. Beatrice as the embodied spirit of religious revelation and pure love replaces Vergil, the embodiment of combined conscience and natural reason, for Dante's journey is upwards. Winston likewise has two guides, Julia and O'Brien. The revelation that Julia brings comes before the reason of O'Brien because Winston's journey is downwards, out of purgatory briefly into paradise, with a final descent into the inferno, capped by a 'happy ending'—'He loved Big Brother'— which parallels, but ironically, the 'comedy' of Dante's poem.

Julia, seen as a guide, has therefore an expository rôle in the book, but this claim may seem to be contradicted by her unintellectual nature, her lack, above all, of intellectual curiosity as to the political nature of the society in which she lives. She subverts it by resistance to its theoretically non-existent laws, but she falls asleep when Winston reads Goldstein's book to her. Compared to O'Brien, catechist and expositor, Julia may seem to do little explaining, but her expository rôle is in actuality substantial and defines her function in the book.

First of all, Julia has courage. Winston has taken what he knows to be the ultimately fatal step of starting his diary, but his desire for Julia is frozen into hatred by fear. It is Julia who acts to realize their love, to propel it forward, and she leads in arranging the details of the journeys that enable them to consummate it. When Vergil sees Dante's hesitation in canto II of the *Inferno*, he says that it was Beatrice who impelled him to serve Dante as guide, she having seen that he had turned back from fear. Courage is, axiomatically, the foundation of virtue since one cannot practise virtue without it. Julia teaches this truth by example.

Her other great teaching is her revelation to Winston that it is possible to live life in a manner he believes extinct. Julia shows him that privacy can be stolen from the system, that a private relationship can provide a way of living that nullifies the isolation imposed by the state. Winston has thought about this possibility before knowing Julia, but his thoughts have considered the ultimate implications of such a relationship. He dreams of his mother and sister (Part one, III) who disappeared during a 'purge' years before. 'They were in the saloon of a sinking ship looking up at him through the darkening water.' He is in the light and air, and both his mother and sister know 'that they must die in order that he might remain alive, and that this was part of the unavoidable order of things.' Winston realizes in his dream that his thoughts are being clarified:

> The thing that now suddenly struck Winston was that his mother's death, nearly thirty years ago, had been tragic and sorrowful in a way that was no longer possible. Tragedy, he perceived, belonged to the ancient time, to a time when there was still privacy, love and friendship, and when the members of a family stood by one another without needing to know the reason. His mother's memory tore at his heart because she died loving him, when he was too young and selfish to love her in return, and because somehow, he did not remember how, she had sacrificed herself to a conception of loyalty that was private and unalterable. Such things, he saw, could not happen today. Today there were fear, hatred and pain, but no dignity of emotion, no deep or complex sorrows.

His relationship with Julia is utterly precious to Winston because it offers the possibility of tragedy. Paradoxically, that possibility measures the profundity of their love. Julia offers Winston privacy, love and friendship, and the privacy and friendship are just as important as the love. The passion of the first stage of their love is quickly supplemented by a form of domesticity. Julia makes a 'home' for Winston in their rented room, and she is given a number of maternal traits to link her to the memory of Winston's mother. This love is certainly 'from the ancient time', and that is why it is the last thing that Winston clings to during his re-education at the hands of O'Brien. The latter has boasted that 'We have cut the links between child and parent, and between man and man, and between man and woman. No one dares trust a wife or a child or a friend any longer.' But when he scornfully asks Winston 'Can you think of a single degradation that has not happened to you?' Winston is able to reply 'I have not betrayed Julia'. O'Brien fully understands this answer, since Winston means 'He had not stopped loving her'. And so the final stage of Winston's re-education must lead him to betray Julia, to betray, that is, the possibility of self-sacrifice their love contains, to make pathos of the denial of a tragic ending, as he cries 'Do it to Julia!'

The objection that can be brought against Orwell's use of Julia

Two scenes from the 1954 BBC adaptation of 1984: Winston Smith and Julia (above) and Winston Smith and O'Brien (below)

in this rôle is that it is merely schematic. Many see her as a stereotype, and it is undeniable that within the conventions of what appears to be a novel of realism she seems far too insubstantial to generate true tragic emotion. Once again, however, *The Divine Comedy* helps us understand her position.

Julia's independent existence is subordinated to her rôle as Winston's guide. Like Beatrice, she appears as needed and is removed from the action during those parts of the narrative when another guide—O'Brien—is more appropriate. As in his other realistic novels, Orwell has created a protagonist who is essentially a solitary (a tendency, of course, for which he criticized himself) though here the solitude is part of the book's political meaning: it is an Age of Solitude. Julia and O'Brien are defined by their function as guides, but that limitation on the fulness of their character development is not as acceptable as the similar limitation on Beatrice and Vergil in *The Divine Comedy*. The conventions of the realistic novel within which Orwell has to work criticize that limitation as a fault. The reader's discomfort with the character of Julia may therefore be traceable to her essential rôle as Winston's teacher. Her character exists for the sake of his. As presented in the novel, she seems to claim and deserve the same kind of attention that Winston gets, but in fact Orwell has to keep her in her subordinate role.

Such subordination in the actual—as opposed to the fictional—year 1984 has political meaning Orwell did not anticipate. Nowadays, one is apt to read that Julia is a 'male fantasy', or that Orwell's attitude is 'patriarchal'. In the intended context, this is true. What one can recover of his attitudes to the relationship of the sexes, the rôle of women, and to feminism shows that it is impossible to make Orwell 'politically correct' in the feminist meaning of the term. The function of Julia in *1984* is to serve Winston, and the characterization of her is designed for that purpose. When Winston says that Julia is 'only a rebel from the waist downwards' she thinks the remark brilliantly witty and embraces him in delight. Few of Orwell's female readers now are likely to do the same for him.

The situation is in no way improved by the accurate statement that Orwell believes he is paying Julia the highest of compliments. But though to understand may not be to forgive, it is still right to understand. Despite her sexual promiscuity—indeed, in this context, as we shall see in a moment, *because* of it—Julia is a woman as the angelic mistress, a figure combining the features of the Virgin Mary and the blessed damsel of courtly love. Dante's Beatrice again provides a parallel, though an episode in the *Purgatorio*—where Beatrice is not present—fits best with Julia's function as the bestower of blessedness upon her lover. In canto XXVIII of the

Purgatorio, Dante has regained the earthly paradise, which is depicted as a holy forest, inhabited by the form of Matilda, the female embodiment of humanity unfallen or restored. Dante's desire for her, as he speaks to her across the stream which is one feature of the place, is his purified longing for the blessed life. Her speech of explanation names the place as the dream of the poets.

> Those who in old times sang of the age of gold and of its happy state perhaps dreamed on Parnassus of this place; here the human root was innocent, here was lasting spring and every fruit . . . .

> (trans. Sinclair)

Julia, pressing into his hand the note that reads 'I love you', comes to Winston as the gift of grace. To call this an 'ancient fantasy' is again to apply the criteria of the realistic novel. 'Ancient', however, it certainly is. The undeserved, undeservable gift of God's grace in the form of the mistress's favour completely transforms the man's life. It is his dream come true. His dream of the drowning of his mother and sister, quoted earlier, leads to a dream of a landscape.

> In his waking thoughts he called it the Golden Country. It was an old, rabbit-bitten pasture, with a foot-track wandering across it and a molehill here and there. In the ragged hedge on the opposite side of the field the boughs of the elm trees were swaying very faintly in the breeze, their leaves just stirring in dense masses like women's hair. Somewhere near at hand, though out of sight, there was a clear, slow-moving stream where dace were swimming in the pools under the willow trees.

In this dream Julia—'the girl with dark hair'—comes to him across the field, flinging off her clothes in a gesture that sweeps into nothingness all the oppressive system of the state. Later, Julia guides Winston to a place where they can be alone, and he undergoes 'a curious slow shock of recognition'. It is the Golden Country.

Julia's enactment of the rôles of Beatrice and Matilda is not nullified but endorsed by her 'corruption'. Winston questions her about her previous sexual experience and is told that she has 'done this' often before. Winston's joyous reaction parodies the male lover's pride in the virginal mistress. 'His heart leapt. Scores of times she had done it: he wished it had been hundreds—thousands. Anything that hinted at corruption always filled him with a wild hope.' He hopes it is evidence that the system is a rotten sham. 'Anything to rot, to weaken, to undermine . . . . The more men you've had, the more I love you . . . . I hate purity, I hate goodness! I don't want any virtue to exist anywhere. I want everyone to be corrupt to the bones.'

That Winston should be defining his Beatrice in these terms is absurd, but it is a necessary absurdity in Orwell's critique of totalitarianism. Since the Party has appropriated the idea of chastity, and has made women, wearers of the scarlet sash of the Junior Anti-Sex League, into the enforcers of its policy, then resistance must be in the form of behaviour at the opposite pole from that approved by the Party. And as feminists have noted, Julia's contraband make-up, silk stockings and high heels are emblems of freedom, not the 'capitulation to patriarchy' they might be in another society.

This binary, either/or relation of the resisting individual to the state means that freedom becomes defined by the state. To oppose is to do the opposite, and *only* the opposite, so unchastity becomes the necessary conduct of those who wish to place themselves outside the boundaries of conduct approved by the state. Orwell offers no solution to this dilemma, but it occurs in various forms often enough to be a theme of his book, one of the things he has to say about the shape the total state gives to the lives of its citizens.

Despite O'Brien's statement that Winston Smith is 'the last man', it must be doubtful that his is a terribly rare case in Oceania. After all, three of the people he knows well (Parsons, Syme, and Ampleforth) disappear or are arrested without being implicated in his crime. Enormous amounts of time and money are evidently spent by the state to bring Winston and those like him into conformity. Totalitarian states have been willing to make large expenditures to such ends, as we know, but in *1984* the commitment goes much further. The Thought Police have watched him night and day for seven years, he decides, but he learns that his extermination cannot occur until he has been made right. 'It is intolerable to us that an erroneous thought should exist anywhere in the world, however secret and powerless it may be.' Such totality has no human precedent and submits to no economic constraints. Orwell is investing his Party, parodically and very seriously, with the absolute attention to detail and unconcern about costs that only the deity possesses. Big Brother's eye is on the sparrow that is Winston. O'Brien's fanaticism consequently parodies monotheism. 'There will be no loyalty, except loyalty towards the Party. There will be no love, except the love of Big Brother.' Thou shalt have no other gods before me. In O'Brien's hands, Winston will complete the tuition he has begun with Julia, and Julia's necessary place in Winston's education will feed the paranoia with which Orwell so skilfully infects his reader. Could it be that Julia, too, is part of the apparatus devoted to the remaking of Winston Smith? Is she a Thought Policewoman? Sanity says no, but sanity is made to totter here.

The literary quest for religious understanding, which has been the greatest model of expository literature, has led for Dante (as for Christian of *Pilgrim's Progress*) to final happiness. Final understanding and happiness are the same. Orwell's adaptation of his model involves first enlightening Winston by bringing him, in his experience with Julia in the Earthly Paradise and later with O'Brien in the House of the Interpreter or Ministry of Love, to a full understanding that is a revelation of horror. Happiness, however, awaits Winston, but only when he is allowed to forget what he has learned. The reader, unlike Winston, is allowed to retain the horror. Winston loves Big Brother but we do not. For us the reward of the book is the understanding that Winston is privileged to forget. At the end of *1984*, Orwell believes that there is still some point in explaining things to someone, to us.

Prophecy: 'a novel about the future'

Satire and prophecy, in their respective orientations towards past and future, have in reality closer relations than might appear. The satirist's empirical concern with the effects of human folly leads naturally to a concern with the future increments of those effects, and the satirist is then one step from becoming a prophet. Prophecy, if defined as essentially a matter of prediction, need have none of the satirist's concern with history, with what has happened, but prophecy in religious literature has usually manifested a deep interest in the actualities of past and present. The Hebrew prophets projected the political decline and chaos of the eighth, seventh, and sixth centuries BC into the future, to give weight to their warning of God's displeasure with Israel. Their statements of prediction can be imagined as being implicitly preceded by a conditional clause: 'If present trends continue . . .' and their predictions depend on a careful study of history and current politics. This is prophecy as Orwell practised it, which in turn explains why a knowledge of all his writing before *1984* gives his steady readers the illusion that they themselves could have written *1984* if Orwell had not. His analytic understanding of past and present is the justification for his predictions. He was an empirical prophet.

But *1984* was a best-seller, meaning that perhaps millions of people who had no knowledge of Orwell and the road that led him to Oceania were reading his book. Orwell found himself misinterpreted, politically misread, fortunately while he still had enough life in him to do something about it.

> I do not believe that the kind of society I describe necessarily *will* arrive, but I believe (allowing of course for the fact that the book is a satire) that something resembling it could arrive . . . . The scene of the book is laid in Britain in order to emphasize that

the English-speaking races are not innately better than anyone else and that totalitarianism, *if not fought against*, could triumph anywhere. (4/502)

Orwell's 'sort of *démenti*', as he called it, has been a godsend to the interpreters of *1984*. On its authority, argument is general that *1984* is a warning, not a definite prediction, that it presents a worst-possible, hypothetical case, that Orwell really meant it as a contribution to the political debates of the late 1940s, and consequently that it is as much about tendencies he perceived at work within the democracies as about the nature of actual totalitarianism.

These are valuable as correctives, but if accepted as a complete and major realignment of the purpose of Orwell's book, they conceal the basic truth about it. (For a fine instance of such concealment, there is the Soviet assessment of *1984* as wholly concerned to attack United States' militarism and social structure, in which, since Oceania embraces both Britain and the United States, the President of the USA is clearly Big Brother. But no plans have been made to publish this anti-imperialist work in the USSR.) To deny that *1984* is really 'about the future' is effectively to deny that Orwell's principal model is Soviet totalitarianism.

Orwell's power of prophecy tends to be underrated, because what he predicted has become everyday reality. His greatest prophecy is that politics in the second half of the twentieth century will have as its central problem the spread and containment of totalitarian systems. This is now so mundane a truth as to be quite unsurprising, for even the politics of nuclear armament are a subordinate element within the problem of totalitarianism. Orwell was not the only person to make this prediction, but in 1949 he was the writer who made it come alive for the Western public. A great war had just come to an end with the defeat of three great totalitarian powers. Yet Orwell prophesied in *1984* that the struggle over this unprecedented social form was not finished and that it could come home painfully to the established democracies. He depicted the dramatized existence of an individual within such a system, and people marked what he said. It was a prophet's triumph. He predicted accurately, gave effective warning, and timed it right.

Despite the accidental and deliberate misunderstandings, in *1984* Orwell fulfilled his ambition. He made political writing into an art. It is a book of propaganda that will survive as a work of art in the unlikely event of the disappearance of its political *raison d'être*. 1984 has come and totalitarianism has not covered the globe, but what events show is that the totalitarian will continue to exist, and that ideology and technology provide an increasingly fertile environment for it. It would be pleasant to believe that *1984* might have become an exhibit in the museum of redundant ideas, but history

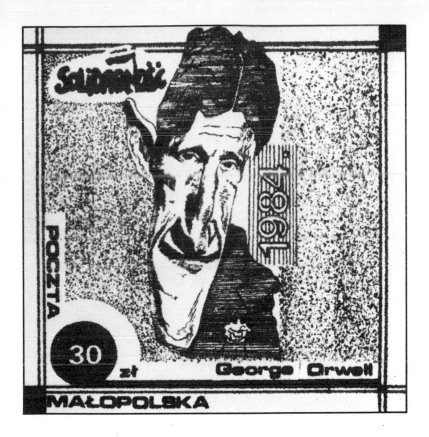

Within the stamp image: Solidarność · 1984 · POCZTA · 30 zł · George Orwell · MAŁOPOLSKA

Clandestine Polish stamp: Cracow Solidarity branch

and politics do not seem willing to let it happen. Orwell prophesied how it would be and how it continues to be.

One of the prophecies of *1984*, however, haunts Orwell's readers strangely, and contributes substantially to the debate over the ultimate pessimism of the book. Winston Smith, watching the proletarian woman, who is thus representative of the largest element in society, those who are not party members, hang out her laundry, decides: 'If there was hope, it lay in the proles! Without having read the end of *the book*, he knew that that must be Goldstein's final message. The future belonged to the proles.' Some readers note that O'Brien attacks the belief—'The proletarians will never revolt . . . . They cannot. I do not have to tell you the reason: you know it already'—and argue that Orwell is showing its emptiness. Others—a larger group, perhaps—respond to the indefinable passion of this statement by assuming that it corresponds to Orwell's own strongest beliefs. So Bernard Crick can say, of the things Orwell left unsaid, 'We need to know why hope lies in the Proles'. Orwell does not tell us, and the assumption that he had such a hope is based on the emotion perceived in his identification with Winston at this point. If it is Orwell's belief, it may be dismissed as sentimental socialist mystique, and as it stands it is surely no more than a declaration of faith, and so a rather different form of prophecy from the rest of the book.

But even this mystical hope—if that is what it is—has shown signs of realization. The foundation in 1980 in a totalitarian country of an independent trade union—Polish Solidarity—was an event to fulfil a little of that hope, despite Solidarity's suppression by a military *coup d'état*. It was, perhaps, the most important political event since the Second World War, one that would have absorbed Orwell's interest, and one that would have caused him some surprise. He considered the Roman Catholic Church, for instance, as a prototype of totalitarian organization, but cases are sometimes strangely altered.

> When an official lecture organized by Krakow students on 'Orwell's 1984 and Poland today' was broken up by police, the organizer went in some distress to his parish priest. A few days later there was a meeting in church, with an address, subject . . . 'Orwell's 1984 and Poland Today'. The meeting was not disrupted. Among his many firsts, Pope John Paul II, the Archbishop of Krakow [in 1977], must be the first divine to have ordered *1984* to be read in churches.
>
> (Timothy Garton Ash)

So apparently absurd an event comes about as the result of a long but logical chain of cause and effect. Another such chain runs from the present to the grimly absurd future of *1984*.

Part Three
Reference Section

Gazetteer

United Kingdom

ETON COLLEGE A scholarship to the most famous school in the world was the greatest of prizes for a preparatory school boy. When Orwell won his, St Cyprian's was given a holiday in celebration—and as an advertisement of the school's success. Eton was founded in 1440 by Henry VI, and Henry Longhurst recalled that Mrs Wilkes punished any aspersion on that unfortunate king, since '*He founded Eton!*'

Orwell was a King's Scholar, one of seventy 'Collegers', paying fees of £25 a year, whereas 'Oppidans', about 900 non-Collegers, paid £100. Collegers lived in the central Tudor buildings of the school, whereas Oppidans lived in sundry houses in the town. Orwell entered the school in May 1917 and left at Christmas 1921.

'I did not work there and learned very little', he wrote. About his work there is no disagreement. His reaction to the cramming of St Cyprian's was to work as little as possible. In his last year he was placed 138th out of 167. He had made sure that a scholarship hunt at Oxford or Cambridge, necessary if he was to go to university, was out of the question.

But he seems in his own way to have enjoyed Eton. 'It . . . has one great virtue . . . and that is a tolerant and civilized atmosphere which gives each boy a fair chance of developing his own personality', he wrote. Eton was secure enough to leave him a good deal alone, and the general impression he made on his contemporaries is summarized in the nickname Cyril Connolly gave him: 'Cynicus'. He was sardonic, half-withdrawn, and sometimes and somehow seemed older than the others of his year. 'I don't feel that Eton has been much of a formative influence on my life', he wrote, but many who met him recognized its stamp on his manners. And though it was used to unusual ends, the Old Etonian network—Richard Rees, John Lehmann, Cyril Connolly, Anthony Powell, David Astor—certainly helped him.

That Orwell should have gone to the school always considered to stand at the summit of privilege and snobbery seems to be one of the many ironies of his life. But Eton can claim some credit for forming him, if only by its tolerance of eccentricity. To claim him as typical of it, however, is rather like describing Voltaire as a typical product of Jesuit schooling.

HENLEY-ON-THAMES, OXFORDSHIRE Henley has the best claim to be

Orwell's home town since it was his family's home from 1904 until 1921. The town and the landscape of the Thames valley are the setting of *Coming Up for Air*. For his account of the world of inner peace before the First World War, he drew on his memories of growing up in Henley, but for the ghastly transformation of 'modernity' when George Bowling returns, Orwell seems to have applied his imagination and what he had seen elsewhere, since there seems to be no record of a return to Henley after 1921.

The first of several Blair homes in Henley was 'Ermadale', Vicarage Road, from 1904 to April 1905. Thereafter they moved to 'The Nutshell', Western Road until 1912, when they moved to 'Roselawn' in Station Road, Shiplake, three kilometres from Henley. They moved back to Henley in 1915, to number 36, St Mark's Road, which they gave up in 1921 to move to Southwold in Suffolk.

JURA, ARGYLLSHIRE (now STRATHCLYDE)   In his wartime diary, 20 June 1940, he wrote: 'Thinking always of my island in the Hebrides, which I suppose I shall never possess nor even see.' But he did. The family of David Astor, son of the proprietor of the *Observer*, and a generous benefactor to Orwell, owned land on Jura in the Inner Hebrides, and Astor introduced him to another land-owner who eventually rented to Orwell the farmhouse called Barnhill, where much of *1984* was written.

Barnhill was not a holiday cottage. Orwell meant it to be his home and tried seriously to farm there. As with his stay in Paris, his retreat to the island was a conventional thing done in an unconventional way.

Jura, says the guidebook, 'boasts magnificent scenery but is seldom visited on account of the scanty accommodation'. Longitude 6 degrees west and latitude 56 degrees north intersect on the island, forty-five kilometres by thirteen, south of Mull. In 1946 it had about 250 inhabitants. As Orwell insisted, the climate is surprisingly mild (it is said that tropical plants once grew on Jura, carried there by the Gulfstream), so as far as that goes he was not 'courting death' by going there. But Barnhill, at the north end of the island, was remote from the ferry at the south end, and the journey at that time from London to Jura is exhausting even to read about (Orwell gives instructions for it in a letter to Sonia Brownell, 12 April 1947). The farm work was hard, and medical aid was a long way off, even though Glasgow was only ninety-seven kilometres away as a hardy crow flies. Orwell was not courting death, but neither did he strive officiously to stay alive.

Between the top of Jura and the small, mountainous island of Scarba to the north lies the Gulf of Corryvreckan, with its famous and legendary whirlpool, 'a tiderace dangerous to small craft', which in the summer of 1948 nearly claimed the author of *Animal*

Farm and put paid to *1984*. Returning by boat from a camping expedition to the other side of the island, with his son Ricky and his much older niece and nephew, Lucy and Henry Dakin, Orwell miscalculated the tides and they were swept away and stranded on a rock island until rescued by a lobster boat a couple of hours later. 'He seemed to keep his normal "Uncle Eric" face the whole time, no panic from him or from anyone . . . He almost seemed to enjoy it.'

LONDON   Orwell said he detested London, and he was certainly a reluctant Londoner, but the city and its life were essential—though perhaps in a negative sense—to his work, much of which draws from and contributes to the *mythos* of town versus country in English literature.

He first lived in London in the autumn and winter of 1927 when he was learning painfully to write in a room in the Portobello Road, Notting Hill. After returning from Paris, in September 1931, he stayed in a lodging house in Bermondsey, and in October and November had a room at 2 Windsor Street, Paddington. His periods of schoolmastering at Hayes and Uxbridge, Middlesex, were followed in 1934 by a part-time job in a bookshop, Booklovers' Corner, 1 South End Road, Hampstead. Orwell lived first in a room at 3 Warwick Mansions, Pond Street, Hampstead, and later (March 1935) in a room at 77 Parliament Hill, Hampstead. In August 1935, he moved again to a flat at 50 Lawford Road, Kentish Town. He left this flat and the job in the bookshop in January 1936 to make his journey to the industrial north.

After his marriage and several years at Wallington, Orwell came back to London during the war. He and his wife had a fourth-floor flat at 18 Dorset Chambers, Chagford Street, near Regent's Park. Orwell's Home Guard service was with the St John's Wood company, C Company, 5th County of London Battalion. Bomb damage apparently forced the Orwells to move in April 1941 to a fifth-floor flat at 111 Langford Court, Abbey Road, St John's Wood. Orwell worked for the BBC at Portland Place and Oxford Street from August 1941 until November 1943. In the summer of 1942, the Orwells moved to 10a Mortimer Crescent, Maida Vale. In June 1944, a flying bomb forced them to move again, to a third-floor flat at 27B Canonbury Square, Islington. He kept this flat after Eileen's death until December 1948. There is now a George Orwell School in Islington. The London of *1984* is the London of Orwell's war years.

ST CYPRIAN'S SCHOOL, EASTBOURNE, SUSSEX (NOW EAST SUSSEX)   St Cyprian's had been founded in 1899. It occupied two Victorian houses near Eastbourne, and not far from Beachy Head. When

Plaque in Hampstead unveiled in 1969

Orwell went there, there were twelve teachers, including the proprietors, Mr and Mrs Wilkes, and about a hundred boys who paid £180 a year (Orwell, as an undeclared 'scholarship boy', paid half fees, still £65 a year more than his Eton fees would be.) The school continued until after the Second World War. Mrs Wilkes lived in her retirement at the Master's Lodge on the St Cyprian's grounds, visited by many former pupils, Orwell not among them: 'it is a fact that for many years I could hardly have borne to look at [the school] again. Except upon dire necessity I would not have set foot in Eastbourne. I even conceived a prejudice against Sussex, as the county that contained St Cyprian's, and as an adult I have only once been in Sussex, on a short visit. Now, however, the place is out of my system for good. Its magic works no longer, and I have not even enough animosity left to make me hope that Flip and Sambo are dead or that the story of the school being burnt down was true.' It was, and 'Flip' outlived Orwell by several years.

SOUTHWOLD, SUFFOLK   Orwell's parents moved to Southwold, on the coast between Aldburgh and Lowestoft, in 1921, and it was there that he returned from Burma. It was not quite Orwell's home, but rather, as Bernard Crick suggests, 'his main base camp' until he got married in 1936. Southwold was a resort town with many Anglo-Indian retirees. It was not the kind of scene Orwell wanted for his social and literary investigations, but it had its uses. His sister Avril's job in a tea-shop became, suitably darkened, Gordon Comstock's sister's job in *Keep the Aspidistra Flying*, and Hilda, George Bowling's shrewish wife in *Coming Up for Air*, has had her character warped by the genteel poverty of the 'Anglo-Indian colony in Ealing'.

Orwell was developing as a writer and a character in the period of his visits to Southwold and many reminiscences and anecdotes of him are connected with the place. He was asked to be holiday tutor to three brothers, one of whom, Professor R. S. Peters, published in 1974 an affectionate memoir of him. The Orwell of the Peters brothers was

> a thoroughly lovable and exciting companion. . . . He was a mine of information on birds, animals, and the heroes of boys' magazines. Yet he never made us *feel* that he knew our world better than we knew it ourselves. . . . And it was as if he entered unobtrusively. . . into our world and illuminated it in a dry, discursive sort of way without in any way disturbing it. He never condescended; he never preached; he never intruded. . . . His attitude to animals and birds was rather like his attitude to children. He was at home with them. He seemed to know everything about them and found them amusing and interesting. . . . He

infused interest and adventure into everything we did with him just because of his own interest in it. Walking can be just a means of getting from A to B; but with him it was like a voyage with Jules Verne beneath the ocean.

He took them bird watching and, of course, fishing, and calmly demonstrated home-made explosives.

I can still remember the smell of wild peppermint or spearmint which formed a background to his exposition on the properties of marsh gas. . . . His attitude to Nature was symbolised in the prodding of his stick. There was nothing of the romantic about him. If he had met Wordsworth's leech-gatherer he would have been interested in the leeches and in how the old boy made a living.

Southwold did not offer the country life that was Orwell's deepest desire, but its coastline and the River Blythe clearly gave him something he needed. He named himself, after all, for one of the slow rivers of East Anglia.

On perhaps his last visit to Southwold, when his father died in 1939, Orwell found himself with a problem that is revealing simply because it was a problem. In his pocket when he left his father's deathbed were the pennies that had weighted down Richard Blair's eyes. But what to do with them? He could not spend them. So he carried them down to the seafront and threw them into the waves.

SUTTON COURTENAY, BERKSHIRE   Orwell's will stated: 'And lastly I direct that my body shall be buried (not cremated) according to the rites of the Church of England in the nearest convenient cemetery, and that there shall be placed over my grave a plain brown stone bearing the inscription "Here lies Eric Arthur Blair born June 25th, 1903, died . . . ." But 'the nearest convenient cemetery' proved a problem for Orwell's friends, since he had no link with any particular church. The problem, like a number of others, was solved for Orwell by David Astor. He arranged for him to be buried in the beautiful churchyard at Sutton Courtenay, near the Astor estate. Crick draws a thoughtful analogy. 'As once the atheist Thomas Hobbes had needed the power of territorial magnate, of a Duke of Devonshire, to get him buried in sacred ground, so now the Left-wing sceptic needed the power of a friendly newspaper proprietor, one of the magnates of our time.' Orwell now lies in the Thames valley he loved, under his plain stone, recently scrubbed for its appearances in the commemorative documentary films, white, not brown.

WALLINGTON, HERTFORDSHIRE   Orwell's wish for a country life had its longest fulfilment at Wallington. After his time in Hampstead,

Blair's grave

156

he wanted to get away from London, and on the recommendation of friends rented—for seven shillings and six pence a week—a small house in this village, sight unseen, while on his journey to Wigan in February 1936. The village, about half-way between London and Cambridge, is five kilometres from Baldock, where there was a railway station and an infrequent bus service to Wallington. The place was 'small, unspoiled, dull, remote in feeling if not in actual distance from London, and free of the dangerous quaintness that might attract tourists and stockbrokers' (Stansky and Abrahams).

The house was called 'the Stores' (it had housed a village shop) and like the other homes of Orwell's choosing it had its penitential aspects. It was a very small, 300 year-old lath and plaster house of two storeys. Upstairs were two small bedrooms, and a bathroom (there was only a cold-water tap, and in the winter the lavatory frequently froze over). The house's frontage was only eleven feet. It stood next to the pub, the Plough, and had a chaotic garden at the back where Orwell claimed to have dug up twelve boots in a week. Again typically of an Orwell house, it soon acquired a menagerie. Orwell kept ducks, hens, and goats (Kate and Muriel), grazing them on the Wallington common, and later they had a standard poodle ('dirty white' say Stansky and Abrahams; black' says Crick) called 'Marx' (more likely *côté de* Karl than *côté de* Groucho).

Orwell revived the village shop in his front room (so allowing him to put himself down as a 'grocer' on his papers in the Spanish militia) but did very small business, mostly selling sweets— interestingly priced at seven for a penny, four for a halfpenny—to the local children. On his trip to Wigan he had apparently considered making the Stores into an antique shop. Orwell selling antiques is an interesting idea.

In the parish church of St Mary on 9 June 1936, Orwell married Eileen O'Shaughnessy, and, with some long absences to accommodate the Spanish War, a stay in a sanatorium, and a holiday of convalescence in Morocco, lived at Wallington until 1940, longer than anywhere else in his adult life. At Wallington he did most of the writing of *The Road to Wigan Pier, Homage to Catalonia, Coming up for Air*, and *Inside the Whale*. In May 1940, Orwell went back to live in London, but kept the house at Wallington as a country cottage until 1947.

WIGAN, LANCASHIRE (NOW GREATER MANCHESTER) Orwell's journey to the industrial north lasted from 31 January to 30 March 1936. *The Road to Wigan Pier* is based on three weeks in Wigan, and shorter stays in Barnsley and Sheffield in Yorkshire, but Orwell also visited Manchester, Liverpool and Leeds, where his sister and brother-in-law lived.

Orwell wanted to study and experience conditions of hardship, and he went to Wigan because it suffered high unemployment as the result of closures and short-time in coal mines and cotton mills. After staying a while at 72 Warrington Lane, Orwell felt he should experience rougher conditions, and put up at the tripe shop (22 Darlington Road) which gave his book so striking a beginning and which was remembered by neighbours in the 1970s as 'a specially filthy hole' (Crick). He watched the unemployed coal-picking at Fir Tree Siding, and went down one coal mine, Cribbens, where the roofs were very low and the travelling hard. The experience literally knocked him out several times. He did not investigate the cotton mills.

For him, though, this journey was symbolic as well as social scientific. The title of his book carefully parodies his road to Mandalay, and its final form, incorporating a lot of autobiographical reflection, emphasizes the importance of the journey for him.

Orwell explained the Wigan Pier joke in a broadcast in 1943.

Wigan has always been picked on as a symbol of the ugliness of the industrial areas. At one time, on one of the little muddy canals that run round the town, there used to be a tumble-down wooden jetty; and by way of a joke, someone nicknamed this Wigan Pier. The joke caught on locally, and then the music-hall comedians got hold of it, and they are the ones who have succeeded in keeping Wigan Pier alive. . . .

It lives now, of course, only in Orwell's title.

There is now a George Orwell pub in the Town, more 'up-market' than those locally in the 1930s.

Abroad

BURMA The Socialist Republic of the Union of Burma now has a population of about 38 million in a land area of more than half a million square kilometres. It occupies the northwest part of the Indochina peninsula on the Bay of Bengal, bordering on Bangladesh, India, China, Laos, and Thailand. By 1886, the whole of Burma was under British rule. It gained its independence after the Second World War, and chose not to become a member of the Commonwealth.

During Orwell's period of service there, and despite geographical, economic and cultural distinctiveness, Burma was annexed to India. Hence Orwell served in the *Indian* Imperial Police.

Orwell arrived in Burma in November 1922, and went for training to Mandalay. He had postings to several stations in the delta around Rangoon, and one at Insein, north of Rangoon, where there was a large prison, which may have been where he saw a hanging. In April 1926 he was posted to Moulmein, where his grandmother Limouzin and one of his aunts were still living. (Family connections had helped him to choose Burma, but in writing about his time there he generally avoided mentioning the fact.) His final posting, before he went home on leave in the summer of 1927, was to Katha in upper Burma, whose distinctive landscape is that of *Burmese Days*.

There is no objective evidence to support Orwell's claims (in two of his best essays) that he witnessed a hanging and that he shot an elephant during his service in Burma. To friends who asked him about 'A Hanging' he described it as 'only a story', but he twice repeated in print that he had witnessed an execution. During Orwell's Burmese service, there were more than seven hundred hangings, so there was plenty of opportunity. Orwell placed the elephant shooting in Moulmein.

CATALONIA   Orwell's Spain was a pair of battlefields, the trenches near Saragossa and the streets of central Barcelona. When he arrived in Spain in December 1936, Madrid was under siege, the Republican Government had its capital at Valencia, and the Aragon front was fairly quiet. After his initial training in Barcelona, Orwell's unit, part of the 20th Division, moved into the trenches on the Aragon front, at Alcubierre, between Saragossa (in Nationalist hands throughout the war) and Huesca. Orwell was in the trenches there for 115 days. His wife came to Spain in mid-February 1937, but Orwell got only a few days leave with her while being treated at Monflorite for a poisoned hand.

After his 115 day stint, Orwell was able to take a longer leave in Barcelona, in May 1937, but found himself in the middle of another kind of war. The antagonism between the Republican Government, much influenced by the Communists, and their critical, leftist allies, particularly the Anarchists and the POUM, came to shooting with a government attempt to take over control of the Telephone Exchange from the Anarchist unions. Barricades were built and there was fairly extensive street fighting.

Eileen Blair was staying at the Hotel Continental in the Ramblas, one of the main avenues of Barcelona. Because of the shooting, Orwell was stuck in the Hotel Falcon, farther down the street on the same side, a building used by the POUM. A few doors down was the Café Moka, where some government Assault Guards had holed up. Orwell was issued a rifle by the POUM, and for much of the time during the 'May days' he stood guard on the building across the Ramblas that housed the Poliorama cinema and, on its upper floor, the Science Club of Barcelona. On the roof was a two-domed observatory, from where Orwell observed the Assault Guards on the roof of the Moka across the street, read Penguin books, and waited for an attack that never came.

When things quietened down and a truce between the factions was established, Orwell went back to the trenches on 10 May. On 20 May, near Huesca, he was wounded in the throat and shipped down to Lérida, where his wife found him. He was then moved to Tarragona, on the coast, and a week later to suburban Barcelona to convalesce. By 20 June Orwell had completed his discharge from the militia and returned to the Hotel Continental, on the very day when the Government had turned on the Anarchists and the POUM, which was banned. Orwell was suddenly a political fugitive. Dodging the police, he, Eileen, and two friends crossed the border into France.

PARIS   Orwell went to Paris, as so many have done, to be a writer, living off his savings and (in 1928–29) enjoying a good rate of exchange for his pounds. He was unusual, however, in that he really did write (two novels, several short stories—all destroyed unpublished—and some journalism, several items of which got into print) and in that he did not lead the typical literary life of 1920s Paris. (The Scott Fitzgeralds were living not far from Orwell at the time.) Orwell supplemented his savings by giving English lessons, and it was not until his money ran low, particularly when he was robbed, that he lived in poverty and took the job as dishwasher in a hotel—experiences that make up so much of *Down and Out in Paris and London* though covering only ten weeks of Orwell's stay. Thus he came to these 'typical Orwell' experiences largely without previous intention and found that he possessed a method of study —the sharing of poverty—that determined his literary direction.

Orwell's 'bohemian' Aunt Nelly Limouzin was living in Paris during his stay. Typically, he suppresses the existence of this family lifeline in writing about the experience. He had to choose solitude.

Orwell's hotel was at number 6, rue du Pot de Fer, in the fifth *arrondissement*, the Latin Quarter. (Since the street had in reality the perfect Orwell name, he had to give it the transparent disguise of 'rue du Coq d'Or'.) Though a somewhat tough, squalid yet picturesque district, it was not the 'representative slum' Orwell called it. The rue du Pot de Fer is a two-block street, running from the rue Mouffetard to the rue Lhomond, and crossing the rue Tournefort. The rue d'Ulm, with the Ecole Normale Supérieure, is a couple of blocks away. The hotel is now offices, workshops, and flats.

When Orwell became ill, he want to the Hôpital Cochin, in the Faubourg St Jacques, to the south of the fifth *arrondissement*, and with the Santé prison as its immediate neighbour—rather suitably in the light of 'How the Poor Die'.

160

Orwell's time as a hotel worker produced one mystifying anecdote. In her splendid memoirs, *Grace and Favour*, Loelia, one of the several duchesses of the second Duke of Westminster, records meeting 'at a party . . . a frail-looking man' who told her he had once worked at the Hotel Lotti where the Westminsters stayed in Paris. The Duke, late one night, had asked for a peach. Orwell, the 'frail-looking man', was sent out to get one—or else. Everything was shut, but he eventually found a small greengrocer's with peaches in the window. He could rouse nobody, and in desperation smashed the window and carried a peach back to his fellow Etonian, the Duke of Westminster.

MOROCCO   Orwell's last journey abroad followed his sanatorium stay of the spring and summer of 1938. The doctors advised a winter in a warm, dry climate. The Orwells could not afford it, but the novelist L. H. Myers, who admired Orwell's work and had visited him, anonymously gave Orwell £300 for the trip. (The money was a gift, but Orwell considered it a loan, and later repaid it. He never knew who his benefactor was.)

George and Eileen sailed to Morocco on 2 September 1938. They visited Tangier and Casablanca, and stopped in Marrakech. They rented a house, acquired the usual menagerie (goat and hens) and stayed for nearly seven months. During this time, Orwell's energies went into *Coming Up for Air*, which he delivered to Gollancz on his return. After Christmas, the couple spent a week at Taddert, in the Atlas Mountains. They returned to England on 30 March 1939.

It is true, as Bernard Crick says, that on this journey Orwell remained 'intellectually remote' from the life of the country, and that his one specifically Moroccan essay, 'Marrakech' (1/153), is 'overwritten . . . somewhat contrived and external'. But the experience did make a contribution to the body of Orwell's political ideas. It was a late reminder, a 'booster shot', of the anti-colonialism he had brought back from Burma. He could not overlook Morocco's colonial society and the lives of its poor: 'it's the first place I've seen where beggars do literally beg for bread and eat it greedily when given it.' (1/140)

Eileen Blair

Short biographies

EILEEN MAUD (O'SHAUGHNESSY) BLAIR, 1905–1945   Orwell's first wife was born in South Shields and educated at Sunderland High School and St Hugh's College, Oxford, where she got a second class degree in English in 1927. After university, she had several jobs, including teaching and running a typing agency, but when Orwell met her, in the spring of 1935, she was taking an MA course in psychology at University College London.

When they got engaged, the plan was to get married after Eileen had finished her thesis on child psychology and had a job. In the event, they were married in June 1936, and Eileen never got her degree, accepting instead the rôle of the writer's wife. Six months after they were married, for instance, she followed Orwell to Spain, and to be near him took a secretarial job at the ILP headquarters. She too disliked London and was happy at Wallington. She shared Orwell's wish to move to the Hebrides and helped make the arrangements.

When war broke out in 1939, Eileen took a job in the government censorship department. Later she worked for the Ministry of Food, preparing recipes and scripts for the 'Kitchen Front' series of broadcasts on the BBC (she was a good cook). In June 1944 she gave up the job since they had decided to adopt a child, Richard, born 14 May 1944.

During the war, Eileen's health had deteriorated, and in March 1945, while Orwell was in Germany as a war correspondent for *The Observer*, she went into hospital in Newcastle for a hysterectomy, for she seems to have had cancer. She died under the anaesthetic of heart failure. Orwell himself was in hospital in Cologne when he got the news. Eileen had downplayed the seriousness of her condition to her husband, and he had permitted himself to believe her when the available facts should have told him otherwise.

SONIA (BROWNELL) BLAIR, 1918–1980   After Eileen's death, Orwell was eager to marry again and made a series of rapid proposals to various women friends. He was gently rejected by all, including Sonia Brownell, with whom he had a brief affair in late 1945. In 1950, however, during his last illness, he proposed to her again, and she accepted. They decided not to wait until he got well: 'I really think I should stay alive longer if I were married . . . . Sonia thinks we might as well get married while I am still an invalid, because it would give her a better status to look after me . . . ' (Crick). The ceremony took place at University College Hospital, London, on

13 October 1949. Orwell died there on 21 January 1950. They were married for ninety-five days.

Like Orwell, Sonia had been born in India. She rebelled against a convent upbringing by involving herself in the literary artistic world of London. She had been assistant editor to John Lehmann on *New Writing*, and later became Cyril Connolly's 'extraordinarily beautiful assistant' on *Horizon*. In the 1960s she was co-editor of *Art and Literature*, based in Paris as a translator from the French.

We will never know what kind of marriage Orwell and Sonia would have had, but Sonia undeniably became a very efficient author's widow, guarding Orwell's reputation and his archive. Though she was legally Sonia Blair, she always signed herself, and was named in copyright notices, as Sonia Orwell. There is a portrait of her (in which Orwell is referred to only once) in David Plante's *Difficult Women: A Memoir of Three* (New York: Atheneum, 1983, London: Futura, 1984).

CYRIL VERNON CONNOLLY, 1903–1974   Connolly was at school with Orwell, both at St Cyprian's and at Eton, but he proceeded to Balliol College, Oxford, and later had a career as a writer rather more conventional than Orwell's. From 1927 he wrote articles, especially book reviews, for the *New Statesman* and the *Sunday Times*, though his most important journalism was his founding and editing of *Horizon*, from 1940 to 1950, where much of the best British writing of the period, including some of Orwell's, was published. He wrote novels (*The Rock Pool* was reviewed with friendly severity by Orwell in 1936) and his most famous book is *The Unquiet Grave*: *A Word Cycle*, published in 1944 under the pseudonym 'Palinurus'. It is part anthology, part meditation. Connolly was made CBE in 1972.

In *Enemies of Promise* (1938) Connolly began the literary career of St Cyprian's (which he called St Wulfric's), giving an account that Orwell elaborated on and darkened in 'Such, such were the joys'. The two had lost touch at Eton but Connolly rekindled their friendship by reviewing *Burmese Days* in 1935. At their re-union, he reported, Orwell gave 'his characteristic wheezy laugh, "Well, Connolly, I can see that you've worn a good deal better than I have." I could say nothing, for I was appalled by the ravaged grooves that ran down from cheek to chin. My fat cigar-smoking persona must have been a surprise to him.' The friendship was sustained, despite a divergence of beliefs and attitudes that went very deep, as may be indicated by some comments of Connolly's on the same war that convinced Orwell of the necessity of politics.

But for us the Spanish war was the crux of everything, and it was such a disaster to our hopes: it was so awful to see the side we

Sonia Orwell

were convinced was right totally defeated, with the democracies looking on, either sadly or cheering. It made one feel nothing could be done by politics. You had to give up all that side. And then go back into the ivory tower . . . .

VICTOR GOLLANCZ, 1893–1967 Victor Gollancz Ltd published Orwell's first book, *Down and Out in Paris and London*, in 1933, followed by several others, and would doubtless have published all his books were it not for a highly revealing dispute between author and publisher which led to Orwell turning to the firm of Secker and Warburg for the publication of *Homage to Catalonia*.

Victor Gollancz had left New College, Oxford, to fight in the First World War. He had proved himself a successful and innovative publisher as Managing Director of Ernest Benn Ltd and founded his own firm in 1928. Victor Gollancz Ltd rapidly established itself with a striking list of authors and a successful line of detective novels. Gollancz put his books into yellow jackets with black and magenta lettering and went in for lavish and forceful advertising. Orwell was an instance of his skill at picking talent, though almost everything of Orwell's he published gave him trouble. With the early books there were persistent fears of libel suits. Despite grave aesthetic doubts, he published *A Clergyman's Daughter*. Then he had the simply brilliant idea of commissioning a book from Orwell about conditions in the depressed areas of the industrial North. The £500 advance Orwell got for *The Road to Wigan Pier* enabled him to get married and changed the direction of his career, but when Gollancz got the manuscript he had yet another problem. Orwell's comments on Socialism and Socialists in the second half of his book were cutting and painful to Gollancz, who had decided to issue it in his newly-founded Left Book Club. After kicking about such ideas as issuing only the first half in the Left Book Club edition, Gollancz decided to put it out complete in both club and public editions but with a dissenting introduction by himself. Over 40,000 copies appeared in this odd manner. Gollancz took as one of his principles the refusal to publish books that militated against his own beliefs (he refused, for instance, the highly profitable memoirs of German generals), and this first clash with Orwell was the prelude to a more disruptive one over *Homage to Catalonia*. As a fellow-traveller of the Communists at the time of the Spanish War, Gollancz accepted many of the views (of the POUM, for instance) that Orwell attacks in his book. Seeing Orwell's direction, Gollancz refused the book before it was written, and thus aligned himself with Orwell's opponents. He was contracted to publish Orwell's novels and did publish *Coming Up for Air*, but the attack on Stalin's Russia in *Animal Farm* was quite impossible for him (and for a number of other publishers, including

166

T. S. Eliot for Faber and Faber). This book, too, went finally to Secker and Warburg, and that firm's loyalty made Orwell decide they should publish all his work thenceforth. Gollancz still had rights to Orwell's next three novels, but in 1947 Orwell's agent, Leonard Moore, got him to agree to relinquish those rights—'your generous action', Orwell called it.

Gollancz's career as a political activist survived his disillusionment with Stalinism. As a Jewish humanitarian, he did relief work for Arabs in Israel and for Germans after the Nazi defeat. He took prominent parts in the campaigns in Britain against capital punishment and for nuclear disarmament. He was knighted in 1965.

ARTHUR KOESTLER, 1905–1983   Born in Budapest and educated at the University of Vienna, Koestler lived a life of turbulent change that was strangely characteristic for a mid-European intellectual in the twentieth century. His well-off Jewish family was ruined in the financial crisis that followed the First World War, and Koestler became converted to Communism, joining the Party in 1931. He worked for the Ullstein newspapers as a foreign correspondent, then in Berlin, writing often on scientific subjects. In 1932 he was invited to the Soviet Union, where he spent six months travelling and six months writing a book about his visit, leaving in the autumn of 1933 and moving to Paris, since Hitler had come to power in Germany. In 1936, Koestler managed to get accredited to visit Franco's headquarters in Spain, but was soon recognized and denounced as a Communist and had to escape. Later in the war, when operating undercover as a Comintern agent, he was captured by the Nationalists, condemned to death, and, after four months' imprisonment, released when the British Government intervened in his case and he was exchanged for a prisoner held by the Republic. In 1938, at the period of the Moscow trials, Koestler left the Communist Party. In 1939, after the war began, he was imprisoned in France, was released in 1940, briefly joined the Foreign Legion, escaped to England, was imprisoned in Pentonville, was released, served in the Pioneer Corps, and then worked for the Ministry of Information.

After his rejection of Communism, Koestler became one of the most effective of anti-totalitarian writers, but he abandoned political writing in the 1950s ('Cassandra has gone hoarse . . . .') and pursued instead his interests in science, philosophy, and parapsychology. He was a principal figure in the campaign to abolish capital punishment in Britain. Later he campaigned to make euthanasia legal and when he discovered that he himself was terminally ill, committed suicide in 1983.

Orwell and Koestler met in the winter of 1940–41, though each had read and—in Orwell's case—reviewed the other's books.

Koestler's earlier books were written in German and translated into English. Among these, *Darkness at Noon* is a modern classic. In the person of its protagonist, Rubashov, the novel dramatizes the processes that in Koestler's view caused Old Bolsheviks to confess, at the Moscow purge trials, to crimes they had not committed.

Koestler's contribution to *The God that Failed* (1950, edited by Richard Crossman) is one of his masterpieces. His working title for it was 'memoirs of a tight-rope walker', since it describes, with fine wit and irony, the mental balancing act he had to perform to retain his Communist faith against the increasing evidence of his senses. Orwell died just before it was published, but the essay offers illuminating commentary on the mental world depicted in *1984*. His name was given to a chair in parapsychology at Edinburgh from 1985.

HENRY VALENTINE MILLER, 1891–1980   Miller was a New Yorker, raised in Brooklyn, and like another Brooklyn boy, Whitman, he made his work a stream of autobiography. (Orwell was one of the first critics to draw the comparison, to Whitman's disadvantage.)

Miller had little formal education and had all kinds of jobs in the United States. His writing career began in earnest in 1925 when he determined to be nothing but a writer. From then on his biography is largely made up of the titles of his prolific output. From 1930 until 1940 he lived mostly in Paris. *Tropic of Cancer* was published there in 1934, *Black Spring* in 1935, *Tropic of Capricorn* in 1939. In his later years, Miller lived in California. He was six times married, five times divorced.

Orwell's great disagreement with Miller centered on what Orwell labelled his 'nihilistic quietism', in particular his refusal to see any importance in politics or to assign himself any political responsibility. When Orwell called on Miller in Paris in December 1936, en route to Spain, Miller ridiculed Orwell's purpose but admired his steadfastness. They parted friends, Miller giving Orwell a jacket to wear in the trenches.

Orwell's reviews of Miller's books and letters to him are included in the *Collected Essays, Journalism and Letters*, as is his most elaborate piece on Miller, 'Inside the Whale'.

STEPHEN HAROLD SPENDER, 1909–   During the 1930s, Spender—together with MacNeice, Auden, and Day Lewis ('MacSpaunday')—was part of what Orwell called 'the movement', the defining literary grouping of the period, its characteristic manifestation in literature, in this instance a group of anti-Fascist poets, proclaiming their political commitment in their work.

Spender left University College, Oxford, in 1931 without a degree. He was then sympathetic towards Marxism, though a member of the Communist Party for only a few weeks in 1936–37.

Revulsion from Fascism in Germany and support for the Spanish Republic were defining events in his 1930s, though his poetry at its most political was always lyrical and strongly neo-romantic. In 1937 he published *Forward Liberalism* in a Left Book Club edition, arguing the case for Communism. To Orwell, until he met him, Spender was conveniently representative. 'I had always used him and the rest of that gang as symbols of the pansy Left, and in fact I don't care for his poems to speak of, but when I met him in person I liked him so much and was sorry for the things I had said about him.'

Spender and Orwell became friends after that meeting. During the Second World War, in which he served in the Auxiliary Fire Service in London, Spender broke from Communism, and later contributed a chapter to *The God that Failed*. He co-edited *Horizon* with Cyril Connolly in 1940–41, and was co-editor of *Encounter* from 1953–65, when he resigned on discovering that the magazine received covert support from the American Central Intelligence Agency. Besides his poetry, he has written fiction, criticism, translation, autobiography, and political commentary. He has been Professor of English at University College London, and was made CBE in 1962.

HERBERT GEORGE WELLS, 1866–1946 In Orwell's lifetime, and in his thinking, H. G. Wells was an unavoidable literary presence. He came from the shabby-genteel world of the nineteenth century. His father, a failed small-businessman, had been a professional cricketer; his mother, a housemaid and housekeeper, was a fundamentalist Protestant. Wells fought free of their world, which for him took the form of employment as a draper's and chemist's assistant, by means of a scientific education and a powerful literary imagination. He wrote over a hundred books in which he recreated the dominant images he had absorbed from his mother's religion, actions of destruction and regeneration. For Wells, the Last Judgement took the form of invaders from outer space or of inhuman future dystopias, while the New Jerusalem was brought about by Fabian Socialism, sexual liberation, scientific progress, and idealistic utopianism.

Of the utopian and dystopian writers Orwell studied so carefully, it was to Wells that he owed most. 'Orwell's work contains scarcely a topic related to politics and social systems which cannot be found in Wells's books', says William Steinhoff. He points out that even Orwell's pseudonym echoes Wells's name.

After the First World War, Wells's reputation with the younger generation that included Orwell underwent a sharp decline, and in Chapter XII of *The Road to Wigan Pier* Wells is evoked as the great representative of the inhuman machine-world that many Socialists actually. hold up as a positive ideal: 'machines to save work, machines to save thought, machines to save pain, hygiene, efficiency, organization, more hygiene, more efficiency, more organization, more machines—until finally you land up in the by now familiar Wellsian Utopia, aptly caricatured by Huxley in *Brave New World*, the paradise of little fat men.' Orwell trusted neither Wells's optimism nor his pessimism, but the critique offered has undoubtedly an oedipal element, for he admitted that it might be 'a sort of parricide' for someone of his generation to attack Wells. 'The minds of all of us, and therefore the physical world, would be perceptibly different if Wells had never existed.'

Orwell's books, certainly, are in Wells's debt. Wells claimed that his scientific-poetic romances were meant to exemplify his political beliefs—exactly the situation of *Animal Farm* and *1984*. *Coming Up for Air* is Orwell's tribute to the success of Wells's 'little man' novels: *Love and Mr. Lewisham* (1900), *Kipps* (1905), and especially *The History of Mr. Polly* (1910). Wells supplied more particular details, too. *Mr. Blettsworthy on Rampole Island* (1928) has been found to anticipate 'double think'. Most of all, *The Island of Dr. Moreau* (1896) fed both *Animal Farm* and *1984*.

Parties, movements, ideologies and events

ANARCHISM 'I worked out an anarchistic theory that all government is evil, that the punishment always does more harm than the crime and that people can be trusted to behave decently if only you will let them alone. This of course was sentimental nonsense. (*The Road to Wigan Pier*, IX) Thus in 1936 Orwell dismissed the 'anarchism' he had evolved to deal with his experiences in the Burma Police. His time in Spain, however, introduced him to a more political form of anarchism for which he retained afterwards a muted and critical sympathy.

The first great schism of Communism was that between Marx and Mikhail Bakunin (1814–76), between authoritarian and libertarian socialism within the First International (organized in 1864 by Marx and Engels to associate the trades unions of all nations). Bakunin's anarchism had its largest following in Spain, and the Anarchist groups took a leading part in the revolution within Republican Spain that followed Franco's uprising in 1936. The Anarchists, like the POUM, were at the left extremity of the Republican political spectrum, so Orwell stood beside them in their opposition to the Communists.

The Anarchists' beliefs and their appeal to Spaniards are summarized by Hugh Thomas in a manner that reveals their attraction for Orwell.

The state, being based upon ideas of obedience and authority, was evil. In its place, there should be self-governing communes—municipalities, professions, or other societies—which would make voluntary pacts with each other. All collaboration with parliaments, governments, and organized religion was to be condemned. Criminals would be punished by the censure of public opinion. Bakunin was influenced, like Tolstoy, in forming such views, by a nostalgia for the Russian village life which he had himself known in childhood. The Spaniards . . . can also be represented as hankering for a similar simplicity of the days before the grasping modern state, of the medieval village societies and provincial autonomous units which had flourished in Spain as in the rest of Europe. Money in much of Spain was then still an innovation. Anarchism was thus more a protest against industrialization than a method of organizing it to the public advantage.

Like these Spaniards, Orwell too was suspicious of the power of the state, nostalgic for a simpler village life he believed had existed before the First World War, and very reluctant to embrace what he called 'machine civilization'. Yet his sympathy was insufficient to make him an Anarchist, and he was not really a fellow-traveller. He deplored the general English ignorance that equated anarchism with anarchy (1/110) and that was unaware of the 'remarkable things' that Spanish anarchism had achieved, but later, when Spain had come into perspective, he asked some hard questions of anarchism in reviewing a book by Herbert Read:

> how are freedom and organization to be reconciled? If one considers the probabilities one is driven to the conclusion that Anarchism implies a low standard of living. It need not imply a hungry or uncomfortable world, but it rules out the kind of air-conditioned, chromium-plated, gadget-ridden existence which is now considered desirable and enlightened. The processes involved in making, say, an aeroplane are so complex as to be only possible in a planned, centralised society, with all the repressive apparatus that that implies. Unless there is some unpredictable change in human nature, liberty and efficiency must pull in opposite directions. (4/14)

Orwell saw, too, that anarchism could bestow on the believer a psychological licence for the pleasures of power. Like pacifism, it was a self-denying belief, seeming to renounce power, a creed free from 'the ordinary dirtiness of politics . . . surely that proves you are in the right? And the more you are in the right, the more natural that everyone else should be bullied into thinking likewise' (4/76).

BURNHAMISM   In the 1940s, the writings of the American political philosopher and political sociologist James Burnham (born 1905) had sufficient popularity and stimulated sufficient criticism to give currency to such terms as 'Burnhamite' and 'Burnhamist'. Orwell wrote on five occasions about James Burnham's ideas, and in a highly characteristic manner. He opposed and refuted many aspects of Burnhamism, yet he also adopted some of Burnham's ideas, so that it is quite correct to say that *1984* would be markedly different without the influence of James Burnham.

Burnham had excelled as a student at Princeton and had studied English literature at Oxford. He became a professor of philosophy at New York University in 1930. For much of the next ten years he gave his allegiance to the ideas of Leon Trotsky. He helped found the American Workers Party and co-edited *The New International*, but towards the end of the decade he began to dissent from Trotskyism, and in 1940 broke with the movement. His 1941 book,

The Managerial Revolution, is a refutation of Trotsky's predictions and was immensely popular. One hundred thousand copies of the hardback edition alone were published during the war, and one of its readers was Orwell.

The Managerial Revolution argues that capitalism has failed but that its replacement will not be Marxist Socialism but a form of totalitarianism administered by and serving the interests of a 'new class', that of the managers—the guides, organizers, and administrators of the production processes. Orwell's view was that Burnham gave an acute and reliable account of current trends— Stalin's Russia was clearly neither Socialist nor reverting to Capitalism, and it was oligarchal—but that he was a defective prophet. He declared Burnham to be infected with the intellectuals' disease, the worship of power, which led him in prophecy to assume that what had happened must continue to happen. Burnham predicted the triumph of Germany and Japan and the defeat of the USSR. Orwell could thus deride his predictions and seek their origin in the seductions of power worship. Orwell's model of a future totalitarianism in *1984*, however, clearly owes a great deal to *The Managerial Revolution,* and while it would be easy and comforting to suggest that therefore Orwell intended to expose Burnham's model to ridicule and refutation, the truth is more complex and painful. Burnham appealed strongly to the pessimistic side of Orwell, so when he encountered Burnham's ideas in open intellectual debate, he strove vigorously against them. But that vigour did not produce a final defeat for the appeal of Burnhamism. The lust for power as the original sin of politics is alive, though a mystery, in *1984*, several years after Orwell had poured scorn on it in writing about Burnham. 'The strangest aspect of Orwell's relation to Burnham', says Alex Zwerdling, 'is how many of his criticisms could also be levelled against his own vision in *1984.*'

COMINTERN The Comintern (from 'Communist International') was the Third International, founded in 1919 by the Russian Bolsheviks to promote revolutionary Marxism rather than the reformist Socialism of the Second International. Until 1925 it was dominated by Zinoviev. Its policies produced severe defeats for the German Communist Party in 1923 and for the Chinese Communist Party in 1927. After 1928, leftist influence, particularly Trotsky's, was eliminated and the Comintern's function became that of promoting Stalin's foreign policies. It was dissolved in 1943.

INDEPENDENT LABOUR PARTY In the late nineteenth century, working-class candidates stood for Parliament under the 'Liberal-Labour' name. Keir Hardie established the Independent Labour Party in 1893 to sever the Liberal connection. From 1900 to 1932 the ILP was in uneasy partnership with the Labour Party, refusing to affiliate with the Communists or to join the Comintern. The party had three parliamentary seats in 1945, but has been unrepresented since 1947.

Bernard Crick sums up the ILP of 1934, when Orwell first encountered it, as 'Left-wing, egalitarian, a strange English mixture of secularized evangelism and non-Communist Marxism'. This was the only political party to which Orwell ever belonged. He joined on 13 June 1938, after his return from Spain. He had asked the party to sponsor him in going to Spain, and this connection led to his joining the militia of the POUM, the ILP's Spanish sister-party.

After the experience of Spain, Orwell's views were for a time those of the ILP. He opposed the Popular Front, Fascism, *and* preparation for war against Germany (a sort of 'left pacifism'). 'If one collaborates with a capitalist-imperialist government in a struggle "against Fascism", i.e., against a rival imperialism, one is simply letting Fascism in by the back door.' (1/105) Being opposed to Hitler and re-armament was a contradiction Orwell shared, as Crick points out, with most of the Labour Party at that time (1937). It was identical, too, to the Trotskyite view of things. But when war came in 1939, and Hitler and Stalin made their pact, Orwell gave up this attitude. The ILP leadership continued to call the war a capitalist-imperialist conspiracy, and Orwell, without publicity, left the Party.

INGSOC   The name of the ideology of the Party in *1984* obviously derives—in the modified spelling of Newspeak—from 'English Socialism'. This has encouraged some misinterpretation of Orwell's meaning, well exemplified by the report on *1984* that Frederic Warburg, Orwell's loyal but sometimes obtuse publisher, wrote for his staff.

> The political system which prevails is Ingsoc-English Socialism. This I take to be a deliberate and sadistic attack on socialism and socialist parties generally. It seems to indicate a final breach between Orwell and Socialism, not the socialism of equality and human brotherhood which clearly Orwell no longer expects from socialist parties, but the socialism of Marxism and the managerial revolution. *1984* is among other things an attack on Burnham's managerialism; and it is worth a cool million votes to the Conservative Party; it is imaginable that it might have a preface by Winston Churchill after whom the hero is named. *1984 should be published as soon as possible, in June 1949 . . . .*

But the analogy on which the term 'Ingsoc' is constructed ought to dispel such misunderstandings. Both the great totalitarianisms of the twentieth century—Soviet Communism and Nazism—have named themselves 'Socialist'. (Nazism was 'National Socialism'.) Neither, in Orwell's view, was Socialist at all. He therefore gives his Party in the novel the character trait of having stolen the name of Socialism while spurning its meaning.

MOSCOW PURGE TRIALS   The Moscow trials of 1936 to 1938, and the massive purges that accompanied them throughout the USSR, were Stalin's means of making himself absolute master of the State. The trials presented a crisis of belief for Communists outside the USSR, since they had either to believe the intrinsically incredible or to renounce their faith, as Arthur Koestler did

On 1 December 1934, Kirov, a member of the Central Committee and a popular protégé of Stalin, was assassinated. (In 1956, Kruschev apparently confirmed that Stalin was implicated in the murder.) In the repression that followed, Stalin's leftist rivals, Zinoviev and Kamenev, were arrested. Eighteen months later, Stalin announced that a huge plot existed, directed from abroad by Trotsky, whereby tens of thousands of Soviet military and political officials, in concert with Fascists and foreign capitalists, were to overthrow and dismember the state. In 1936, Zinoviev, Kamenev, and fourteen others were tried, confessed, and were executed. Trials of leftists and rightists within the Party, including Old Bolsheviks like Bukharin, followed. All made refutable confessions to amazing crimes. Of fifty-four defendants, seven were imprisoned (though none survived); the rest were killed. Trotsky and his followers were the cause of all.

In the purge, seven million arrests were made, followed by half a million executions. As many as two-and-a-half million of the prisoners died in the camps. Ninety-eight out of one hundred and thirty-nine members of the Central Committee of 1934 were purged. In 1937–38, a purge of the army eliminated nearly half of the officer corps, and seventy-five out of eighty members of the Supreme Military Command. Stalin was left with absolute power, the latest of the czars.

Orwell's presentation of these events is given in the seventh chapter of *Animal Farm*.

POPULAR FRONT   The Popular Front was a movement to unite parties of the Left against Fascism. It was launched in 1935 after the Comintern, which earlier had denounced other left parties as 'Social Fascists', switched its tactics and encouraged co-operation and electoral pacts between Communists, social democrats, radicals, and liberals. In 1936 a Popular Front Government came to power in France. The victory of the Popular Front in the Spanish election of February 1936 helped precipitate the Spanish Civil War. The Republic's governments, until its defeat in 1939, were Popular Front alliances.

After the suppression of the POUM and the actions against the Anarchists by the Communist-dominated Popular Front Government in 1937, Orwell became vigorously opposed to the concept of the Popular Front, which he found to be self-contradictory.

> For even when the worker and the bourgeois are both fighting against Fascism, they are not fighting for the same things; the bourgeois is fighting for bourgeois democracy, i.e., capitalism, the worker, in so far as he understands the issue, for Socialism .... This uneasy alliance is known as the Popular Front. It is a combination with about as much vitality, and about as much right to exist, as a pig with two heads. . . . (1/100)

Orwell saw that for orthodox, Stalinist Communists, the Popular Front was an element of Soviet foreign policy, and argued that the Communists' participation was anti-revolutionary, since events in Russia made them wish to suppress 'Trotskyists'.

The alliance between the democracies and the Soviet Union to defeat Nazi Germany was for Orwell a version of the Popular Front. The alliance was necessary, but the Western allies should not wishfully suppose that Stalin's Russia was anything but an anti-revolutionary, totalitarian state.

POUM   The Partido Obrero de Unificación Marxista (Workers United Marxist Party) was founded in 1935 by Joaquín Maurín (1896–1973), a Marxist with no illusions about Soviet Communism. Maurín argued that only an alliance of workers and peasants could bring about revolution in Spain, the bourgeoisie being too weak. The POUM's base and strength was in Catalonia, and the Party took a Catalan nationalist line.

On Franco's insurrection, the POUM, although a very small party (it grew with the Revolution, but not enormously) formed its own militia, and Orwell's ILP credentials placed him in its ranks, though he never joined the Party. The POUM's hostility to Stalinism never abated during the war, and was proclaimed publicly in its newspaper, *La Batalla*, which gave nearly unique publicity to the Moscow purge trials—to the fury of the Communists. As Russian influence (based on weapons supplies) increased in the Republican Government, and as the Spanish Communists became the dominant element in the ruling alliance, the extermination of the POUM—'Trotskyists' like those being hunted down in Russia—became inevitable. A campaign was launched to depict the POUM as in active collaboration with Franco, and after the May 1937 troubles in Barcelona, the party was banned, and many members and adherents arrrested. Nin disappeared into a secret Communist prison, where he was murdered.

The suppression of the POUM, and particularly the tactics

employed, educated Orwell about totalitarianism. He put the POUM case (rather uncritically, he admitted) in *Homage to Catalonia*, and for a while proclaimed rather POUMist attitudes, such as this diary comment: 'Within two years we shall either be conquered or we shall be a Socialist republic fighting for its life, with a secret police force and half the population starving' (18 May 1941). But the war and the revolution were not as inseparable as he at first believed.

SOVIET MYTH (sometimes RUSSIAN MYTH)   This was Orwell's term for the fiction or mistaken belief of Western intellectuals and workers that the Soviet Union was truly a Socialist State.

> ... it was of the utmost importance to me that people in western Europe should see the Soviet regime for what it really was. Since 1930 I had seen little evidence that the USSR was progressing towards anything that one could truly call Socialism. On the contrary, I was struck by clear signs of its transformation into a hierarchical society, in which the rulers have no more reason to give up their power than any other ruling class. ...
>
> And so for the past ten years I have been convinced that the destruction of the Soviet myth was essential if we wanted a revival of the Socialist movement. (3/110)

Animal Farm is Orwell's main attack on this myth.

SPANISH CIVIL WAR   Spain's history in the late nineteenth and early twentieth centuries is of great political turbulence and of rapid and multi-directional change. At various times, Spanish governments were Republican, restored monarchist, and military dictatorship. There were wide divisions of wealth and class antagonisms, urban and industrial unrest, colonial wars, rival monarchist movements, movements of provincial autonomy or separatism, an aggressively conservative Church opposed by savage anti-clericalism, a politicized army, a working class and peasantry considerably committed to anarcho-syndicalist politics, Fascists, Communists—in fact every variety of social and political antagonism. In 1931, the monarchy again fell and the Second Republic replaced it. In the election of February 1936, a Popular Front won a majority in support of a Republican, though non-Socialist, government. In July, in reaction to the policies of the government and social unrest, a long-prepared military revolt began in Morocco. Garrisons in Spain joined it, and the largely Moorish Army of Africa, commanded by General Franco, was airlifted by the Germans and Italians to southern Spain. The government armed the working-class militias and other groups and in several big cities, notably Madrid, Barcelona, and Valencia, the uprisings were defeated. The Socialists and Communists entered the government, and a *coup d'état* became a civil war.

By the end of 1936, Franco's Nationalists controlled half of Spain, the south and west. Franco's attempt to divide Republican territory by advancing on Valencia at first failed, but in June 1937 the Nationalists captured Bilbao in the north. In 1938, they reached the Mediterranean coast between Barcelona and Valencia, the Republic's capital. Late in the year, the Nationalists broke through on the Catalan front. In January 1939, Barcelona fell, followed in March by Valencia and Madrid. Franco remained *caudillo*, in effect king, of Spain until his death in 1975. In 1969 he had nominated as his successor Prince Juan Carlos of Borbon.

The Spanish Civil War was a battlefield for the polarized politics of the whole world of 1936. Despite a 'non-intervention' treaty signed in 1936, Hitler sent an air force, the Condor Legion, and Mussolini's Italy 50,000 troops to help Franco. The Soviet Union helped the Republic with weapons and advisers. Britain and France, meanwhile, tried to enforce non-intervention by means of naval patrols. The Republic was aided by foreign volunteers, chiefly the International Brigades, which were Communist-dominated. Orwell's Spanish experience was limited to north-east Spain, Catalonia and its capital Barcelona, and the Aragon front—the most revolutionary of the areas under Republican control.

STALINISM *Stalinism* is a term of abuse for policies and attitudes of Stalin (Josef Vissarionovich Djugashvili, 1879–1953) or for policies and attitudes that the speaker wishes to condemn by association with the name of 'this disgusting murderer', as Orwell once called him.

At the Twelfth Congress of the Soviet Communist Party in 1923, Stalin combined with other old Bolsheviks to isolate Trotsky. By means of a Five-Year Plan, ruthlessly enforced, Stalin began his campaign for 'Socialism in One Country', a policy opposed to Trotsky's international Socialism. By means of the purges of the 1930s, Stalin made himself absolute dictator of the USSR. He led the country through the Second World War, adding the conquered states of eastern Europe to the Soviet Empire. In 1956, at the Twentieth Party Congress, Kruschev gave the first official Soviet acknowledgement of Stalin's 'cult of personality' and crimes. In 1961, his embalmed body was removed from Lenin's tomb and reburied near the Kremlin wall.

Stalinism implies a foreign policy devoted solely to the interests of the Soviet Union, and at home a rigid police state with vigilant supervision of all social activities and unyielding economic central-ization. Periods of 'deStalinization' are significantly called 'thaws'.

In *Animal Farm*, Stalin (the pseudonym means 'Steel') is represented by Napoleon, the name chosen by Orwell to suggest the emergence from revolution of a military dictator whose regime eventually assumes the form of an empire, with quasi-religious veneration of the emperor. Eisenstein's film, *Ivan the Terrible* is one of the visions of Stalinism personally approved by Stalin.

TOTALITARIANISM   *Totalitarian* denotes a political system in which a party or leadership, subject to no power greater than itself within the state, is the sole source of authority and of change, enforcing its decisions by police and military power so as to bring all sectional interests and all institutions—political, social, religious, and cultural—into conformity with its own will. Totalitarian systems permit the existence of no autonomous institutions within the state. They allow no freedom of association, and enforce complete state control of the means of communication. Every aspect of life is assigned political significance, so in a totalitarian system there are effectively no non-political activities, albeit that the great mass of the people is denied a genuine political rôle in the state.

Orwell's greatest claim to originality as a political thinker is his presentation, especially in *1984*, of the model of a totalitarian state. He perceived, after his experiences in Spain, that

> common factors were emerging in Stalinism and in Nazism concerned with the retention and extension of power by the inner party elite. These lead the State to mobilize all society as if for perpetual and total war, a common process more important than the vestigial and nominally antagonistic ideologies. Koestler, Borkenau, Silone, Malraux and Orwell all established this usage and began to develop the theory at about the same time, 1936 to 1940 (as far as I can discover, quite independently of each other). . . . They set out this theory and acted upon it. It was to be a decade and a half before the scholars and academics 'invented' or 'discovered' the totalitarian thesis and elaborated it at length. . . .

> (Crick)

TROTSKYISM   *Trotskyist* is used to designate the version of Communism associated with Trotsky (Lev Davidovich Bronstein, 1879–1940) who, after the death of Lenin in 1924, was, with Stalin, one of the claimants to the leadership of the Soviet Communist Party. A brilliant orator and talented writer, Trotsky was chairman of the Petrograd Soviet during the October Revolution (1917), the main organizer of the Bolshevik seizure of power and Lenin's closest associate. Trotsky enjoyed great prestige as the founder of the Red Army and the organizer of its victories in the Civil War, but during Lenin's last illness he was occupied with foreign and military affairs, allowing Stalin, who like the other old Bolshevik leaders distrusted Trotsky, to isolate him. After Lenin's death,

Trotsky was discredited in the Bolshevik Party and the Comintern. He was expelled from the Party in 1927 and exiled from the USSR in 1929. He lived in exile in Turkey, France, and Norway, and finally in Mexico, generally a vigorous critic of Stalin and his policies. In 1940 he was murdered by one of Stalin's agents.

In *Animal Farm*, the character and activities of Snowball are meticulously based upon Trotsky's. It should be noted that Orwell is careful to implicate Trotsky in the creation of social privilege to benefit the revolutionary hierarchy. In chapter three, the milk and apples are not shared equally but are retained for the pigs only. 'All the pigs were in agreement on this point, even Snowball and Napoleon.'

In 1937, Orwell pondered the meaning of 'Trotskyist'—'This terrible word'—in light of his Spanish experience.

> The word . . . is generally used to mean a disguised Fascist who poses as an ultra-revolutionary in order to split the left-wing forces. But it derives its peculiar power from the fact that it means three separate things. It can mean one who, like Trotsky, wished for world revolution; or a member of an actual organiz-ation of which Trotsky is head (the only legitimate use of the word); or the disguised Fascist already mentioned. The three meanings can be telescoped one into the other at will. (1/100)

H. G. Wells once called Orwell 'that Trotskyist with the big feet'.

Bibliography

This list divides into three parts. The first is of reading recommended for the further study of Orwell, while the second part identifies work referred to or cited in the text. The third part provides a small selection of prophetic books and other texts which may be consulted as precursors of *1984*.

Further reading

EDITION OF ORWELL'S WORKS   All of Orwell's books are in print. In Britain, Penguin Books offers paperback editions, and in the USA Harcourt Brace and Jovanovich does so (Harvest Books).

A new edition of *The Complete Works of George Orwell* is now being prepared by Peter Davison. Orwell's nine books will be newly edited, and the collection will include the complete *Essays, Journalism and Letters*. The current edition (the *Collected Essays, Journalism and Letters*, four volumes, edited by Sonia Orwell and Ian Angus) will be expanded to six volumes, incorporating material not previously published or reprinted. His radio scripts have been published in Orwell (ed. W. J. West), *The War Broadcasts* (London: Duckworth, BBC, 1985).

BIBLIOGRAPHIES   There is as yet no separately published Orwell bibliography, but the journal *Bulletin of Bibliography* (published by the F. W. Faxon Co., Boston, Massachusetts) has published several lists which together make up a very detailed bibliography of works by and about Orwell. The exact references are: by Zoltan G. Zeke and William White, vol. 23, no. 5, May–Aug. 1961, 110–114; vol. 23, no. 6, Sept.–Dec. 1961, 140–144; vol. 23, no. 7, Jan.–Apr. 1962, 166–168; by M. Jennifer McDowell, vol. 23, no. 10, Jan.–Apr. 1963, 224–229; vol. 24, no. 1, May–Aug. 1963, 19–24; vol. 24, no. 2, Sept.–Dec. 1963, 36–40; by Ian Willison and Ian Angus, vol. 24, no. 8, Sept.–Dec. 1965, 180–187; by Jeffrey Meyers, vol. 31, no. 3, July–Sept. 1974, 117–121. Jeffrey Meyers has supplemented this last item in the journal *Modern Fiction Studies*, vol. 21, 1975, 133–136.

Jeffrey and Valerie Meyers have compiled *George Orwell: An Annotated Bibliography of Criticism* (New York and London: Garland, 1977). This lists books, articles, chapters in books, and reviews about Orwell's work from all over the world. Each item is accompanied by a brief synopsis and occasionally evaluative comment. This list is very helpful but rather difficult to use, since items are given only in alphabetical order of the authors' names; no other indexing method is employed.

BIOGRAPHIES 'I request that . . . no biography shall be written.' These are the last words that Bernard Crick quotes from Orwell's will. A good writer who prohibits a biography seems to assure that he will get one (or more, authorized or unauthorized) as Kipling, Hardy, Eliot and Auden have discovered. Orwell's prohibition has been no more effective than theirs. (Such is the interest generated by Orwell's request that rumours have gone around that the will really contained no prohibition, that it was invented by Sonia Orwell.)

The principal biography of Orwell is Bernard Crick's *George Orwell: A Life* (revised edition, London: Secker and Warburg, 1981, and Boston: Little Brown, 1981. Penguin Books edition, 1982) which Crick undertook when Malcolm Muggeridge, Sonia Orwell's first choice as biographer, gave up. This is the basic resource for anyone needing information on Orwell's life and work. Without it, books such as this one would be very hesitant and uninformed.

Peter Stansky and William Abrahams published *The Unknown Orwell* in 1972 (London: Constable, and New York: Knopf) and its sequel *Orwell: The Transformation* in 1979. The authors did not have Crick's access to Orwell's papers, and they sometimes fall into error (instances conscientiously recorded by Crick), but they carefully followed Orwell's footsteps, sometimes giving more detail than Crick can, and they were able to interview some persons, such as Mrs Vaughan Wilkes, who had died before Crick began his study. So Stansky and Abrahams usefully supplement Crick's biography, although their story ends with Orwell's return from Spain.

CRITICISM There are now many books about Orwell's writing, some concentrating on individual aspects of it. The following short list is of recommended books that deal with Orwell's work in general.

Two books by friends of Orwell, combining memoir with criticism, are: Richard Rees, *George Orwell: Fugitive from the Camp of Victory* (London: Secker and Warburg, 1961) and George Woodcock, *The Crystal Spirit: A Study of George Orwell* (Boston: Little Brown, 1966; Penguin Books, 1970; New York: Schocken, 1984).

William Steinhoff's *George Orwell and the Origins of '1984'* (Ann Arbor: University of Michigan, 1975) shows how Orwell's last book is the accumulation and culmination of his thinking and experiences from his very earliest work.

Richard Voorhees's *The Paradox of George Orwell* (Lafayette, Indiana: Purdue University, 1961) is the earliest and still one of the best scholarly studies of Orwell, despite being written before the publication of the *Collected Essays, Journalism and Letters.*

Alex Zwerdling's *Orwell and the Left* (New Haven and London: Yale University, 1974) is very reliable.

Jeffrey Meyers has edited *George Orwell: The Critical Heritage* (London and Boston: Routledge and Kegan Paul, 1975), gathering over one hundred reviews of Orwell's work from 1933 to 1968.

References and citations

1 WRITING

Moral is political
Lionel Trilling, 'Introduction' to George Orwell, *Homage to Catalonia* (New York: Harcourt, Brace & World, 1952) p. xviii.

The pleasures of reading Orwell
V. S. Pritchett, review of *1984, New Statesman and Nation,* 18 June 1949.

2 LIFE

The good fit: Orwell and Adlerian psychology
Sheldon T. Selesnick, 'Alfred Adler: The Psychology of the Inferiority Complex', in *Psychoanalytic Pioneers,* eds. F. Alexander, S. Eisenstein, and M. Grotjahn (New York: Basic Books, 1966) p. 81.
Hertha Orgler, *Alfred Adler: The Man and His Work* (New York: Capricorn Books, 1965) p. 55.

3 REPUTE

'Orwellian': a mythology
Language and Public Policy, ed. Hugh Rank (Urbana, Illinois: National Council of Teachers of English, 1974).
Lionel Trilling, *op. cit.,* p. viii.

Unofficial history
Peter Stansky and William Abrahams, *Orwell: The Transformation* (London: Constable, 1979) p. 203.
Hugh Thomas, *The Spanish Civil War,* revised and enlarged edition (New York: Harper and Row, 1977) p. 653 and pp. 646–74.
Raymond Carr, 'Orwell and the Spanish Civil War', in *The World of George Orwell,* ed. Miriam Gross (London: Weidenfeld and Nicolson, 1971) p. 66.

Paul Fussell Jr, *The Boy Scout Handbook and other observations* (New York: Oxford University Press, 1982) p. vii.

Socialism
T. R. Fyvel, *George Orwell: A Personal Memoir* (New York: Macmillan, 1982) pp. 146–7.

Language and style
George Steiner, *After Babel* (New York and London: Oxford University Press, 1975) pp. 81–2.
Edward Sapir, cited in Steiner, p. 87.
Richard Lanham, *Literacy and the Survival of Humanism* (New Haven and London: Yale, 1983) p. 123.
See also W. F. Bolton, *The Language of 1984: Orwell's English and Ours* (Oxford: Blackwell, 1984).

The religious sense of life
Two critics who have considered Orwell in relation to religious ideas are Christopher Small, *The Road to Miniluv: George Orwell, the State, and God* (London: Gollancz, 1975) and Alan Sandison, *The Last Man in Europe: An Essay on George Orwell* (London: Macmillan, 1975).

5 NOVELS, ESSAYS AND CRITICISM

Essays
On documentary in the 1930s, see Donald Mitchell, *Britten and Auden in the Thirties: The Year 1936* (London: Faber and Faber, and Seattle: University of Washington, 1981) pp. 57–62.

'From an anthropological point of view'
Arthur Calder-Marshall, *Wish You Were Here: The Art of Donald McGill* (London: Hutchinson, 1966).
Philip Thody, *Roland Barthes: A Conservative Estimate* (Atlantic Highlands, New Jersey: Humanities Press, 1977).

6 THE GREAT FICTIONS

Allegorical ingenuity
Jeffrey Meyers, *A Reader's Guide to George Orwell* (London: Thames and Hudson, 1975) chapter seven, 'The political allegory of *Animal Farm*'.

Hard questions
Alex Zwerdling, *Orwell and the Left* (New Haven and London: Yale University Press, 1974) pp. 86–90.

Julia
Elaine Hoffman Baruch, "'The Golden Country": Sex and Love in *1984*', in *1984 Revisited*, ed. Irving Howe (New York: Harper and Row, 1984) pp. 47–56.

Prophecy: 'a novel about the future'
Timothy Garton Ash, *The Polish Revolution: Solidarity* (New York: Scribner's, 1984) p. 21.

GAZETTEER

Eton College
Henry Longhurst, *My Life and Soft Times* (London: Cassell, 1972) p. 34.

Southwold, Suffolk
R. S. Peters, *Psychology and Ethical Development* (London: Allen and Unwin, 1974) pp. 460–3.

Paris
Loelia, Duchess of Westminster, *Grace and Favour* (London: Weiden-feld & Nicolson, 1961) p. 225.

SHORT BIOGRAPHIES

Cyril Vernon Connolly
Contemporary Authors: Permanent Series, ed. Christine Nasso (Detroit, Michigan: Gale, 1978) vol. 2, p. 133.

PARTIES, MOVEMENTS, IDEOLOGIES, AND EVENTS

Anarchism
Hugh Thomas, *op. cit.*, pp. 61–2.

Burnhamism
John P. Diggins, *Up from Communism: Conservative Odysseys in American Intellectual History* (New York: Harper and Row, 1975).

Ingsoc
Frederic Warburg, cited in Bernard Crick, *George Orwell: A Life* (London: Secker and Warburg, 1981) p. 396.

Before 1984: utopias and prophecies of political doom

Between Thomas More's *Utopia* of 1516 and Orwell's *1984* of 1949 lie many works within these two genres, imaginary country and prophetic nightmare, a number of which are given below.

Thomas More, *Libellus vere aureus nec minus salutaris quam festivus de optime reip. statu. deq nova insula Utopia* (Aloist, Thierry Martin, 1516).

Francis Bacon, *New Atlantis* (London: I. H. for W. Lee, 1627).

James Harrington, *The Common-wealth of Oceana* (London: J. Streater for L. Chapman, 1656).

Samuel Butler, *Erewhon, or, Over the Range* (London: Trübner, 1872).

William Morris, *News from Nowhere* (London: Reeves & Turner, 1891).

H. G. Wells, *A Modern Utopia* (London: Chapman & Hall, 1905).

A selection from a range of books of political prediction, several of which in their own day created a further sub-literature of sequels not here listed, and many of them anonymous.

The Reign of George VI (London: W. Nicoll, 1763).

Private Letters from an American in England to his Friends in America (London: J. Almon, 1769).

[Louis Sebastien Mercier] *Memoirs of the Year 2500* (London: Robinson, 1772).

—— *Astraea's Return; or, The Halcyon Days of France in the Year 2440: a Dream* (London, 1797).

1829, or, Shall it be so? (London: Stockdale, 1819).

[John Banim] *Revelations of the Dead-alive* (London: Simpkins & Marshall, 1824).

The Rebellion of the Beasts: or, The Ass is Dead! Long Live the Ass! (London: Hunt, 1825).

[Mary Shelley] *The Last Man* (London: Colburn, 1826).

[Jane London] *The Mummy!* (London: Colburn, 1827).

[R. F. Williams] *Eureka: a Prophecy of the Future* (London: Longman, 1837).

[Richard Walker] *Oxford in 1888: a Fragmentary Dream* (Oxford: Slatter, 1838).

1945: a Vision (London: Rivington, 1845).

[C. F. Henningsen] *Sixty Years Hence* (London: Newby, 1847).

The Last Peer (London: Newby, 1851).

The History of the English Revolution of 1867 (London: King, '3867' i.e. 1867).

Henry O'Neil, *Two Thousand Years Hence* (London: Chapman & Hall, 1868).

[Chesney, Sir George] *The Battle of Dorking* (Edinburgh: Blackwood, 1871).

The Cruise of the Anti-Torpedo (London: Tinsley, 1871).

What Happened after the Battle of Dorking, or, The Victory of Tunbridge Wells (London: Routledge, 1871).

Bracebridge Hemyng, *The Commune in London, or, Thirty Years Hence* (London: Clarke, 1872).

Gortschakoff and Bismarck, or Europe in 1940 (Oxford: Parker, 1878).

[W. F. Butler] *The Invasion of England; Told Twenty Years After* (London: Sampson Low, 1882).

Walter Besant, *The Revolt of Man* (Edinburgh: Blackwood, 1882).

Richard Jefferies *After London* (London: Cassell, 1885).

[W. H. Hudson] *A Crystal Age* (London: Unwin, 1887).

Walter Besant *The Inner House* (Bristol: Arrowsmith, 1888).

H. G. Wells *The Time Machine: an Invention* (London: Heinemann, 1895).

—— *The War of the Worlds* (London: Heinemann, 1898).

—— *When the Sleeper Wakes* (London: Harper, 1899).

[E. E. Mills] *The Decline and Fall of the British Empire 'Tokio, 2005'* (Oxford: Alden, 1905).

William Le Queux, *The Invasion of 1910: with a Full Account of the Siege of London* (London: Eveleigh Nash, 1906).

Jack London, *The Iron Heel* (London: Everett, 1908).

Owen Gregory, *Meccania, the Super-State* (London: Methuen, 1918).

Rose Macaulay, *What not; a Prophetic Comedy* (London: Constable, 1919).

Evgeny Ivanovich Zamyatin *We*, trans. into English by Gregory Zilboorg before publication in Russia (New York: Dutton, 1924).

Aldous Huxley, *Brave New World* (London: Chatto & Windus, 1932).

James Burnham, *The Managerial Revolution* (New York: John Day, 1941).

Aldous Huxley, *Ape and Essence* (London: Chatto & Windus, 1949).

George Orwell, *1984* (London: Secker & Warburg, 1949).

General index

Adler, Alfred, 37–44
Amis, Kingsley, 7

Bagehot, Walter, 14
Barthes, Roland, 122–3
BBC Eastern Service, 8
Berlin, Isaiah, 128
Blair, Eileen (wife), 44, 157, 159–60,
    161–3
Blair, Richard (father), 155
Blair, Sonia (wife), 163–5, 182
Brave New World (Huxley), 76–7, 170
Burma, 44, 52, 63–6, 158

Carr, Raymond, 58–9
Churchill, Winston, 16, 82, 174
Connolly, Cyril, 56, 61, 104, 150,
    164–5
Crick, Bernard, 66, 75, 148, 155,
    158, 161, 174, 179, 182

Dante, 139–45
Dickens, Charles, 120

Eliot, T.S., 119, 167
Eton College, 44, 47, 52, 68, 89, 91,
    150, 164

Freud, Sigmund, 37–8, 42
Fussell, Paul, Jr., 61
Fyvel, T.R., 76

Gollancz, Victor, 57, 166–7

Hazlitt, William, 111
Houseman, A.E., 107
Humboldt, Wilhelm von, 86
Huxley, Aldous, 76, 170

Independent Labour Party, 72,
    173–4

Joyce, James, 95, 101–3
Jung, Carl Gustav, 37–8

Koestler, Arthur, 3, 57, 58, 79,
    132–3, 167–8, 175

Lamb, Charles, 111

Lanham, Richard, 91
Look Back in Anger (Osborne), 7
Lucky Jim (Amis), 7

Meyers, Jeffrey, 65, 129, 183–4
Miller, Henry, 23, 105–5, 168
Morris, Wright, 50

Osborne, John, 7

POUM, 59–60, 79, 159–60, 166,
    174, 176
Pound, Ezra, 119
Priestley, J.B., 22, 119
Pritchett, V.S., 22

Rowlandson, Thomas, 10–12
Ruskin, John, 107

St Cyprian's School, Eastbourne,
    34–44, 47, 52, 75, 150, 152, 154,
    164
Sapir, Edward, 86
Secker and Warburg (publishers),
    57, 166–7, 174
Smollett, Tobias, 100, 102, 111
Solzhenitsyn, Aleksandr, 3, 5, 45
Spender, Stephen, 48, 168–9
Stalin, Joseph, 104, 129, 130, 173,
    175, 178
Steiner, George, 84–5, 86
Swift, Jonathan, 39, 138

Thody, Philip, 122
Thomas, Hugh, 58–9, 171
Tribune, 8, 44, 117
Trilling, Lionel, 14, 48
Trotsky, Leon, 57, 129, 132, 172,
    175, 178, 179

Wain, John, 7
We (Zamyatin), 76
Wells, H.G., 107, 138, 169–70, 180
Whorf, Benjamin Lee, 86

Yeats, W.B. 119, 127

Zamyatin, Evgeny, 76
Zwerdling, Alex, 24, 62, 78, 132, 173

Index of Orwell's Works

Animal Farm, 4, 5, 20, 46, 69, 104, 124–33, 166, 170, 175, 177, 178, 180
'The Art of Donald McGill', 121–2

'Boy's Weeklies', 121
Burmese Days, 44, 65, 110, 159

A Clergyman's Daughter, 4, 96
Coming up for Air, 4, 7, 105–9, 121, 151, 154, 161

Down and Out in Paris and London, 5, 24, 41, 71–2, 110, 112, 160, 166

'England, Your England', 7
The English People, 8–22, 81

'A Hanging', 44, 69–71, 159
Homage to Catalonia, 5, 22, 41, 48, 50–60, 68, 73, 112, 166, 177
'How the Poor Die', 112–17, 160

'Inside the Whale', 105, 168

Keep the Aspidistra Flying, 4, 7, 154

The Lion and the Unicorn: Socialism and the English Genius, 8, 74–6
'Looking Back on the Spanish War', 60

'Marrakech', 66

'New Words', 83–5
1984, 4, 5, 18, 20, 22, 24, 45, 46, 69, 77, 80–1, 82, 83, 84, 85, 87, 93, 95, 97, 124, 134–48, 168, 170

'Politics and the English Language', 47, 82, 87–93
'The Prevention of Literature', 80–1

'Raffles and Miss Blandish', 121
'Reflections on Gandhi', 49
The Road to Wigan Pier, 5, 24, 41, 62, 68, 71, 73, 109, 112, 157, 169, 171

'Shooting an Elephant', 44, 66, 159
'The Spike', 69–72
'Such, such were the joys', 37–42, 111

'Why I Write', 3, 22–3, 121